RENEWALS 458-4574

DATE DUE

Gender and the Public Sector

Managerial change has had a significant impact on professionals working in the public sector in recent years. This collection of essays examines claims about the pervasiveness of the 'new' public management and its impact on public sectors in countries such as England, France, Greece, India, South Africa and Sweden. It also considers the changing character of professional identities, with a particular focus on the gendered implications within the fields of welfare provision and social policy and inter-relationships in the governance of public sector organisations.

Contributors draw upon the disciplines of sociology and social policy from a variety of perspectives and approaches and a range of theoretical resources, including insights from the work of Lyotard, Foucault, Bourdieu and Gramsci, and the recent interest in biography. The volume presents empirical research findings with international coverage, extending to countries where the new managerialism has had varying degrees of impact, from Sweden at one extreme, thought to be at the forefront of the reforms along with Britain, to Greece, the 'new' South Africa and India, where public administration predominates.

Topics covered include gender and local government in India, the process of management reform within the South African public services since 1994, how issues such as privatisation, marketisation and managerialism have affected female public sector managers from the social services, the NHS, higher education and local government. The gendered construction of nursing identity and the management of care homes are also considered.

Gender and the Public Sector will be essential reading for advanced students and academics in the fields of Sociology, Social Policy, Social Work, Health Studies, Organisation Studies and Gender Studies as well as practising professionals and managers in the public sector.

Jim Barry is a political sociologist and Reader at the University of East London, based in the East London Business School. His current research interests include gender and managerialism in higher education as well as in the public sector more generally. **Mike Dent** is Professor of Health Care Organisation at Staffordshire University. Currently, his main research interest is the comparative study of medical and nursing work, professional and health care organisations and accountability across Europe. **Maggie O'Neill** is Reader in Sociology at Staffordshire University. Her main research interest focuses upon developing participatory action research with marginalised communities and integrating theory and praxis through renewing methodologies by the use of visual and creative methods.

Routledge Advances in Management and Business Studies

Gender and the Public Sector

Professionals and managerial change

Edited by **Jim Barry, Mike Dent and Maggie O'Neill**

LONDON AND NEW YORK

First published 2003
by Routledge
2 Park Square, Milton Park, Abingdon, Oxon, OX14 4RN

Simultaneously published in the USA and Canada
by Routledge
270 Madison Ave, New York NY 10016

Routledge is an imprint of the Taylor & Francis Group

Transferred to Digital Printing 2006

Typeset in Baskerville by
Prepress Projects Ltd, Perth, Scotland

British Library Cataloguing in Publication Data
A catalogue record for this book is available from the British
Library

Library of Congress Cataloging in Publication Data
Gender and the public sector : professionals and managerial
change / edited by Jim Barry, Mike Dent, and Maggie O'Neill.
    p. cm.
  Includes bibliographical references and index.
  1. Women government executives. 2. Public welfare
administration. I. Barry, Jim, 1950– II. Dent, Mike, 1944– III.
O'Neill, Maggie
  HQ1390 .G44 2003
  306.2–dc21   2002013228

ISBN 0–415–25819–7

Contents

Notes on contributors

Jim Barry is a political sociologist and Reader based in the East London Business School at the University of East London. He is an associate of the Mega-Cities Project, co-director of the Organisation Studies Research Group and a member of the European Network on Managerialism and Higher Education. He has published on gender and politics, gender and public service, gender and organisations, gender and business ethics, lone parenting and employment, and gender, managerialism and higher education.

Elisabeth Berg is a Docent (Reader) in Sociology in the Department of Human Work Sciences at Luleå University of Technology in Sweden. Her earlier research considered organisation, gender and social politics. Her later research concerned women in female-dominated organisations and explored the ways in which they handled their careers. Some of her findings are published in her book *Kvinna och chef i offentlig förvaltning* [*Woman and Management in Public Service*] (Liber, 2000). More recently her research has involved gender and organisation in academia in Sweden, England and The Netherlands. She is a member of the European Network on Managerialism and Higher Education.

Joanna Brewis works in the Department of Accounting, Finance and Management at the University of Essex. Her research interests centre around the exploration of organising processes through the lenses of gender, sex, sexuality and identity. These interests are reflected in works such as 'Unpacking Priscilla: Subjectivity and identity in the organization of gendered appearance' (with co-authors Stephen Linstead and Mark P. Hampton; *Human Relations*, 50 (10), 1997) and 'Who do you think you are? Feminism, work, ethics and Foucault' in *The Ethics of Organisations*, edited by M. Parker (Sage, 1998).

John Chandler is a sociologist teaching Organisational Studies in the East London Business School at the University of East London. His current research interests include gender and managerialism in higher education and the 'new careers'. He is a co-director of the University's Organisation Studies Research Group, based in the East London Business School, and his publications include *Organisation and Identities*, co-edited with Jim Barry and Heather Clark (International Thomson, 1994) and *Organization and Management: A Critical Text*, co-edited with Jim Barry, Heather Clark, Roger Johnston and David Needle (Thomson Learning, 2000). He is a member of the European Network on Managerialism and Higher Education.

Mike Dent is Professor of Health Care Organisation in the School of Health at Staffordshire University. His main research interest recently has been the comparative study of medical and nursing work and professional organisation and accountability across Europe. He also retains an interest in health care computing and information systems. He has published a number of articles on these topics as well as three books: *Professions, Information Systems and Management in Hospitals* (Avebury, 1996), *Professions, New Public Management and the European Welfare State*, co-edited with Maggie O'Neill and Carl Bagley (Staffordshire University Press, 1999) and *Managing Professional Identities*, co-edited with Stephen Whitehead (Routledge, 2002).

Hans Hasselbladh is an Assistant Professor at the School of Economics and Commercial Law, University of Gothenburg. He gained his PhD from Uppsala University in 1995. He has a particular interest in Foucault-inspired and institutional approaches to organisational and societal change. His current research includes a study of the quality movement in Sweden with co-workers from the National Institute of Working Life.

Trudie Honour gained degrees from the Universities of Leicester and Sussex and then became the ICI Research Fellow at the University of Sussex researching the effectiveness of various forms of management training. Her academic career has focused on management development and she is currently Head of Special Projects at East London Business School. She has developed and managed a number of certificated postgraduate management programmes, both in the UK and abroad, for example in Singapore, Malaysia and the People's Republic of China. In addition she has worked for Boston University in London on some of its management programmes and has extensive experience of writing, editing and tutoring distance-learning material for one of the largest providers of distance-learning in the UK. She has had over 20 years consultancy experience in organisational and managerial development in change situations – especially, but not exclusively, in the National Health Service (NHS). Her research publications have focused around issues of change, gender and corruption in India and London, which attracted funding from The British Council in Mumbai. She is an associate of the Mega-Cities Project.

Heather Höpfl is Professor of Organisational Psychology and Head of the School of Operational Analysis and Human Resource Management at Newcastle Business School, Newcastle upon Tyne, UK. She is known for her original research in organisational culture, management development and organisational theory. She completed her PhD in Organisational Psychology at Lancaster University in 1982 and has since worked in the theatre, in research and in teaching. She has undertaken research with a number of large companies including British Airways, the Prison Service, the Department for Education and Employment (DfEE), and the Land Transport Authority in Singapore. She has a particular interest in the relationship between structures and processes and this has been an important part of her work on the design of systems environments both for the analysis of airline safety information and for the development of learning organisation approaches for management development.

Deborah Kerfoot is a lecturer in Organizational Behaviour at Keele University. Her research interests and publications are in the field of sociology and critical study of management, empirical research on employment, poststructuralism, and gender and sexuality in organizations. She is Joint Editor of the journal *Gender, Work and Organization* and Book Review Editor for the *Journal of Management Studies* (both published by Blackwell).

Janet Newman is at the Open University. She is co-editor (with Cathy Itzin) of *Gender, Culture and Organisational Change* (Routledge, 1995). She is the author of 'The limits of management: Gender and the politics of change', in *Managing Social Policy*, edited by J. Clarke, A. Cochrane and E. McLaughlin (Sage, 1994) and 'Managerialism, modernisation and marginalisation: Equal opportunities and institutional change', in *The Changing Politics of Gender Equality in Britain*, edited by E. Breitenbach, A. Brown, F. Mackay and J. Webb (Palgrave, 2002). She is also the co-author (with John Clarke) of *The Managerial State: Power, Politics and Ideology in the Remaking of Social Welfare* (Sage, 1997). She is currently researching and writing about the implications of the modernisation agenda for public services.

Maggie O'Neill is a Reader in Sociology at Staffordshire University. Her 'woman-centred' action research in Nottingham in 1990 led to the development of a multi-agency forum (1991–4), which involved sex workers as key players. Committed to participatory action research, she was involved in the management committee and early development of POW! (Prostitute Outreach Workers) and has worked with the Sex Workers Project in Stoke-on-Trent, as well as researched routes into prostitution from Care and conducted comparative research (funded by the British Council) with colleagues in Spain. She has published on: prostitution and feminism; ethnographic, participatory action research with 'hard to reach' populations; male violence against women and children involved in prostitution; multi-agency responses to prostitution; the social role of art, cultural theory and feminisms; and refugees and asylum seekers. Her publications include *New Public Management and the European Welfare State*, co-edited with Mike Dent and Carl Bagley (Staffordshire University Press, 1999); *Adorno, Culture and Feminism*, an edited text of papers by leading feminists/critical theorists (Sage, 1999); *Prostitution and Feminism* (Polity Press, 2001); *Prostitution: A Reader*, edited with R. Matthews (Ashgate, 2002).

Jenny Owen works at the University of Sheffield. She coordinates an MA in Applied Research and Quality Evaluation in the Department of Sociological Studies, teaching specific modules on qualitative data analysis, team project research and the research/policy relationship in public services. She is also employed in the Institute of General Practice and Primary Care in the University, providing support for health care staff in developing collaborative research proposals and projects. Originally a community education tutor, she has also worked on organisational development and management development projects both for Sheffield Health and also for the NHS Management Education Scheme by Open Learning (MESOL). Jenny has carried out research on information technology (IT), and gender and organisations, and her current research interests are in health services policy and management, within the broad area of changes in public sector organisation and management. She retains an active interest in patterns of IT use and development, including innovative approaches to the use of the Internet for collaborative teaching and learning.

Sneha Palnitkar is a Professor and Director of International Relations and Research at the All-India Institute of Local Self-Government (AIILSG), based in Mumbai (formerly Bombay), India. After gaining qualifications from the University of Bombay, the Training Institute for Child Welfare and the Chetna Institute of Management and Research, she worked for the Ambedkar Institute for Labour Studies before joining the AIILSG. She has undertaken a large number of national and international research projects, specialising in urban, labour, health and community studies. She is a coordinator for the Mega-Cities Project.

Martin Selander is a PhD candidate in Business Studies at the Department of Business Administration at Göteborg University in Sweden. He is currently writing his dissertation, which uses a discursive perspective to understand the introduction of new public management (NPM) reforms in the care of elderly people.

Stephen Whitehead is Lecturer in Education in the Department of Education at Keele University. His research interests and publications concern the critical study of men and masculinities; gender and education management; post-structuralism; and subjectivities, epistemologies and identities in organisations. He is author of *Men and Masculinities: Key Themes and New Directions* (Polity Press, 2002) and co-editor of *Transforming Managers: Gendering Change in the Public Sector* (with Roy Moodley; UCL Press, 1999), *The Masculinities Reader* (with Frank J. Barrett; Polity Press, 2001), and *Managing Professional Identities: Knowledge, Performativity and the 'New' Professional* (with Mike Dent; Routledge 2002).

Ann Young is currently Head of Strategic and International Management at the East London Business School, University of East London. Her previous experience consisted of nearly 30 years in the health service, many of these in nurse education. For the last 3 years of her NHS career she moved from senior education manager to head of business and administration. She has written extensively on legal, ethical and management issues in nursing. Her current research and publications examine the effect of imposed change on middle managers' power relations in health care organisations and, on this subject, she has presented a number of papers at international conferences.

Acknowledgements

This volume originates from the Third International Research Conference, *Dilemmas for Public Sector Professionals, Managers and Users in the Millennium*, organised by Staffordshire University in 1999, at which a number of the chapters were first presented as papers. We are especially grateful to participants at the conference, whose insights and enthusiasm sparked our initial interest and a belief that an undertaking of this kind was not only important but also possible. In addition to papers presented at the conference the volume contains other, specially commissioned, chapters. Our thanks go to all the contributors.

Jim Barry, Mike Dent and Maggie O'Neill

Introduction

Jim Barry, Mike Dent and Maggie O'Neill

The purpose of this collection is twofold. First, to consider various aspects of gender and professional identities in the face of managerial change within the field of welfare provision and social policy. Second, to explore their interrelationships in the governance of public sector organisations. A new public sector managerialism, it has been argued, has had an impact across many parts of the world in recent years (e.g. Hood 1991, 1995), especially in Britain (Clarke and Newman 1997), where England is situated and a number of the authors locate their study. The contributors discuss the impact and implications, particularly in relation to gender, drawing on the disciplines of sociology and social policy from a variety of perspectives and approaches.

England, along with other northern European countries, including Sweden, has been in the forefront of what Hood *et al.* (1999: 189–90; see also Osborne 1999) have called a 'managerial reform movement' in the public sector, more commonly referred to as a 'new' public management or NPM (e.g. Hood 1991; Pollitt 1993). Australia and the Pacific rim have also come under its sway as its influence has spread (Pollitt 2001; Pollitt and Bouckaert 2000). Yet the literature has only recently begun to consider the impact of the NPM (e.g. Exworthy and Halford 1999). And there has been little examination, beyond the volume by Itzin and Newman, which appeared back in 1995, of the implications of the 'new' managerialism for the study of gender and professionalism across different public sector sites.

Instead, texts have tended to consider gender and organisations more broadly, seeking to contribute to what is becoming a burgeoning literature on women – and latterly men – in management (Gherardi 1995; Collinson and Hearn 1996a; Alvesson and Due Billing 1997). Texts such as these reflect the influence of conventional wisdom (Gilligan 1982), which recounts differences in managerial style between women and men in both the private (e.g. Rosener 1990) and public sectors (e.g. White 1995), or the significance of context in helping to shape behaviour (e.g. Wajcman 1998). More recently power, as a complex, multidimensional phenomenon, has been reintroduced into gender and organisation discourses (Halford and Leonard 2001). Power is also central to Hearn and Parkin's work (1987; 1993). They have recently examined oppression, violence and bullying in organisations, which is structured and practised through 'unspoken forces'.

Where texts have focused on gender and professions they have had a specific policy focus, as, for example, in Whitehead and Moodley's (1999) exploration of gender identity in education, Morley and Walsh's (1995; see also Morley 1999) examination of women in Academe and Langan and Day's (1992) treatment of women and social work. Recently, texts have been reorienting studies of management and organisation to reflect a growing recognition that identities are multifaceted and, whether or not fractured (Bradley 1997), continuously remade. This is notable in the management of professional identities, in which there is acknowledgement of the implications for gender (Dent and Whitehead 2002). There have, nonetheless, been few accounts of international experiences or of the variable global impact of managerialism on those involved, beyond the exploratory work of Hood (1995) himself and Olson *et al.* (1998), whose consideration is restricted to the new public *financial* management.

In contributing to and extending the literature, this volume draws on the experience of a number of authors who have already made significant contributions in their respective fields. In this text they focus their attention on the impact of the new managerialism on gender and identity in the governance of welfare and social policy. In selecting authors, we were careful to include those with particular expertise in professional and managerial identity and a research interest in gender, in order that the implications for gendered identity in the wake of the recent changes could be teased out and set in context. Moreover, in examining the implications from a rich variety of perspectives and approaches, in a number of countries, our intention has been to provide insights into the processes at work.

The authors draw on a range of theoretical resources, including insights from the work of Lyotard, Foucault, Bourdieu and Gramsci, as well as from the recent interest in biography, which attempts to explore the fluid and dynamic character of identity through lived experience (Chamberlayne *et al.* 2000). Most of the contributors report on empirical research findings, with international coverage extending to countries where the new managerialism has been having an impact to varying degrees – from Sweden at one extreme, thought to be at the forefront of the reforms along with England, to Greece, the 'new' South Africa, and India, where public administration predominates. This is not to imply a convergence model for the NPM reforms (Pollitt 2001), suggesting that public sectors worldwide are likely to be somehow overwhelmed by a *logic of managerialism* reminiscent of the earlier prognostications by Burnham (1945) or Kerr *et al.* (1960). It is instead to acknowledge the widespread influence of what we will call the *managerial turn*, in order to set the scene for an examination of the changing character of *gendered subjectivity*.

There are a number of ways of organising the chapters into themes, an issue that confronts all editorial groups. Although acutely aware that there are always alternative ways of ordering any text, we have nonetheless decided to arrange the contributions into the following three parts: contexts and networks; managing professional work; and identity and biography.

Part I: Contexts and networks

Janet Newman takes as her starting point 'New Labour's' concern for reshaping relations between state and civil society around notions such as active citizenship, which offers a 'joined up' approach and effective delivery of policy based on 'what works'. And in conceptualising the public realm as a gendered and racialised domain, she uses theories of governance to explore state–society interconnections and issues of diversity. In showing how earlier, post-war approaches to equal opportunity gave way to a concern with effective utilisation of staff, she identifies a shift from coordination, through hierarchy and competition, to networks and partnerships, as elements of New Labour's 'Third Way'. This reflects, she argues, its emphasis on inclusion and underpins its holistic approach to governance, resulting in the dissolution of old hierarchies and power blocs. It nonetheless depends on a new system of patronage, which raises a number of issues. For in attempting to empower the people or the community, in effect little more than disembodied abstractions, questions of who is and who is not 'included' are raised, with related issues of tokenism and incorporation unresolved. Janet Newman concludes by identifying a new research agenda to explore the 'politics of inclusion'.

Trudie Honour, Jim Barry and Sneha Palnitkar provide a contrasting public administrative perspective from India in a chapter that considers gender and local government. The authors discuss the implications of a 1992 policy adopted in Mumbai (formerly Bombay) that guarantees a 30 per cent seat reservation or quota system for women politicians in comparison with London, where women councillors are present in similar numbers. The research is timely for a number of reasons, not least because concerns have been expressed worldwide in recent years about the under-representation of women in positions of responsibility and decision making. There have also been questions concerning what has been called 'good governance' and worries expressed about clientelism and corruption, issues addressed more fully in Mike Dent's chapter. Trudie Honour, Jim Barry and Sneha Palnitkar accordingly examine the experience of the women and the significance of, first, *critical acts* such as social movement activity and the quota and, second, the role of the *critical mass* in initiating an irreversible 'chain reaction'. In short, whether women, when present in sufficient numbers, might make a lasting difference to urban governance. They consider issues of welfare and policy provision as well as gendered ways of working. Interestingly, they find that the women in both cities are respected, seen as highly competent and as fair and even-handed in their dealings with others, managing their identities and focusing their energies on the most disadvantaged and socially excluded in their respective communities.

Jenny Owen's chapter discusses the processes of management reform within the South African public service since 1994. She identifies the distinctive features of public service and management in South Africa and the implications this has for the adoption of Western public management concepts. From a review of the available literature on management it becomes clear that there are two distinct differences between South African and Western texts. First, there is a much heavier emphasis on community over individualism. Second, gender does not appear to register as a priority issue. There is much evidence of difficulties obstructing the public service transformation originally envisaged by the African National Congress (ANC). The challenge of overcoming the massive inequalities and problems left after the collapse of apartheid and white-dominated rule is considerable. One consequence is that gender issues are commonly viewed as being of lesser significance in relation to other policies, at least for the present. It is only within small-scale initiatives and innovations that we find women's issues, rather than gender per se, beginning to be addressed.

The main strength of Mike Dent's chapter lies in his grasp of the political and social context of the French and Greek public sectors and understanding of the dynamics of professional identity. He considers four issues and examines their interconnection in order to draw out the gendered implications. These are the organisation and funding of the respective health care systems, gender and welfare state regimes, governmentality and state/profession relations, and the role of the family in relation to official and unofficial co-payments. After outlining the organisation and funding systems in the two countries in question he moves on to consider the gendered character of welfare regimes, identifying variations between those that treat women primarily as 'wives and mothers' and those that view them as 'workers'. It is in this context that Mike Dent considers the French and Greek medical professions, through the Foucauldian lens of governmentality. This analysis enables him to point up the role of the different medical systems in sustaining gendered 'difference'. He concludes by showing how the 'modified male breadwinner' model in France has led to women there benefiting on the one hand from natalist policies while on the other being accepted into a somewhat unfriendly labour market. This stands in contrast to the more traditionally patriarchal, but equally paradoxical, approach found in Greece, which implicates the family in the discourse of health care and empowers women to manipulate the health care system and secure favourable medical treatment for their families – through the questionable practice of illicit payments (*fakelakia*).

Part II: Managing professional work

Stephen Whitehead examines professionalism in relation to gendered subjectivity and identity, coming to similar conclusions to Deborah Kerfoot, whose chapter appears in Part III, by a slightly different route. In drawing on poststructuralist perspectives, Stephen Whitehead reviews the literature covering managerial and professional work and examines links between identities, desire and masculinities. He considers labour process debates, from realist to poststructuralist, before moving on to the dilemmas and contradictory demands confronting contemporary managers. These, he argues, lead to the experience of uncertainty, the mitigation of which becomes compelling. And it is in this context that the identity of the professional, albeit unclear and untidy, becomes significant in that it provides a 'seductive set of discourses' for the reduction of uncertainty and the enhancement of personal and organisational legitimacy. Moreover, he argues, it is 'identity work with political implications', as this concern with the attainment of professional, managerial and ontological security is framed by notions of masculinity that underscore, following Lyotard, the contemporary discourse of performativity.

Elisabeth Berg's chapter examines middle managers' career opportunities in a female-dominated work environment in the public sector in Sweden, identifying factors that encourage women to gain managerial positions and noting the complexity of career options for women and men with different educational backgrounds. She makes use of the concepts habitus and positioning, drawing on the work of Bourdieu and Foucault, extended through the insights of Alcoff, in order to show how gender is shaped through interaction. She considers the situation of women and men in the public sector in two organisational divisions that operate within the same administration – the 'division of individual and family care' and the 'division of elderly and the handicapped' – and identifies a power structure within the social welfare service in Sweden that results in the prioritisation of certain types of competence. Elisabeth Berg's research shows that women and men have different strategies when they apply for higher appointments and that women keep their children at the centre of their concerns even if they have followed traditional career paths. Despite the dominance of women in this sector, it is contended that the activities are structured according to a traditional model that benefits men, who secure most of the managerial positions.

Hans Hasselbladh and Martin Selander's chapter is an in-depth case study of two nursing homes, carried out in Gothenburg in Sweden, organisational sites that are also dominated by women. Their study is concerned primarily with the impact of NPM-inspired reforms on the organisation and delivery of nursing care for elderly people in Sweden. The strength of their work lies in their understanding of the processes at work for the professionals involved, which, they argue, introduce ambiguity into the status of the 'patient' as well as the role and identity of the nurses. They outline three frames for structuring the work and its meaning. These are the medical frame (dominated by rules and routines), the nursing care frame (emotional labour) and the service orientation frame (patients as customers), which are reconfigured in the light of the increased emphasis currently being placed on a fourth frame, namely economic rationality (budgetary control and accountability). What is interesting about this is the implications it has for gender relations at work as the nurses in the study are all female. Although it might appear likely that the introduction of a service-oriented frame in the wake of the NPM would have undermined the previously dominant and masculine medical frame, it transpires that this frame also undermines the care frame. The case study documents the nurses' responses to the organisational changes and offers explanations for why they choose one masculine mode of framing over another, and why, in effect, there is little choice anyway.

Jo Brewis draws on interviews conducted with twelve female public service managers across social services, the National Health Service (NHS), higher education, the probation service and local government. Her focus is on the key changes, from privatisation to marketisation and managerialism, introduced into the public sector by the respective Conservative regimes that held power in Britain between 1979 and 1997. In considering their accounts in depth, she explores their experiences of the changes within the public sector and their interpretation of the impact on managerial roles, as well as exploring the ways in which the changes were thought to affect the quality of provision to the public and to public sector workers. Her findings indicate a number of significant changes, including the demand for more managerial skills and a concern with accountability and performance measurement, alongside an emphasis on the three E's of economy, efficiency and effectiveness to achieve value for money, and customer responsiveness. While acknowledging that the old 1970s system had its flaws – seen as 'wasteful and somewhat arrogant' by one respondent – she shows how the new has failed, nonetheless, to improve the quality of provision to either public sector workers or the public. With increased pressure on staff, a variable impact on service provision and the raising of consumer expectations to unrealistic levels, the result is less than promising. In examining the gendered implications Jo Brewis uses Weber's work on rationality, showing how *means* rationality is structured around stereotypical masculine values (including control, quantification, objectivity, linear logic and competitiveness) in contrast to *ends* rationality, which can invoke perceived feminine qualities of reflection, care, non-materialism and community-centred holism. She concludes that, according to her interviewees, *means* rationality (and associated masculinity) continues to prevail over *ends* rationality (and associated femininity) in the public services.

Ann Young's chapter explores the implications of a contractual and managerialist approach to health care for middle managers in a British context using interview data from three contrasting groups of middle managers: NHS nurse managers; NHS finance managers with an accounting background; and nurse managers from private hospitals. These groups were selected as it had been thought initially that the first two would illustrate how the introduction of general management and managed markets into the NHS affected the managerial mode of operating, with an increase in finance managers' overall power and a marked shift for the nursing managers away from a traditional mode of influence. It had been expected in addition that the third group, the independent sector managers, would be more hard-nosed and business oriented in a marketised organisational setting. The results, however, were not quite as expected. To begin with, she found that all three groups had faced frequent and considerable change alongside repeated restructuring, with the last affecting her 'piggy in the middle' managers the most. Moreover, she found that, again in all three groups, the managers, with very few exceptions, were nonetheless able to exercise some degree of choice in adaptation and response – in particular, over whether they played what Ann Young calls the 'pink and fluffy' card or the 'hard business' one in their 'gender games'. In short, whether they engaged in feminine or masculine behavioural displays. But not only was gender significant in all this, so too was context, with interaction influenced by the uncertainty over boundaries of professional identity and the strategy of identifying a number of different 'bosses'.

Part III: Identity and biography

Heather Höpfl's chapter examines the gendered construction of nursing identity and the inherent ambiguities and contradictions this contains. In considering the profession's roots in charity and religious orders, she shows how nursing has traditionally been seen as 'dirty work with a noble significance'. Then, by following the changing images of the profession in Britain from the post-war period onwards, as represented in recruitment literature and popular culture through the medium of film, she shows how the idea of nursing as vocation altered in the 1950s to nursing as service to the nation, through the NHS. After this the image underwent further changes from 'petty authoritarian' to 'handmaiden' or 'sexual spectacle'. The expression of collective dissatisfaction through trade union action came later, along with the bifurcation of the nursing profession at senior levels with the development of specialist and managerial identities. Heather Höpfl argues that the recent pressure on nurses, to care more for the abstract categories of 'care management' than people and thereby emphasise the masculine over the feminine, has resulted in their seeking to distance themselves from the lingering image of 'ministering angel' in order to emphasise their situation as workers with professional competencies and skills. To break, as she puts it, 'the association between service and subservience' for nurses.

John Chandler considers the gendered implications raised by the management of care homes using life-history and narrative research, a growing area of enquiry in the social sciences (Rustin 2000) and a field of study in its own right, which has been characterised as the biographical turn (Chamberlayne *et al.* 2000). In using this approach John Chandler bases his research, drawn from a wider study, on two distinct biographies of people involved in managing private residential care homes in what is becoming, in this sector, a mixed economy of welfare. The accounts of one male and one female interviewee are used to construct two managerial ideal-types. The first draws on an identity that sees management as a highly rationalised activity and managers as preoccupied with measurement, assessment and efficiency. The second is more concerned with relationships, processes and effectiveness. The accounts begin with each respondent appearing to conform to gendered stereotype: the man resolutely rational as he cites the importance of quality control and the influence of managerial gurus such as Peters and Waterman, the woman concerned about the people who work for her and those for whom she cares. Yet as the chapter unfolds it becomes clear that the man is employing managerial techniques to ensure the delivery of a high level of care, to make the difference to people's lives that he felt unable to when working for the NHS, even if he remains ultimately managerialist. Whereas the woman sees her caring role as just that, a role to be superseded when she moves on and seeks more lucrative work outside of the care service, despite her enacting relational management at present. John Chandler thus shows the multi-layered character of gendered identity as women and men shift between their regions of experience at work, raising questions in the process about any differences in the public and private delivery of 'care'. His concern with the changing biography of two characters is something shared with the chapter by Deborah Kerfoot which follows.

Deborah Kerfoot develops a Foucauldian analysis of professional identity and its links with management, which draws on empirical research in order to examine aspects of gendered identity. In examining the ways in which professional identity is constructed, she reports on a series of in-depth semi-structured interviews, supplemented by ongoing informal contact, with two women, Brenda and Karen, over a period of months. The women were working in different organisational public sector sites, Brenda in a local authority residential care unit and Karen in education welfare. Both had worked in the public sector for many years, both were experiencing a period of change and/or difficulty in their work situations and both drew on notions of being 'professional' to deal with the problems they faced. In identifying how they construct their identities from competing discourses, which include 'wife/mother/carer/manager/woman/professional', Deborah Kerfoot shows how identity is gendered, precarious and subjected to a process of continuous change.

From these chapters, which explore managerialism, gender and professional identity, we see in sharp relief the complexities of interaction in contemporary organisational life in the public sector. The chapters reveal a variety of identities – professional, gendered and managerial – in play and in flux, together. In all this it is perhaps tempting to see the shifts in the relationship between gender and professionalism as epiphenomenal, as somehow following the emergence of a 'new' managerialism. But this would be too simplistic a conclusion since we see similar shifts in Honour *et al.*'s Indian case study (Chapter 2), in which gender is a live issue but public administration rather than managerialism predominates.

Nonetheless, to suggest gender as a prime mover of public management reform may be equally problematic. The role of women's movements as a social and political force for change internationally may have played a part in the changing character of the public sector, but this is not always the case as, for example, in the 'new' South Africa, where gender has yet to appear on the managerial agenda. This contrasts with the Indian case, in which it has become clearly established as an issue. What this suggests is that while ideas and influences associated with the new public management spread worldwide, they are received, interpreted and operationalised in a variety of ways in different contexts (Pollitt 2001). This is also evidenced clearly in the case study of Greece, which indicates a complex interplay in the field of social and organisational relations as pressures to make the workings of the public sector transparent run aground on the rock of historically embedded social arrangements (Granovetter 1989). This casts doubt on arguments about convergence or isomorphism, of whatever variety (Powell and DiMaggio 1991). Indeed it would seem that, if anything, a variety of settlements are being forged in different public sectors in different parts of the world, even if the pressures for change often appear similar.

But what is clear in respect of gender, and this is one of the major conclusions of the contributions in the collection, is that in the present context the intersubjectivities of identity work and the sometimes contradictory managerial changes in organisational life offer opportunities for participants to cross boundaries and confound stereotypes and conventional wisdom – at least as (re)presented in everyday life and many academic texts. In short, the readings raise questions not about women and men per se but about the constitution of feminine and masculine identities and their associated behavioural displays.

It is in this sense that individual experience assumes significance, since it is through the study of narrative that the intersection of identity through human experience can be seen – in line with what has been called the biographical turn (Chamberlayne *et al.* 2000). The implications for studies of gender are thus considerable, not least in the public sector, as appreciation of the complexities becomes increasingly acknowledged. What this suggests is a need for painstaking scholarly work in the attempt to understand the significance of these insights.

References

Alvesson, M. and Due Billing, Y. (1997) *Understanding Gender and Organisations*, London: Sage.

Bradley, H. (1997) *Fractured Identities: Changing Patterns of Inequality*, Cambridge: Polity Press.

Burnham, J. (1945) *The Managerial Revolution,* Harmondsworth: Penguin.

Chamberlayne, P., Bornat, J. and Wengraf, T. (eds) (2000) *The Turn of Biographical Methods in Social Science*, London: Routledge.

Clarke, J. and Newman, J. (1997) *The Management State*, London: Sage.

Collinson, D. and Hearn, J. (eds) (1996a) *Men as Managers, Managers and Men: Critical Perspectives on Men, Masculinities and Managements*, London: Sage.

Collinson, D. and Hearn, J. (1996b) ' "Men at work": Multiple masculinities in multiple workplaces', in Mac an Ghail, M. (ed.), *Understanding Masculinities: Social Relations and Cultural Arenas*, Buckingham: Open University Press, pp. 61–76.

Dent, M. and Whitehead, S. (eds) (2002) *Managing Professional Identities: Knowledge, Performativity and the 'New' Professional*, London: Routledge.

Exworthy, M. and Halford, S. (eds) (1999) *Professionals and the New Managerialism in the Public Sector*, Buckingham: Open University Press.

Gherardi, S. (1995) *Gender, Symbolism and Organisational Cultures*, London: Sage.

Gilligan, C. (1982) *In a Different Voice: Psychological Theory and Women's Development*, Cambridge, MA: Harvard University Press.

Granovetter, M. (1989) 'The strength of weak ties', *American Journal of Sociology*, 78: 1360–80.

Halford, S. and Leonard, P. (2001) *Gender, Power and Organisations: An Introduction*, London: Palgrave.

Hearn, J. and Parkin, W. (1987) *'Sex' at 'Work': The Power and Paradox of Organisation and Sexuality*, Hemel Hempstead: Prentice Hall/Harvester Wheatsheaf.

Hearn, J. and Parkin, W. (1993) 'Organisations, multiple oppressions and post-modernism', in Hassard, J. and Parker, M. (eds), *Postmodernism and Organisations*, London: Sage, pp. 33–52.

Hearn, J. and Parkin, W. (2001) *Gender, Sexuality and Violence in Organizations: The Unspoken Forces of Organizational Violence*, London, Sage.

Hood, C. (1991) 'A public management for all seasons?' *Public Administration*, 69 (1): 3–19.

Hood, C. (1995) 'The "new public management" in the 1980s: Variations on a theme', *Accounting, Organizations and Society*, 20 (2/3): 93–109.

Hood, C., Scott, C., James, O., Jones, G. and Travers, T. (eds) (1999) *Regulation Inside Government: Waste-Watchers, Quality-Police and Sleaze-Busters*, Oxford: Oxford University Press.

Itzin, C. and Newman, J. (eds) (1995) *Gender, Culture and Organisational Change: Putting Theory into Practice*, London: Routledge.

Kerr, C., Dunlop, J. T., Harbison, F. and Myers, C. (1960) *Industrialism and Industrial Man*, Harmondsworth: Penguin.

Langan, M. and Day, L. (1992) *Women, Oppression and Social Work: Issues in Anti-discriminatory Practice*, London: Routledge.

Morley, L. (1999) *Organizing Feminism: The Micropolitics of the Academy*, London: Macmillan.

Morley, L. and Walsh, V. (eds) (1995) *Feminist Academics: Creative Agents for Change*, London: Taylor & Francis.

Olson, O., Guthrie, J. and Humphrey, C. (eds) (1998) *Global Warning: Debating International Developments in the New Public Financial Management*, Oslo: Cappelen Akademisk Forlag as.

Osborne, S. (1999) 'Editorial: Public management in the new millennium', *Public Management*, 1 (1): 1–4.

Pollitt, C. (1993) *Managerialism and the Public Services: Cuts or Cultural Change in the 1990s*, 2nd edn, Oxford: Basic Blackwell.

Pollitt, C. (2001) 'Convergence: The useful myth?' *Public Administration*, 79: 993–47.

Pollitt, C. and Bouckaert, G. (2000) *Public Management Reform: A Comparative Analysis*, Oxford: Oxford University Press.

Powell, W. W. and DiMaggio, P. J. (1991) *The New Institutionalism in Organzsational Analysis*, Chicago: The University of Chicago Press.

Rosener, J., (1990) 'Ways women lead', *Harvard Business Review*, 68 (6): 119–215.

Rustin, M. (2000) 'Reflections on the bibliographical turn in social science', in Chamberlayne, P., Bornat, J. and Wengraf, T. (eds), *The Turn to Biographical Methods in Social Science*, London: Routledge.

Wajcman, J. (1998) *Managing Like a Man: Women and Men in Corporate Management*, Cambridge: Polity Press.

White, J. (1995) 'Leading in their own ways: Women chief executives in local government', in Itzin, C. and Newman, J. (eds), *Gender, Culture and Organisational Change: Putting Theory into Practice*, London: Routledge, pp. 193–210.

Whitehead, S. and Moodley, R. (eds) (1990) *Transforming Managers: Gendering Change in the Public Sector*, London: UEL Press.

Part I

Contexts and networks

1   New Labour, governance and the politics of diversity

Janet Newman

Debates about gender and management have typically been concerned with the organisational domain. The literature has highlighted the organisational practices that reproduce unequal representations of women and men in management posts; the ways in which cultural norms and values constrain opportunities for women; and the gendered knowledges and practices of managerialism. In terms of the public sector this is, however, only part of the story. The gendering of organisational life in public services is inextricably tied to the way in which the public realm is constituted as a gendered and racialised domain.

'Governance' provides one set of theories through which the public realm can be understood. Governance in its broadest sense denotes issues concerning the changing role and powers of the state; the relationships between the public, private and voluntary sector in emerging patterns of service delivery; and expectations about the role of citizens, communities, families and households. In this chapter I use the term governance to embrace such state–society interactions and to open up debates about issues of diversity in the public realm.[1] I deliberately focus on issues of diversity rather than gender alone because of the problem of isolating gender from other forms of social identity and other lines of social division. However, my analysis has been shaped both by drawing on the experience of women working in public services in the UK and by feminist forms of analysis and praxis.

Governance can be viewed as a gendered and racialised domain at a number of different levels of analysis. The most straightforward is the question of 'who governs'? – the representation of different groups in the council chamber, in parliament and government. This has long been an issue of major concern to those concerned with equality agendas, who have repeatedly pointed to the under-representation of women and of black and ethnic minorities in government and local government. More recent concerns have been expressed about the constitution of the new quangocracy – the boards of public bodies that govern key institutions set up at arms length from the state itself, from school governing bodies to health trusts. While this chapter touches on such issues, they are not a major concern. I focus rather on key dimensions of emerging patterns of governance, especially those that characterise the policies and practices of the current Labour government in the UK. Labour's attempts to develop a more inclusive, participatory approach to state–society interactions and its increasing emphasis on networks and partnerships have major implications for the policies and practices of public service organisations. These developments are shaped within and articulated through Labour's attempt to remould the relationship between the state and 'civil society'. They require a rethinking of the way in which public sector organisations understand their contribution to the reproduction of, or challenge to, embedded patterns of inequality in the societies they serve. There is, in particular, a need to refocus attention beyond the boundaries of internal organisational structures and policies to embrace wider conceptions of the governance processes – the patterns of state–society interaction – which are mediated through the public sector itself.

Understanding governance

Rhodes claims that governance has become the 'defining narrative of British government at the start of the new century' (Rhodes 2000a: 6). Work within the UK political science tradition highlights issues such as the 'hollowing out' of the state (Rhodes 1994; Gamble 2000) or the 'decentring' of state power (Pierre and Peters 2000). It is argued that the capacity of governments to control events within the nation-state has been influenced by the flow of power away from government institutions, upwards to transnational bodies, downwards to regions and localities. The development of market mechanisms and contracting through the 1980s and 1990s broke up the old state bureaucracies, and there was a proliferation of quasi-state bodies (quangos) fulfilling many of the functions previously carried out by government. All of these shifts have created problems of coordination and control by the centre. The old mechanisms of control-through-hierarchy have, it is argued, been superseded, first, by the rise of markets and, second, by the increasing importance of networks as a mode of coordinating the public domain. (e.g. Rhodes 1997; 1999; 2000a; 2000b; Stoker 1999; 2000). Governments, it is argued, can no longer achieve their goals through traditional methods of control because of their dependence on a wide range of actors across the public, private and voluntary sectors. They are increasingly obliged to govern at a distance by influencing, persuading and providing incentives for action. At the same time they are developing stronger roles in building partnerships, steering and coordinating, and providing system-wide integration and regulation.

New patterns of governance have become more significant, not only because of the fragmentation of the public domain but also because of the growing complexity of social problems and the changing nature of civil society. Kooiman (1993), for example, views government as only one of many actors in a field in which other institutions have a great deal of autonomy. The role of government is to address the problems of guiding and influencing, rather than making, public policy. This produces patterns of state–society interaction based on 'co-' arrangements – collaboration, cooperation, co-steering, and co-governing. This form of analysis shifts the focus of attention beyond economic structures or processes towards a much broader concern with issues of citizenship, concepts of community, and social and cultural formations.

These different strands of theory provide insights into the style of governance developed by the 1997 Labour government in the UK. Its emphasis on 'joined up' or 'holistic' government and working in partnership reflects ideas of network-based governance and the development of partnerships across the public, private and voluntary sectors. Labour has also stressed the need for an inclusive policy process that can draw multiple actors into the development and delivery of policy. It has sought to involve citizens in co-governance arrangements, seeking, for example, to bring public bodies and communities together to develop solutions to the problems of social exclusion, neighbourhood renewal, crime and disorder, low educational attainment among some categories of young people, long-term unemployment and other problems. None of these developments was invented by Labour, but Labour has placed much more emphasis on the need to modernise government in order to address these so called 'wicked' issues. This term captures a range of problems that are complex, have multiple strands of causation and a number of possible forms of policy intervention. Each cuts across the main departmental 'silos' of government and involves interaction between different tiers of government (international, national, regional, local and community based). Labour has also sought to remake the relationship between state and civil society, seeking the active involvement of citizens in the rebuilding of 'community' and encouraging them to act as 'responsible' users of welfare services.

However, rather than suggesting a fundamental shift from old-style government to new forms of governance, Labour's policies and strategies suggest a complex interface between different forms and styles of governing. The strong centralised control exerted by Labour – over the Party as well as over public services – suggests a continuing theme of hierarchical governance. Labour is also a strongly managerial administration, emphasising the search for 'what works' and unrolling a range of 'modernising' policy reforms. In *Modernising Governance: New Labour, Policy and Society* (Newman 2001a) I set out a framework through which the interaction between multiple models of governance might be explored. This depicts four models of governance, representing different flows of power and authority, forms of relationship, and conceptions of social action (Figure 1.1). Each model is based on distinctive discourses, embodying specific forms of language, practice and relationship. Each is associated with particular logics of decision making, which guide and coordinate action, and with specific forms of authority and conceptions of responsibility and accountability. Each, as I argue below, raises distinctive questions about how notions of equality and diversity are to be understood, and presents particular challenges for the scope and focus of equality policy and practice.

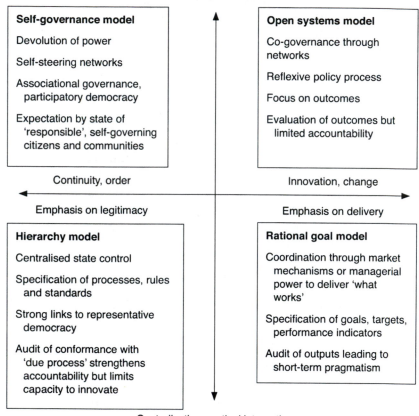

Figure 1.1 Models of governance.

Trajectories of change: bureaucracy and managerialism

This framework can help illuminate the forms in which notions of equality and diversity became institutionalised in the UK public sector. This section briefly discusses the discourses of equality that characterise 'hierarchical' and 'managerial' forms of governance.

Governance through hierarchy

The post-war welfare state was characterised by bureaucratic and hierarchical modes of governance: the bottom left-hand quadrant of my model. This was based on a liberal model of equality, strongly linked to notions of equality of citizenship and enshrined in the institutions of representative democracy. The 1960s and 1970s produced a host of procedural and legislative safeguards for the individual, and the model became institutionalised in a plethora of organisationally based policies, rules and guidelines. Its dominant discourse is that of equality of opportunity. The limitations of this model are well known: its refusal to deal with injustices experienced by groups rather than individuals, its incapacity to deal with issues of culture, and its ultimate failure to deliver substantial organisational or social change.

The debates and arguments around how to ensure equality within the constraints of the liberal model live on, not least in the institutions of representative democracy itself, as political parties argue about how to address the unequal representation of women and members of black and ethnic minority groups in parliament. As Phillips argues, 'Embodiment matters. By their presence in decision-making assemblies, members of a previously marginalised group can better guarantee that their interests and perspectives will be articulated' (Phillips 2000: 61). But the sites at which embodiment matters are proliferating as new forms of governance grow in importance. At the same time, patterns of economic and political change have resulted in a flow of power away from national political institutions. Women and other excluded groups, groups that have been knocking on the doors of parliament and other institutions for many years, may be gaining entry (however conditionally and temporarily) precisely at the point at which power is flowing away from those institutions themselves.

Managerial governance

During the 1980s and early 1990s, however, the development of 'new right' politics and the introduction of managerialism and markets into public services led to significant shifts in the discourses and practices of equal opportunities. One consequence of state and economic restructuring was the opening up of huge economic differentials between different social groups and the deepening of social divisions. A second was a demise of legitimacy for the notion of equality itself: public service organisations struggling to contain social problems, while undergoing profound transformation through the application of market mechanisms and radical downsizing, were little concerned about such 'old-fashioned' notions, which seemed to belong to a previous era. At the same time, however, rational management offered a new technology of equality strategies. Rather than policies and procedures, attention shifted to the potential of target setting, performance indicators and other tools to redress workforce imbalances. The discourses of culture change and of creating 'ownership' of equality policies seemed to offer the potential to deliver real change. As organisations adopted the language and practices of human resource management there was a new emphasis on maximising the capacity of all staff to contribute to organisational effectiveness, and good equality policies and practices began to be viewed by some as positive drivers of organisational performance and success.

These 'rational management' equality discourses remain dominant in the UK public sector. Indeed, they have become more significant as public service organisations such as the police have struggled to respond to charges of institutionalised racism, following *The Macpherson Report*, by setting goals and targets for the recruitment of under-represented groups. Such strategies are inevitably limited in their potential to deliver sustained change because the managerial ethos strips notions of equality away from their political roots. 'Race', gender and other issues may now be on the agenda of many organisations, especially in recruitment policies, but addressing deeply patriarchal and racist cultures is another matter. The intractability of organisational cultures leads to severe problems of retention for those groups newly recruited, especially those in which marginalised workers are not able to challenge the existing culture through collective forms of struggle and engagement. Equality in these circumstances remains an individualised concept, constrained by the consensual ethos of the new managerialism (Newman 1994; 1995).

I have done little more than briefly sketch some of the ways in which equality is understood and institutionalised in 'hierarchical' and 'managerial' forms of governance: the story of the 'long march' of equal opportunities in the post-war welfare state and under the new-right transformation of the public sector is relatively familiar (see, for example, Cockburn 1991). In what follows I want to spend rather more time on the questions raised by the proliferation of networks and partnerships and by the development of various forms of 'co-' or 'self-'governance arrangements. I do not wish to suggest that these are displacing the established forms of governance described above: these remain very much the focus of the continuing agenda of struggle and debate. However, I do want to shift the analysis beyond the confines of traditional equality agendas in order to illuminate some concerns flowing from emergent patterns of state–society interaction.

Open system governance: networks and partnership

The governance literature suggests a move away from coordination through hierarchy or competition and towards network-based forms of coordination. This theme is strongly represented in the current public policy system. A focus on networks and partnership forms a central element of the Third Way, which seeks to transcend old ideologically based preferences for delivering services through state bureaucracies, on the one hand, and competition, on the other. It underpins Labour's discourse of 'joined-up government' through which it has attempted to move towards a more holistic approach to public policy, an approach that transcends the vertical, departmental structures of government itself. Partnership also represents a powerful discourse of inclusion and collaboration that is central to Labour's attempt to forge a consensual style of politics. Such a discourse masks the patterns of inclusion and exclusion in network-based modes of governance. Who is invited into the new collaborative arrangements is not an issue that tends to be subject to scrutiny or to be judged against formal criteria of equality. It all depends on who you know and the powers of patronage and sponsorship. Access to the elusive centres of network-based decision making is not the only issue. The discourse of partnership speaks of equality, shared values and high trust, creating an illusory unity within partnerships that directs attention away from the political realities of divergent interests and conflicting goals. Naive or optimistic views of partnership focus on what the parties have in common and ignore power differences and inequalities.

This does not mean that groups are deliberately excluded: indeed many of the new forms of partnership and network-based decision-making structures are explicitly linked to questions of social inclusion and exclusion. For example Labour has sought to draw voluntary and community organisations into partnership with the public and private sectors to deliver social policy objectives on crime and disorder, social exclusion, neighbourhood renewal and so on. Not all of this activity can be characterised as an 'open system' approach: strong elements of centralisation and control cut across many of the new initiatives. But networks and partnerships do represent an attempt to deal with the complexity of many areas of public policy and the incapacity of hierarchical governing to deliver long-term, sustainable policy outcomes.

This form of governance does not, however, sit easily with traditional concepts of equality. When agencies engage in 'partnership' with community or voluntary organisations with radical agendas the result is often a profound clash of politics and culture. 'Presence' at the decision-making table is not enough: as Razzaque, a black woman involved in a regeneration partnership, expresses it in a tellingly titled paper, 'Men in suits make me fall silent' (Razzaque 2000). Issues of gender and race, then, are fundamental to the analysis of partnerships and network-based forms of decision making in a number of ways. First is the question of presence – the inclusion of women, of black and ethnic minorities and other social groupings, in the new partnership arrangements. Second is the question of power – the capacity of such groups to shape the agenda. It is evident that in many cases their presence is based on an attempt to enhance the legitimacy of the partnership to external funders or stakeholders. Such tokenism does little to build trust across lines of difference. Third is the possibility of incorporation. From the perspective of the voluntary and community sectors, involvement may represent 'dangerous liaisons', a term that Taylor and Craig (2002) use in relation to the involvement of voluntary and community groups in partnerships with statutory bodies. But such questions tend to be sidelined within the dominant discourse of equality and the consensual politics within which the new partnership arrangements are framed.

Self- and co-governance: the politics of 'citizenship' and 'community'

By no means can the politics of New Labour be conceptualised as one that fosters any substantial measure of self-governance in the sense of the delegation of real power to citizens and communities. Yet Labour has drawn extensively on communitarian philosophy in its approach to the renewal of civil society. Such a philosophy underpins the calls for responsible, active citizenship and for community-based responses to social problems. It is also represented in Blair's own discourse of 'the people', a people invoked repeatedly as a source of legitimation for political statements. 'The people', 'the community' and even 'citizenship' tend to be depicted as natural, unchanging and unproblematic representations and images. These suggest that to be a citizen is to belong to a nation-state, with the loyalties, expectations and responsibilities that go with it (but see Soysal 1994). They equate membership of a community with relationships of mutuality and reciprocity. They conceptualise 'the people' as a disembodied unity through which a multiplicity of views, interests and identities are channelled neatly into a homogenised whole

Yet the unifying imagery of the people, the immutable conception of citizenship and the nostalgic imagery of community are all deeply contested images. Each is imbued with deeply sedimented layers of meaning. Each is readily appropriated by left and right, radicals and conservatives, to suit their own purposes. Each concept is also deeply imbued with racialised and gendered meanings, though these are masked by the seeming neutrality and inclusiveness of the discourse. Notions of 'the people', 'community' and 'citizenship' are structured around particular (gendered) conceptions of the family and work and (racialised) conceptions of nation. Tensions around each of these conceptions repeatedly undermined the Labour government's attempt to remake a social settlement around the imagery of a modern society and modern citizenship.

This has important implications for the ways in which issues of equality and difference are understood by politicians and public service organisations seeking to devolve power to communities, to engage the public in decision making or to build the capacity of citizens to participate in a measure of self-governance. As well as challenging the consensual and homogeneous notions of the public, there is a need to recognise ways in which self-governance and the 'responsibilisation' of citizens may have profoundly gendered consequences. First, participation and self-governance raises questions about time as a dimension around which gender inequalities are structured. Second, such processes may shift the boundaries between what is constituted as the public sphere – areas that are the responsibility of the state and state agencies – and the private spheres of household and community.

How far might such issues be recognised in the politics and polices of New Labour? It is possible to trace twin strands running through its approach. The first is an acknowledgement of issues of diversity. Labour has undoubtedly been more attentive to notions of difference and diversity than Conservative governments had been. There is a greater degree of acknowledgement of changes in gender relations, of 'multiculturalism' and anti-racism, of sexuality, disability and other issues raised by the new social movements of the 1960s, 1970s and 1980s. The existence of ethnic minorities is acknowledged in the reforms of health and education services and in policies developed to tackle social exclusion. Labour has also given a public commitment to deal with issues of racism. For example, it has established a new category of racially aggravated crime, set targets for the recruitment of black and ethnic minority police officers, and introduced a Race Relations (Amendment) Act, which outlaws discrimination in public services and places a statutory duty on public bodies to promote race equality. It has adopted a positive public stance on disability, with the establishment of a Minister for the Disabled and the setting up of the Disability Rights Commission. It has also demonstrated a 'liberal' stance on homosexuality in its initial commitment to repeal Section 28 of the Local Government Act (banning the 'promotion' of homosexuality)[2] and to reduce the age of consent for gay relationships. It has celebrated the achievement of greater equality for women, represented in the sharp increase of women members of parliament (MPs) in the 1997 parliament.

The second strand of Labour's approach is, however, based not on overcoming inequality or celebrating diversity but on the attempted installation of a homogeneous, consensual representation of the people. This is based on an image of a modern society in which inequalities have largely been overcome (with residual categories dealt with through policies on social exclusion). It is a society in which the old divisions around class, 'race' and gender have been reconciled; in which old prejudices (for example, around disability or gay lifestyles) have been overcome; and which is characterised by mutual understanding and tolerance. The politics of dissent – of struggles around equal opportunities and social justice – have little place in the dominant discourses of responsible citizenship, self-reliant communities and a consensual nation.

Labour's difficulties in handling questions of difference and dissent derive in part from the way in which the Third Way was discursively constructed in opposition to the class politics of the 'old left'. In the process it also marginalised other forms of politics, which challenged the understandings of inequality and difference embedded in the social composition of the 'nation'. The strands of the left that articulated a politics of difference based on the 'new social movements' are present neither in the image of the 'old' that is being rejected nor in the formulation of the 'new' in the guise of the Third Way. The 'people' can include differences, as long as those differences do not make a difference.

Conclusion

Networks and partnerships, public participation and democratic renewal, are all symbols of the new governance. In themselves they appear to be neutral in terms of issues of diversity – indeed they represent a partial dissolution of the old hierarchies and power blocs, to which women and black and ethnic minorities have struggled to gain access, and suggest the possibility of greater openness and inclusion. But they require new forms of analysis. In the 1980s and early 1990s, work on equality in the public sector tended develop around two key forms of analysis. The first was the analysis of the intractability of organisational cultures and the problems of securing change (e.g. Itzin and Newman 1995). The second focused on the exacerbation of inequality through contracting out and privatisation, especially the worsening situation of low-paid women and members of black and ethnic minorities in the labour market. Both are still highly relevant. But this chapter has highlighted the need for analysis of the politics of inclusion and exclusion in the new forms of governance, and the politics of representation in the drive to open up decision making and stimulate democratic renewal.

A key issue is how far public sector bodies reproduce and sustain the dominant ideology of consensus that strips issues of diversity from any association with radical politics. Rustin (1999) notes the way in which Labour has selectively appropriated some of the ideas emerging from the new left. But the conflicts that produced these movements are now assumed to have been settled. The patterns of inclusion and exclusion in Labour's imagery of the modern people inscribe patterns of *political* inclusion and exclusion, through which alternative visions and forms of political agency may be demobilised and dismissed. Several commentators have highlighted the limitations of Labour's consensus-based, inclusive conception of modernity. Mouffe (1998) suggests that Labour's consensual imagery marks out an apolitical terrain, or a politics without antagonism. Lewis argues that, 'They [Labour] attempt to proceed as if all inequalities deriving from the constitution of differences around axes of "race"/ethnicity, gender, class, sexuality and disability are no longer sources of serious antagonism' (Lewis 2000: 268). Franklin, drawing on Beck (1997), argues that,

> New distinctions have been identified to supplant the politics of difference in late modern society: inclusion and exclusion, insider/outsider, conflict/ consensus, safe/unsafe, rights/responsibilities, order/disorder ... They draw a veil over old configurations that haven't necessarily disappeared and set alternative patterns for decision-making. The acceptable choice of consensus, responsibility and cohesion coincides with the communitarian approach, and leads to a framework that is not conducive to social change and can have a dulling effect on political agency.
>
> (Franklin 2000: 18)

Against this, however, must be set the possibility of social agency on the part of public service professionals within organisations and of citizens, users and communities. Much of Labour's agenda was developed from earlier initiatives and innovations within the public sector. The politics of change around issues of diversity will depend on the balance of forces between the dominant consensual ideology and pragmatic politics propounded by a government concerned with rebuilding civil society, on the one hand, and the possibilities of the enlargement of the space within which public service professionals and staff may engage with more radical agendas, on the other. The opening up of organisations to greater influence by users, citizens and communities – including community activists and politicised user groups – can be a major impetus for change. However, there is also a strong possibility of the incorporation of minority voices into the dominant consensual norms that are inscribed in the cultures and practices of the public sector.

Notes

1 This chapter develops work on governance under New Labour published as Newman (2001a).
2 The repeal of this clause of the 1988 Local Government Act was dropped in response to the potential defeat of the new Local Government Bill in the House of Lords. The clause was, however, repealed in Scotland.

References

Beck, U. (1997) *The Reinvention of Politics*, Cambridge: Polity Press.

Cabinet Office (1999) *Modernising Government* (cm 4310), London: The Stationery Office.

Clarke, J. and Newman, J. (1997) *The Managerial State: Power, Politics and Ideology in the Remaking of Social Welfare*, London: Sage.

Cockburn, C. (1991) *In the Way of Women: Men's Resistance to Sex Equality in Organisations*, London, Macmillan.

Franklin, J. (2000) 'After modernisation: Gender, the Third Way and the new politics', in Coote, A. (ed.), *New Gender Agenda*, London: Institute of Public Policy Research, pp. 15–22.

Gamble, A. (2000) 'Economic governance', in Pierre, J. (ed.), *Debating Governance: Authority, Steering and Democracy*, Oxford: Oxford University Press, pp. 110–37.

Hughes, G. and Lewis, G. (eds) (1998) *Unsettling Welfare: The Reconstruction of Social Policy*, London: Routledge.

Itzin, C. and Newman, J. (eds) (1995) *Gender, Culture and Organsiational Change: Putting Theory into Practice*, London: Routledge.

Kooiman, J. (1993) 'Governance and governability: Using complex dynamics and diversity', in Kooiman, J. (ed.), *Modern Governance*, London: Sage, pp. 35–50.

Lewis, G. (2000) 'Discursive histories, the pursuit of multiculturalism and social policy', in Lewis, G., Gewirtz, S. and Clarke, J. (eds), *Rethinking Social Policy*, London: Sage, pp. 259–75.

Lowndes, V. (2000) 'Women and social capital: A comment on Hall's "Social capital in Britain"', *British Journal of Political Science*, 30.

Mouffe, C. (1998) 'The radical Centre: A politics without adversity', *Soundings*, 9 (Summer): 11–23.

Newman, J. (1994) 'The limits of management: Gender and the politics of change', in Clarke, J., Cochrane, A. and McLaughlin, E. (eds), *Managing Social Policy*, London: Sage, pp. 182–209.

Newman, J. (1995) 'Gender and cultural change', in Itzin, C. and Newman, J. (eds), *Gender, Culture and Organizational Change: Putting Theory into Practice*, London: Routledge.

Newman, J. (2001a) *Modernising Governance: New Labour, Policy and Society*, London: Sage.

Newman, J. (2001b) 'Managerialism, modernisation and marginalisation: Equal opportunities and institutional change', in Breitenbach, E., Brown, A. and Mackay, F. (eds), *The Changing Politics of Gender Equality in Britain*, Basingstoke: Palgrave.

Phillips, A. (1995) *The Politics of Presence: The Political Representation of Gender, Ethnicity and Race*, Oxford: Oxford University Press.

Phillips, A. (2000) 'Representing difference: Why should it matter if women get elected?', in Coote, A. (ed.), *New Gender Agenda*, London: Institute for Public Policy Research, pp. 58–65.

Pierre, J. and Peters, B. G. (2000) *Governance, Politics and the State*, Basingstoke: Macmillan.

Razzaque, K. (2000) 'Men in suits make me fall silent: Black and minority ethnic women in urban regeneration', paper presented to the *7th International Conference on Multi-organisational Partnerships and Strategic Collaboration*, Leuven, Belgium, July 2000.

Rhodes, R. A. W. (1994) 'The hollowing out of the state', *Political Quarterly*, 65: 138–51.

Rhodes, R A. W. (1997) *Understanding Governance*, Buckingham: Open University Press.

Rhodes, R. A. W. (1999) 'Foreword: Governance and networks', in Stoker, G. (ed.), *The New Management of British Local Governance*, Basingstoke: Macmillan, pp. xii–xxvii.

Rhodes, R. A. W. (2000a) *The Governance Narrative: Key Findings and Lessons from the ESRC's Whitehall Programme*, London: Public Management and Policy Association.

Rhodes, R. A. W. (2000b) 'Governance and public administration', in Pierre, J. (ed.), *Debating Governance: Authority, Steering and Democracy*, Oxford: Oxford University Press.

Rustin, M. (1999) 'Editorial: A Third Way with teeth', *Soundings*, 11 (Spring): 7–21.

Runnymede Trust (2000) *Report on the Future of Multi-Ethnic Britain*, London: Profile Books.

Soysal, Y. N. (1994) *Limits of Citizenship: Migrants and Postnational Membership in Europe*, Chicago: University of Chicago Press.

Stoker, G. (1999) 'Introduction: The unintended costs and benefits of new management reform for British local government', in Stoker, G. (ed.), *The New Management of British Local Governance*, Basingstoke: Macmillan, pp. 1–21.

Stoker, G. (2000) 'Urban political science and the challenge of urban governance', in Pierre, J. (ed.), *Debating Governance: Authority, Steering and Democracy*, Oxford: Oxford University Press, pp. 91–109.

Taylor, M. and Craig, C. (2002) 'Dangerous liaisons: Local government and the voluntary and community sectors', in Glendinning, C., Powell, M. and Rummery, K. (eds), *Partnerships, New Labour and the Governance of Welfare*, Bristol: Policy Press, pp. 131–48.

2 Gendered states, critical engagements

Trudie Honour, Jim Barry and Sneha Palnitkar

Introductory comments: contexts and issues

This chapter considers the role of gender in urban governance and reports findings from a research investigation into the 30 per cent seat reservation or quota system for women politicians operating in India in the city of Mumbai (formerly known as Bombay). Some comparison with London, which also has around 30 per cent female local politicians, a figure high by international standards, is made through examination of previously published research. The context in which the research is taking place is important for a number of reasons. To begin with concerns have been expressed worldwide in recent years about establishing what has been called good governance in the face of pressure for market reforms and fears of corruption or clientelism. At the same time interest has grown in the role of gender and the under-representation of women in positions of responsibility and decision making, with calls for empowerment heard worldwide. The experience of the recently empowered women in Mumbai and the degree to which *critical acts* and a *critical mass* can make a difference to welfare and social policy is explored. It is contended that women in Mumbai, as in London, are generally held in high regard and are seen as highly competent and fair and flexible in their dealings with others, focusing their energies on the needs of the most disadvantaged and socially excluded in the community. The women in Mumbai are also far less involved in questionable practices than men. It is further argued that women's increasing presence is bringing enhanced levels of respectability to local governance.

In line with the work of authors such as Wilson (1977) and McIntosh (1978), who drew attention to the disadvantaged position of women in respect of social policy and welfare, a number of texts have turned their attention in recent years to the gendered character of the state and state provision (Johnson 1999: 43; Watson and Doyal 1999: 1). There has also been acknowledgement in the literature of a number of perspectives on gender (for example Williams 1989) and a recognition that inequality is manifested in and through the state in a multitude of ways (Pringle and Watson 1992). Yet despite differences of emphasis, underscored by approaches that favour varieties of postmodernism and raise problems over the essentialism of gender (Hallett 1996: 9–11; Lister

2000: 33), what runs through these texts is a question concerning the running and delivery of state services, should women be represented in greater numbers than traditionally has been the case. In short, would a *critical mass* of women make any difference to the state and to state provision?

Our intention here is not to invest the state, which comprises a complex mix of differing interests, with intention or unitary purpose. But neither is it to embrace the cultural turn and the notion of positioned subjectivity uncritically to the point at which the category 'woman' disappears from view (Alcoff 1988). For in underplaying gender categories, as false dichotomies that invite opposition and reinforce otherness, there is a danger that we lose sight of the relations of historically sustained disadvantage. Furthermore, as Pringle and Watson (1992: 54) observe, '[w]omen might well complain that just at the moment when they are achieving "identity" and articulating "interests", these fundamental categories are being rejected by a group of predominantly male theorists'.

Pringle and Watson's approach (1992: 70) is to conceptualise the state as a 'diverse set of arenas which play a crucial role in organizing relations of power' and which enable the continual (re)construction of a range of subjectivities. Insights of this kind, which in their work draws inspiration from the poststructuralism of Foucault, have much to commend them, enabling a focus on gender relations and the state. Historically located, the contested meaning and changing character of subjectivity thus becomes the site of analysis (Alcoff 1988: 434) as stereotypical representations of gender identity are reconfigured through the play of organisational relations. And it is this approach that we adopt here in order to see if the state and state provision really is any different when women are present in positions of responsibility and decision making in relatively large numbers.

To help us do this we report findings from a research project undertaken in India to examine the 30 per cent seat reservation or quota system, which has been operating for women politicians in Mumbai since 1992.[1] Comparison with London,[2] which also has around 30 per cent local politicians who are female, is possible through a consideration of research undertaken some years previously (Barry 1991). This enables an examination of the impact of a *critical mass* of women on local governance in both cities.

The notion of a critical mass as related to women in politics was developed in the work of Dahlerup (1988), although it was Kanter (1977: 207–9) who discussed the significance of the number of group members necessary to 'transform social interaction' and provided the groundwork for later research, even if she did not use the term herself. Drawing on the earlier work of Simmel, Kanter (1977: 207–9) identified four types of group: first, 'uniform', which had only 'one kind of person'; second, 'skewed', which comprised dominants and tokens with 'a ratio of perhaps 85:15'; third, 'tilted … perhaps 65:35', which represented a majority and a minority; and fourth, 'balanced … at about 60: 40 and down to 50:50'.

Dahlerup (1988: 275 and 280) drew on this typology in developing the notion of the critical mass, a concept 'borrowed from nuclear physics, where it refers to the quantity needed to start a chain reaction ...'. In using the concept to examine the impact of female politicians in Scandinavia, she estimated that the figure for the minority in the tilted group (the critical mass), based on Kanter's own figures, ranged 'from 15 to about 40'. Concerned at Kanter's conclusion that the minority position of women was little different to that of other minority groups, and anxious to keep in view women's subordinate status outside organisations that had an impact on their situation within, she distinguished between the concepts *critical mass* and *critical act*.

This is important because Dahlerup (1988: 296–7) considered that the notion of a *critical act* was 'better suited to the study of human behaviour ... [than *critical mass* since it] is one which will change the position of the minority considerably and lead to further changes'. Examples of critical acts included the recruitment of women by other women and the introduction of quotas, legislation and institutions, as well as female role models in high-profile positions. These, she suggested (ibid.: 287), were more likely to lead to change rather than 'any fixed number of women'. In this chapter we accept Dahlerup's distinction and acknowledge that critical acts – including the use of quotas, in the case of Mumbai, and social movement activity, in both Mumbai and London, as we shall argue – have been significant in helping to bring about increased levels of female representation and awareness of gender inequality. However, we will contend that critical acts, such as Mumbai's quota, are insufficient alone to sustain change because of their fragile and tenuous character. Enduring change, we will argue, based on our research in Mumbai and London, requires the *established presence* of a critical mass (see Hainard and Verschuur 2001: 40).

In considering countries such as India and England, where Mumbai and London respectively are located, we acknowledge cultural similarities as well as differences, although we are also aware that the relationship of colonialism has made it difficult for those both inside and outside India to think beyond categories of Orientalism with images of colonial 'rule' lingering on in historical memory (Ware 1992: 230). The legacy, which derives largely from divide-and-rule policies on the part of the ruling power, has left polarity and opposition, by classification of Indian identity through official record – that between Hindu and Muslim being perhaps the most well known (Ludden 1993; see also Breckenridge and van der Veer 1993: 11). At the same time, however, a shared appreciation of public service and local governance has endured long after India's independence (Kaushik 1993a: 19; Sheth 1995). Yet in the present post-colonial context, as India faces the many challenges bestowed by the legacy of what Nehru called its *tryst with destiny* – and others might see as a *post-colonial predicament* bestowed by imperialism – pressures for change in India, as in England, are considerable.

The wider context in which the research is taking place is important in this respect. To begin with, there have been international concerns voiced in recent years to establish what has been called good governance (Hainard and

Verschuur 2001: 50) and fears expressed in India and England that corruption or clientelism threatens its attainment and sustainability (Pratchett and Wingfield 1996; Khilnani 1997). These have been accompanied by efforts to promote market reforms (Seabrook 1997; see also Fukuyama 1989). At the same time interest has grown in the role of gender and worries have been expressed about the under-representation of women in positions of responsibility and decision making, with calls for empowerment heard worldwide (for example in the *Beijing Declaration and Platform for Action* (1995); see also Pietila and Vickers 1994; Ashworth 1995).[3]

It is in this context that recent interest in local governance in India and England becomes significant, linking to growing international awareness about the rights of women more generally. Current research certainly suggests that women have different concerns relative to men, not least in respect of urban issues (Hainard and Vershuur 2001: 35). It also appears that the role of women's movements, operating locally in civil society through autonomous women's groups and networks *and* the local state (Coote and Campbell 1987; Kumari 1993; Singh *et al.* 1993;), have become *translocal* (Sheth 1995) as public debate links awareness of gender inequality and disadvantage across time and space, redrawing the paramaters of local democracy and questioning the significance of organisational boundaries.

These factors bear directly on the research reported here, with the evidence suggesting that women's movement activity has played no small part in the increased presence *and* impact of women in local politics in Mumbai and London, and with activists in both countries taking the decision to engage directly with the local state, after much debate and soul searching, to see what difference they might make as elected representatives.

The chapter begins by outlining the background of the local politicians in both cities before moving on to an examination of the obstacles and facilitators encountered en route to election. We then consider the experiences of office as the women concerned move from political mobilisation to engendering change through the policy process – from *critical acts* to *critical mass*.

Critical acts: political mobilisation

Female representation in Mumbai and London reached a *critical mass* of around 30 per cent in the 1990s. In Mumbai this came about with a quota system at the 1992 elections, which raised the percentage of women corporators[4] dramatically to 34 per cent (their numbers rose from five to seventy-five, out of a total of 221 (Singh *et al.* 1993: 93). In London the growth of female councillors had evolved more slowly, reaching 27 per cent by 1994 (518 out of 1,914), figures high by international standards (UNDP 1995: 60–2).

The research project with which the authors are currently concerned, which has involved an examination of the implications of these changes in representation, has been in operation for a number of years, beginning in the mid-1980s in London before moving to Mumbai in the early 1990s. In both cities discussions with female and male politicians as well as administrators and managers preceded a questionnaire survey of all women politicians and a random sample of men, followed by an in-depth interviewing programme with over forty politicians. This formed the basis of the empirical work,[5] which revealed a number of parallels in terms of the socioeconomic profile of the two female samples.

To begin with the women were generally well educated in terms of formal qualifications relative to their constituents. In London, for example, over half of the Labour women councillors held a degree or higher, although it should be noted that some of the Mumbai women had no formal qualifications and were illiterate. The majority of the women had either been born in their respective cities or been resident there for many years, and although two-thirds of the women in London were married, it was the norm for their counterparts in Mumbai. In addition, their relatively affluent backgrounds – at least compared with the communities they sought to serve – appeared to be quite marked, something borne out in the subsequent interviewing sessions, the caveat concerning illiterate women in Mumbai notwithstanding.

Another notable similarity in the findings was that the female local authority representatives had generally been asked to stand for office. Not too surprising perhaps in the case of Mumbai, following the introduction of a quota, but true also in London,[6] with women more likely to be approached when children or dependents for whom they were seen as responsible were less in need of care. In both cities this meant that the women participated in local politics at a later stage than their male counterparts. This issue of selection is important because it indicates that there is likely to have been less time available for the women to become 'socialised' or 'sponsored' into the 'private club' of institutional party politics, thereby suggesting a later and potentially weaker assimilation of the associated customs (see Turner 1960), leaving in turn, perhaps, 'space' for the assimilation of other values deriving from the varying life experiences of the women concerned. In this respect, the active involvement of many of the women in both cities, prior to standing for office in autonomous women's groups, women's organisations and campaigns over what were seen as women's issues, is significant and may have something to do with the many expressions of support for their respective women's movements recorded in the survey.

The national and international exchange of people and ideas and the growth of supportive and information-sharing networks to raise awareness about women's continuing disadvantaged position worldwide should not be overlooked in all this. Even where women are not 'active' in women's groups they may, nonetheless, draw on the heightened awareness of gender identity that ensues, especially where discussion is amplified through the media (Crook *et al.* 1992: 130). In this respect it is worth noting that Western 'feminist' texts have circulated in India (Honour *et al.* 1998: 190) – relative poverty being no barrier to the lending and reading of books – and that Indian texts on women and politics have been available in England. This is not to suggest that India and England have experienced the development of what might be termed identical women's movements or feminisms, nor that each is a homogeneous entity. Clearly there have been differences within movements, as social and political movements for change (Melucci 1989; see also Pakulski 1991),[7] leading some scholars to point to disarray and to talk of post-feminism and others to question the usefulness of the 'Western' terms 'women's movement' and 'feminism' for countries such as India (Kishwar 1990).

Yet some parallel developments can be discerned from a reading of the literature in respect of the two countries concerned. In England, through individual and collective action in civil society from the 1960s onwards, a second- or third-wave movement (Dahlerup 1986; Rossi 1973) emerged drawing on then recent US feminist discourse, refracted through a socialist and Marxist cultural prism. The growth of autonomous women's groups followed, with the 1970s seeing the development of a number of feminist perspectives and the 'Seven Demands of the Women's Liberation Movement' (Feminist Anthology Collective 1981: 4), not least through a series of conferences, which articulated concerns about economic and workplace issues, male domination, violence and sexuality. In India, particularly from the 1970s onwards, according to some of our research contacts, agitation in civil society also saw the development of a number of autonomous women's groups, some reflecting left-wing origins, which struggled to raise awareness over inequalities affecting women. In this respect, our interviewees indicated concerns about alcoholism, drugs, family violence, rape and the need for communal empowerment and education. At a rally held at Pune on 28 November 1990, which was attended by over 3,000 women from across Maharashtra, the state in which Mumbai is to be found, the Stree Mukti Andolan Sampark Samiti organised a demonstration with a number of other groups and drew up a manifesto, which included such demands as the right to employment, equal wages, joint ownership of family property and the recognition of domestic work as productive (Lele *et al.* 1993: 161–2).

The parallels are thus quite striking, despite considerable cultural difference between the two countries (see Ware 1992; Devendra 1994).[8] This is no more so than at the present time, when the theoretical challenge of deconstruction and acknowledgement of differences between women (Alcoff 1988) are met with calls for an appreciation of strength through diversity as evidence of dynamic and vibrant women's movement activity. This applies both in India (Desai 1997) and in the West more generally (De Lauretis 1990), where some commentators have referred to what they have seen as the 'illusions of post-feminism' (Coppock *et al.* 1995).

To suggest a causal link between movement activity and the relatively high representation of women in local politics, as they move from informal 'shapers' of welfare provision to 'power' holders (Lister 2000: 30), may seem problematic. Yet there is evidence, not just from our interviews but also from published literature, that considerable discussion and debate took place in a number of women's groups concerning engagement with establishment institutions such as the state, in India (Kumari 1993: 6; Singh *et al.* 1993:

100) as well as in England (Coote and Campbell 1987: 287; and Brueghal and Kean 1995: 150[9]), with Basu (1995: 15) noting similar processes occurring in countries elsewhere in the world. Concerns about tokenism and incorporation were expressed alongside worries that well-educated, privileged women, who were benefiting from processes of modernisation around the world (d'Lima 1984: 22–3), might not address the needs of the more disadvantaged members of society once in office – reminiscent of Michels' (1968) conclusions on the iron law of oligarchy drawn many years previously (in 1911).[10] The decision to enter the bastions of elite male privilege and attempt to make an impact on policy was, nonetheless, taken by a number of groups, their activities and networking helping to raise awareness and pave the way. The literature thus provides examples of *critical acts*, in Dahlerup's terminology (as we have seen), which question the state–civil society distinction.

There was, even so, no easy route to office for the women concerned, who encountered many obstacles along the way, suggesting that their increased presence was not achieved easily, as local government, most notably perhaps in Britain (Davies 1988), came under attack from national politicians. The numbers of female representatives in both cities certainly grew, but there was no untroubled passage to political incumbency. In this respect certain factors stood out as barriers whilst others acted as facilitators.

With respect to obstacles, the women in both cities were less likely to stand for office – or be asked to stand – when responsible for children under 5 years of age or other dependents.[11] They also reported difficulties with unhelpful men in their respective political parties, even though in the case of Mumbai the introduction of the quota required female candidates to stand in reserved wards. It was also the case that, initially at least, the women reported some lack of confidence, especially as politics was seen as an unpleasant business, even at the best of times. In Mumbai the women viewed the 'politicking, dirty manoeuvring, manipulation and squabbling' (Kumari 1993: 3–4) with some distaste, while in London many of the female representatives took an early decision not to get too involved with the in-fighting and left the men to what they saw as their spats and petty intrigues. Once they gained experience of office, however, the style of politics was not deemed a problem, as the women politicians in both cities pressed on with the job at hand.

By contrast three facilitators stood out as significant. To begin with, women in Mumbai and London received encouragement and support from their families. Although this may have been forthcoming from some male partners, concerned to keep a vicarious grip on power, our respondents indicated cases of what they believed were genuine support. In addition, and certainly in London, female role models, either mothers or other female family members who had been involved in politics, played a part. Before jumping to the conclusion that the relative dearth of such role models in Mumbai offers no parallel, however, a cautionary note in respect of the term 'politics' may be in order. This relates to the third facilitator, the involvement of the female representatives in autonomous women's groups and networks, and campaigns that were identified with so-called women's issues prior to standing for office. This was reported by the majority of the women in both cities, indicating involvement in their respective women's movements. On this count, their connection with others in social and 'political' movements for change acted as significant facilitators in mobilisation. *Critical acts* thus made political office a reality for a relatively large number of women in Mumbai and London. But what impact have they made as a *critical mass* in these gendered states?

Critical mass: policy and process

All new incumbents face difficulties when assuming political office. It invariably takes time to learn the ropes and become 'effective'. Initial lack of experience of dealing with administrative rules and procedures, administrators themselves and other politicians can even leave them vulnerable. Because of this, political parties offer induction and initial training in the ways of local authority work, although most of our interviewees said that they preferred to learn from direct involvement with the duties of office. Accordingly there were relatively few politicians we interviewed who had availed themselves of the services on offer.

Even so, it is perhaps no surprise to learn that whereas the female politicians felt that they had achieved some of their objectives, they had experienced problems in realising their aspirations in full. In Mumbai the female corporators reported difficulty in achieving cleanliness of the environment and community participation. They also expressed frustration at their inability to influence the circumstances of low-income groups and to generate employment. In London the women councillors referred to the difficulties not just of achieving change, to benefit the community and advance issues that affected women, but also of maintaining momentum and sustaining the changes that they *had* made. They cited examples in which women's committees had come under hostile review and either been merged with committees dealing generally with equal opportunities or been scrapped altogether, thereby placing strains on the link between local state and autonomous women's groups.

There were, nonetheless, a number of instances cited in both cities in which the female politicians felt that they had been achieving their aims. In Mumbai the women reported success in their ability to redress grievances and to influence service delivery of urban amenities. They had also developed a number of public health campaigns, which had resulted in particular benefits to sex workers. Above all, perhaps, they felt that they had been able to voice their concerns, raise issues and initiate change for the benefit of others by arranging for work to be carried out through corporation officials. They also felt that their purview had not been restricted to dealing with 'women's issues' at municipal level, which a number of them associated with children and health. In London the women indicated that they had experienced some success in establishing equal opportunity policies despite some opposition. They had also been able to go beyond what might be conceived as 'women's issues'. Topics that had been addressed included: social services; education; housing; transport; health and safety on streets and underground walkways through improved lighting; laundries; violence against women; provision of toilets and nappy-changing facilities in town centres; the youth service; entry phones on housing estates, planning; and women's centres. This is, as one female councillor put it, '[a]n incredible number of issues'.

There are thus similarities, as well as differences, between female politicians in the cities of Mumbai and London in respect of the achievement and frustration of policy objectives. The contrasts seem to reflect the differing priorities that clamour for attention in countries at varying stages of 'development'. Yet there are also some interesting comparisons that appear to reflect issues of gender. In particular, the women in both cities have focused their attention on what seem to be the most vulnerable and disadvantaged groups in their communities, which include women, but have moved beyond what might be referred to as 'women's issues' in order to do so. In this it would appear that the women have made a contribution to local governance, that they have made a difference, relative to men. But both samples reported difficulties in realising their aspirations, a number of which were related to the men they worked alongside – not in the bureaucracy but in their respective political parties, a point we will return to presently.

The ways in which the women enacted the duties of office in order to achieve their objectives differed in a number of respects from those of the men in both Mumbai and London. To begin with, the female politicians operated in ways that sought to balance home responsibilities and official duties whereas the men dealt with each sequentially, allocating time to home, paid employment and politics in turn. One male politician put it this way, 'I get furiously involved (it's a gut reaction) in politics for a few days, then the family, then I pick up my politics again.' (male councillor, London).

The reasons for this seemed to be related to the differing life experiences of the women and men involved. The women were deemed to be responsible, ultimately at least, for domestic matters and maintained a balance between their public and private lives. In instances, for example, in which children were taken ill at school it was invariably the mother who was expected to take charge. This also worked in reverse, with cases cited in which women undertook official duties in the evening and had to find child care to 'help them out'. In India the extended family can play an important role in all this, often providing the ready services of a mother-in-law who shares the family home. In one instance in London we came across the case of a husband assuming full responsibility for child care, although this was not common. The prevailing situation was summed up by a female councillor, who commented that her husband would help out, 'providing nobody knew he was doing it, he's got a very chauvinistic attitude though he's very good around the house; but he wouldn't like anyone to know that' (female councillor, London).

The linking of public and private has long been a gender issue, not least for radical feminists (Redstockings 1969)[12] and those concerned with social policy and welfare, and our findings confirm the salience of this. The men in both cities prioritised their responsibilities in ways that seemed abstracted from the narrative of daily experience, whereas the women balanced and juggled theirs in order to meet varying human needs and demands. On the face of it this would seem to confirm the conclusions reached by Gilligan (1982), who argued that in terms of moral development boys developed a logic of justice and girls an ethic of care. It is this kind of reasoning that lies behind recent thinking on leadership, with men seen as favouring transactional styles and characterised as tough and aggressive in contrast to women, who are considered caring and nurturing (Rosener 1990). Whereas this seems somewhat at odds with the recent work of Wajcman (1998), who points to organisational pressures and demands as shaping behaviour, such stereotypes linger on in the literature, as well as in the minds of our interviewees – to some degree at least. The role of context in all this, in helping to shape expectation and stereotypical understanding, appears to be significant.

In our study, for example, instances were recounted by officers and politicians in which women were seen as more approachable than men. In London a number of respondents referred to the positive role played by women's units in this respect, with one female councillor indicating that constituents often preferred women housing officers who were thought more likely to be understanding when it came to housing problems. The belief that women were more approachable than men seemed to be common in both cities. One female councillor in London commented, 'I find a lot of women, particularly older women, will come to see me *because* I am a woman ... my constituents say, "we feel we can talk to you *because* you are a woman"'. While a female administrator in Mumbai put it this way '[women] understand the problems of their subordinates ... they can understand their problems better than a male colleague ... [with housing] transfers for example, for residents, because I have small children ... the [men], will not understand the problems'. Yet although the interviewing programme tended to confirm that men's managerial styles were transactional – with some few exceptions – the women were not characterised *simply* as caring or nurturing. This is captured in the contrasting comments from two of our interviewees in Mumbai, '[men] follow ... the rules and ... [are] ... aggressive' (female corporator), whereas, 'all politicians are rogues. We play cricket, they do not, they play rugby ... [though of course] ... women managers can all play rugby' (male administrator).

Although the second quote conveys the lingering image of an elitist, Oxbridge-dominated, *British* civil service, 'unfailingly polite' and inclined to scatter its prose 'with cricketing terms' (Ponting 1986: 92), there was an overwhelming sense that women politicians and administrators were seen as both caring *and* tough in their dealings with others. They were seen as sympathetic if a constituent or subordinate needed help and resolute and uncompromising when confronted with what were perceived to be unreasonable demands. This had earned the women considerable respect from all quarters. Their ability to work with others extended to making deals, crossing over the party line if necessary, to achieve their aims. This was recognised by female and male politicians alike, as two London interviewees explained when referring to the Tory, or Conservative, and Labour parties, two of the main protagonists in London's local government.[13] The first commented, 'The women on the Tory side could do deals with ... women [from another party]' (male councillor, London). The second, 'we sometimes worked successfully with Tory women (not Tory men) – we could sometimes talk them round' (female councillor, London).

Female politicians also reported that they worked well with officials. The women corporators in Mumbai indicated that on one occasion they had received support from male administrators, who had provided secretarial assistance to help with the drafting of committee documents. To women who were illiterate or inexperienced in the ways of office, this was considered invaluable and, even though it was not seen as a long-term solution, it was nonetheless appreciated. Male officials had also banned the husbands of elected representatives from entering the Municipal Chamber, because they had been observed following their female partners inside to offer 'guidance' when it came to a vote.

This kind of behaviour was not seen as forthcoming from male politicians, however. In London some Conservative male councillors had put their female party colleagues 'in their place', when they thought that they had overstepped the party line during their time on a women's committee. In other cases male politicians generally had acted as if equality of opportunity existed when it had not. In Mumbai we uncovered one instance in which a male corporator, acting as mentor, had proffered misleading advice to a new female politician in order to undermine her credibility. The reason for actions such as these is unclear, although we may speculate that it resides in the men's fear of the women's potential – in line with Faludi's (1992) analysis of the 'backlash'. It certainly appeared that the men had reason to be fearful for their long-term positions given the respect that the women were busy earning. Another factor that emerged from the research, in Mumbai at least, was corruption or clientelism, something about which our interviewees were greatly concerned.

When considering the impact that female representatives might be having on local state governance our interviewees argued that the women were less inclined to engage in corrupt or questionable behaviour than the men. It transpired that a number of male corporators were thought to have entered politics to further their commercial or business interests, when tendering for contracts for example. Women's prior links with civil society, however, were seen as located in networks of female friends and women's groups and the women were thought less likely to be vulnerable to forms of corruption as a result. When first elected, we were told, women lived up to expectation. With the passage of time, however, it seemed that this was beginning to change as stories of women's involvement in corrupt or clientalist practices began to permeate the media. It appeared that the sums of money involved were considered small and related to the needs of the family. And a number of our female interviewees were suspicious of male journalists who were broadcasting the stories. There was, nonetheless, widespread concern as reports emerged of women seen to be driving around in expensive cars and making ostentatious use of mobile telephones. This may be a telling sign, but it remains unclear how far the women will become enmeshed in questionable practices over time as their experience of office grows.

Concluding thoughts

What then can we conclude from the limited research into the two gendered states considered here in which, as a result of *critical acts*, women are represented in relatively large numbers as a *critical mass*? Have they initiated an irreversible chain reaction or have their efforts fizzled out like a damp squib?

The role of critical acts, in respect of social movement activity in both India and England and quotas in India, has been important. These acts have proved to be significant and even necessary in facilitating the establishment of a critical mass, albeit in different contexts. In both countries, however, the use of the quota has proved controversial.

In England quotas have been declared illegal, a situation that looks unlikely to change unless the relevant tribunal ruling is successfully challenged.[14] In India quotas for different groups of people such as scheduled castes and tribes have also had their critics, with conflict and violence in evidence in the past (Kumari 1992; Kaushik 1993b: 51; Maiello 1996: 106–7). Yet a quota for female politicians has been established, despite a stormy passage. Nonetheless, opposition to the extension of the quota for women in the Lower House of Parliament, the Lok Sabha, may be an ominous sign. It is also worth noting that the quota in Mumbai operates on a rotation basis for reserved wards and that in time it will have run its course leaving the field open to all aspiring politicians, female and male alike. Even so the implications of the research into the *critical mass* of female politicians are a little clearer.

At the very least it would seem that the women have made a not insig-nificant contribution to local governance in Mumbai and London. Despite working in different cultural milieux, they have sought to focus on their most disadvantaged constituents through policies – in Mumbai, for example, designed to improve public health and the position of low-income groups – that are considered sensitive to human need. They have operated in ways that can be characterised as both tender *and* tough, calling into question the stereotypical wisdom on gendered styles of leadership and management. And they have succeeded, according to respondents, in earning trust and respect from all concerned, gaining enhanced social standing in the process (Hainard and Vershuur 2001: 49). They have thus had an impact on state and state provision in these two cities.

The future for these gendered states is nonetheless uncertain, particularly at a time when both societies face pressures for change in an international milieu perhaps best described as volatile. Pressures for market reforms and concerns about national identity exist in a global context in which nuclear threats remain a reality, not least in current-day India, alongside a questioning of the verities of political certainties and institutions including the North Atlantic Treaty Organization (NATO), something that affects England very directly at the current time. And in both countries the issue of corruption or clientelism is presently contentious. Such issues seem likely only to exacerbate existing tensions in South Asia and Europe. Whether steps will be taken to sustain relatively large numbers of women in positions of responsibility and decision making in such a context, in which those in elite positions ostensibly concerned about this seem preoccupied with other pressing matters, remains uncertain. But, if the policy objective is to continue to focus on the socially excluded and enhance the respectability of local governance, then a significant female presence is likely to be of considerable importance in the years ahead.

Acknowledgements

The authors would like to record their thanks to Elisabeth Berg of Luleå University and Heather Clark and John Chandler of the University of East London's Organisation Studies Research Group for critical and helpful comments on an earlier draft of this paper. Thanks also to participants in the Third International Research Conference, *Dilemmas for Public Sector Professionals, Managers and Users in the Millennium*, held at the University of Staffordshire, England, 5–7 May 1999, at which the paper was presented. Any errors remain the responsibility of the authors.

Notes

1   The Mega-Cities Project is a worldwide network of action researchers investigating social change and transferable innovation. The team received support and funding from the University of East London and the British Deputy High Commission, British Council Division, Mumbai. The notion of 'governance' is not discussed here. The interested reader is referred to Chapter 1 of this volume.
2   This is despite the absence of a quota and a present array of policy making bodies (Arbrar *et al.* 1998), which includes the recently established Greater London Authority (GLA). The Greater London Authority was established as London's regional body after the research reported here was conducted. It is therefore not considered in the discussion, although interested readers may wish to consult the GLA's website, which towards the end of 2000 revealed five women out of fourteen constituency members (36 per cent) and six women out of eleven London list members (55 per cent). In other words, there was 46 per cent female representation (wysiwyg: //6/http//www.london.gov.uk/assembly/london_assembly_members.htm).
3   The United Nations (UN) website for those interested in checking the follow-up on the Beijing Declaration is www.undp.org/gender/beijing/5.
4   The political representative in Mumbai is known as a corporator, with the equivalent in London referred to as a councillor.
5   Our methodology has followed to some degree the approach of new or neo-institutionalism (Powell and DiMaggio 1991) in acknowledging and privileging our respondents' accounts in the creation of their symbolic and social worlds.

6   It is worth noting that in London this was also the case for men.

7   There are presently two dominant schools of social movement theory, which have developed in recent years, leaving aside neo or post-Marxism (Laclau 1990) and postmaterialism (Inglehart and Rabier 1986). One is known as the resource mobilization approach, and originates in the United States (see Tilly 1985; Zald and McCarthy 1987); the other is the identity-oriented approach, which derives from the research of European scholars (Touraine 1985; and Melucci 1989). The former focuses on visible aspects of mobilisation including resources, movement leaders and routinised organisational activity, whereas the latter concerns itself with less tangible elements.

8   This is not to suggest that the movement in England, or more widely in Britain, triggered or somehow initiated developments in India. We are certainly mindful of Devendra's (1994: 154) cautionary comments concerning the colonial relationship and note Ware's (1992) perceptive analysis in this respect. What we are arguing is that there is an international exchange of people and ideas and that influence can operate in a number of different – even sometimes contradictory – ways. In the present case we are simply noting some of the parallel developments that have been recounted to us through our research investigation and which can be found in published literature.

9   Bruegel and Keane (1995: 147–8) use the term 'municipal feminism', which they see as having roots in the socialism of the early part of the twentieth century and the women's movement of the 1970s. This enables them to consider 'the links – and differences – between municipal socialism and municipal feminism'.

10   Michels (1968) argued that oligarchy, or the rule of the few, was an inevitable development in organisational life, an 'iron law'. The interested reader is referred to Barry (1992: 26–30).

11   This was also the case in Maharashtra, prior to the reservation system. d'Lima (1984: 23–5) notes that where women did enter politics it was often at the behest of husbands anxious to maintain their vicarious hold on power as it shifted from 'caste and land holdings ... [to] ... the political machinery of the government'.

12   The Redstockings Manifesto (1969) is perhaps best characterised as the bedrock for a radical feminist perspective. It enumerates three major principles: that women suffer oppression as a class; that the personal is political; and that women should always stand with women against their male oppressors (the pro-woman line). The insight that the personal is political is not, however, confined to radical feminism. It can be found, from those more sympathic to varieties of liberal, socialist and Marxist feminism, in claims for crèches and the collective provision of child care.

13   This is not to play down the role of the Liberal Democrats, who put considerable efforts into local government in England– according not just to Liberal Democrat interviewees, but Labour and Conservative too.

14   The quota has been used in a number of countries including Germany and The Netherlands (Lovenduski and Norris 1993: 11; Haug 1995; see also Lunneborg 1990). In England it was initiated in 1989 by the Labour Party and used for 'all-women shortlists in half the marginal and vacant seats ... in 1993' (Squires 1996: 73), before it became elected to government in May 1997. The quota was declared illegal in January 1997. Milne (1997: 17) suggests that '[h]alf the new Labour women were chosen from all-women shortlists'.

References

Alcoff, L. (1988) 'Cultural feminism versus post-structuralism: "The identity crisis in feminist theory"', *Signs*, 13 (3): 405–36.

Arbrar, S., Lovenduski, J. and Margetts, H. (1998) 'Sexing London: The gender mix of urban policy actors', *International Political Science Review*, 19 (2): 147–71.

Ashworth, G. (ed.) (1995) *A Diplomacy of the Oppressed: New Directions in International Feminism*, London: Zed Books.

Barry, J. (1991) *The Women's Movement and Local Politics*, Aldershot: Gower, Avebury.

Barry, J. (1992) *Movement and Silence: Critical Reflections on Theories of the New Social Movements*, University of East London Occasional Papers on Business, Economy and Society, Paper No. 9, University of East London, London.

Basu, A. (ed.) (1995) *The Challenge of Local Feminisms: Women's Movements in Global Perspective*, Boulder, CO: Westview Press.

Beijing Declaration and Platform for Action (1995) see www.undp.org/gender/beijing/5.

Breckenridge, C. A. and van der Veer, P. (eds) (1993) *Orientalism and the Post-colonial Predicament*, Philadelphia: University of Pennsylvania Press.

Brueghal, I. and Kean, H. (1995) 'The moment of municipal feminism: Gender and class in 1980s local government', *Critical Social Policy*, 44/45: 147–69.

Coote, A. and Campbell, B. (1987) *Sweet Freedom*, Oxford: Blackwell.

Coppock, V., Haydon, D. and Richter, I. (1995) *The Illusions of 'Post-feminism': New Women, Old Myths*, London: Taylor & Francis.

Crook, S., Pakulski, J. and Waters, M. (1992) *Postmodernization: Change in Advanced Society*, London: Sage.

Dahlerup, D. (ed.) (1986) *The New Women's Movement*, London: Sage.

Dahlerup, D. (1988) 'From a Small to a Large Minority: Women in Scandinavian Politics'. *Scandinavian Political Studies* 11, 4: 275–298.

Davies, H. J. (1988) 'Local government under siege', *Public Administration*, 66 (1): 91–101.

De Lauretis, T. (1990) 'Upping the anti [*sic*] in feminist theory', in Hirsch, M. and Fox Keller, E. (eds), *Conflicts in Feminism*, London: Routledge, pp. 255–70.

Desai, M. (1997) 'Reflections from contemporary women's movements in India', in Dean, J. (ed.), *Feminism and the New Democracy*, London: Sage, pp. 110–23.

Devendra, K. (1994) *Changing Status of Women in India*, 3rd edn, New Delhi: Vikas Publishing.

Faludi, S. (1992) *Backlash: The Undeclared War Against Women*, London: Chatto and Windus.

Feminist Anthology Collective (1981) *No Turning Back: Writings from the Women's Liberation Movement 1975–1980*, London: The Women's Press.

Fukuyama, F. (1989) 'The end of history?', in Ball, T. and Dagger, R. (eds), *Ideals and Ideologies: A Reader*, New York: HarperCollins, pp. 432–41.

Gilligan, C. (1982) *In a Different Voice: Psychological Theory and Women's Development*, Cambridge, MA: Harvard University Press.

Hainard, F. and Verschuur, C. (2001) 'Filling the urban policy breach: Women's empowerment, grass-roots organizations, and urban governance', *International Political Science Review*, 22 (1): 33–53.

Hallett, C. (ed.) (1996) *Women and Social Policy*, Hemel Hempstead: Harvester Wheatsheaf.

Haug, F. (1995) 'The quota demand and feminist politics', *New Left Review*, 209: 136–45.

Honour, T., Barry, J. and Palnitkar, P. (1998) 'Gender and public service: A case study of Mumbai', *International Journal of Public Sector Management*, 11 (2/3): 188–200.

Inglehart, R. and Rabier, J. R. (1986) 'Political re-alignment in advanced industrial society: From class-based politics to quality-of-life politics', *Government and Opposition*, 21 (4): 456–79.

Johnson, N. (1999) *Mixed Economies of Welfare: A Comparative Perspective*, Hemel Hempstead: Prentice Hall Europe.

Kanter, R. M. (1977) *Men and Women of the Corporation*, New York: Basic Books.

Kaushik, S. (1993a) *Women and Panchayati Raj*, New Delhi: Har-Anand Publications.

Kaushik, S. (1993b) 'Women and political participation', in Kumari, R. (ed.), *Women in Politics: Forms and Processes*, New Delhi: Har-Anand Publications, pp. 35–53.

Khilnani, S. (1997) *The Idea of India*, London: Hamish Hamilton.

Kishwar, M. (1990) 'Why I do not call myself a feminist', *Manushi: A Journal About Women and Society*, 61 (November–December): 2–8.

Kumari, D. (1992) 'The Affirmative Action Debate in India', *Asian Survey*, XXXII, 3: 290–302.

Kumari, R. (ed.) (1993) *Women in Politics: Forms and Processes*, New Delhi: Har-Anand Publications.

Laclau, E. (1990) *New Reflections on the Revolution of Our Time*, London: Verso.

Lele, M. K., Sathe, N., Maydeo, A. and Singh, S. G. (1993) 'Stree Mukti Andolan Sampark Samiti, Maharashtra', in Kumari, R. (ed.), *Women in Politics: Forms and Processes*, New Delhi: Har-Anand Publications, pp. 133–76.

d'Lima, H. (1984) 'Participation of women in local self-government', in Kaushik, S. (ed.), *Women's Participation in Politics*, New Delhi: Vikas, pp. 21–30.

Lister, R. (2000) 'Gender and the analysis of social policy', in Lewis, G., Gerwitz, S. and Clarke, J. (eds) *Rethinking Social Policy*, London: Sage and the Open University, pp. 23–36.

Lovenduski, J. and Norris, P. (eds) (1993) *Gender and Party Politics*, London: Sage.

Ludden, D. (1993) 'Orientalist imperialism: Transformations of colonial knowledge', in Breckenridge, C.A. and van der Veer, P. (eds), *Orientalism and the Post-colonial Predicament*, Philadelphia: University of Pennsylvania Press, pp. 250–78.

Lunneborg, P. (1990) *Women Changing Work*, New York: Bergin & Garvey.

McIntosh, M. (1978) 'The state and the oppression of women', in Kuhn, A. and Wolpe, A. (eds), *Feminism and Materialism: Women and Modes of Production*, London: Routledge and Kegan Paul, pp. 254–89.

Maiello, A. (1996) 'Ethnic conflict in post-colonial India', in Chambers, I. and Curti, L. (eds), *The Post-colonial Question: Common Skies, Divided Horizons*, London: Routledge, pp. 99–104.

Melucci, A. (1989) *Nomads of the Present: Social Movements and Individual Needs in Contemporary Society* (eds J. Keane and P. Mier), London: Hutchinson Radius.

Michels, R. (1968) [1911] *Political Parties*, New York: Free Press.

Milne, K. (1997) 'Labour's quota women are on a mission to modernise', *New Statesman*, 16 May: 16–18.

Pakulski, J. (1991) *Social Movements: The Politics of Moral Protest*, Melbourne: Longman Cheshire.

Pietila, H. and Vickers, J. (1994) *Making Women Matter: The Role of the United Nations*, London: Zed Books.

Ponting, C. (1986) *Whitehall: Tragedy and Farce*, London: Hamish Hamilton.

Powell, W. W. and DiMaggio, P. J. (eds) (1991) *The New Institutionalism in Organizational Analysis*, Chicago: The University of Chicago Press.

Pratchett, L. and Wingfield, M. (1996) 'Petty bureaucracy and woolly-minded liberalism? The changing ethos of local government officers', *Public Administration*, 74 (4): 639–56.

Pringle, R. and Watson, S. (1992) 'Women's interests and the post-structuralist state, in Barrett, M. and Phillips, A. (eds), *Destabilising Theory: Contemporary Debates*. Oxford: Blackwell, pp. 53–73.

Redstockings (1969) 'Redstockings Manifesto', in Tanner, L. B. (ed.), *Voices from Women's Liberation*, New York: Mentor, New American Library, pp. 109–11.

Rosener, J. B. (1990) 'Ways women lead', *Harvard Business Review*, 90 (November/ December): 119–125.

Rossi, A. (ed.) (1973) *The Feminist Papers: From Adams to de Beauvoir*, Toronto: Bantam Books.

Seabrook, J. (1997) 'Still searching for Gandhi', *New Statesman*, 15 August: 26–7.

Sheth, D. L. (1995) 'Democracy and Globalization in India: Post- Cold War Discourse', The Annals of the American Academy of Political and Social Science: Local Governance Around the World 540, July: 24–39.

Singh, S. G., Lele, M. K., Sathe, N., Sonalkar, W. and Maydeo, A. (1993) 'Participation of women in electoral politics in Maharashtra', in Kumari, R. (ed.), *Women in Politics: Forms and Processes*, New Delhi: Har-Anand Publications, pp. 63–107.

Squires, J. (1996) 'Quotas for women: Fair representation?', in Lovenduski, J. and Norris, P. (eds), *Women in Politics*, Oxford: Oxford University Press, pp. 73–90.

Tilly, C. (1985) 'Models and realities of popular collective action', *Social Research*, 52 (4): 717–47.

Touraine, A. (1985) 'An introduction to the study of social movements', *Social Research*, 52 (4): 749–87.

Turner, R. H. (1960) 'Modes of social ascent through education: Sponsored and contest mobility', in Halsey, A. H., Floud, J. and Arnold Anderson, C. (eds), *Education, Economy and Society*, New York: Free Press, 121–39 (previously published in *American Sociological Review*, XXV: 5).

UNDP (United Nations Development Programme) (1995) *Human Development Report 1995*, Oxford: Oxford University Press.

Wajcman, J. (1998) *Managing Like a Man: Women and Men in Corporate Management*, Cambridge: Polity Press.

Ware, V. (1992) *Beyond the Pale: White Women, Racism and History*, London: Verso.

Watson, S. (1999) 'Introduction', in Watson, S. and Doyal, L. (eds) *Engendering Social Policy*, Buckingham: Open University Press.

Watson, S. and Doyal, L. (eds) (1999) *Engendering Social Policy*, Buckingham: Open University Press.

Williams, F. (1989) *Social Policy: A Critical Introduction*, Cambridge: Polity Press.

Wilson, E. (1977) *Women and the Welfare State*, London: Tavistock.

Young, K. and Rao, N. (1994) *Coming to Terms with Change? The Local Government Councillor in 1993*, London: Joseph Rowntree Foundation.

Zald, M. and McCarthy, J. D. (ed.) (1987) *Social Movements in an Organizational Society: Collected Essays*, New Brunswick, NJ: Transaction Publishers.

3 Managing transformation?

Health and welfare management in South Africa

Jenny Owen

Introduction

A magazine advert during the early years of the Mandela government in South Africa vividly illustrates the ambiguities and the scale of the transition under way at that time. Published in a business magazine, it featured African National Congress (ANC) militants who had used their experience in Umkhonto we Sizwe, the armed wing of the ANC, to go into business as security guards for supermarkets and other companies. Long after Nelson Mandela's release from prison in 1992 and election as president in 1994, debate continues about the transformation process in government policies, services and communities. Early excitement about the peaceful transition symbolised by the security guards' advert has been eclipsed by debates about enduring levels of poverty and inequality among black communities. Do current policies reflect concessions to neo-liberalism and to marketisation which negate the radical impetus of the ANC-led government (Bond 2000)? Or has the maintenance of sufficient stability to allow reforms to proceed, however unevenly, been a major achievement in itself (Ncholo 2000)?

Within this broad picture, commitment to public service transformation has been at the heart of South African government policy since 1994, which is focused on reducing inequalities both in public sector employment patterns and in service delivery and on creating accountable, transparent systems. Reducing gender inequality in employment and in access to services has been a specific aim, with targets and monitoring processes developed accordingly; acknowledging and tackling the high rates of rape and domestic violence have also become priorities. Western governments and donor agencies have become prominent players, through initiatives in policy development, management consultancy, staff training, twinning and other schemes (Bevan 2000; Bond 2000). This period has also seen an important transition in approaches to public sector management from UK government agencies such as the Department for International Development. The Conservative government language of internal markets and customer relations of the early 1990s has been eclipsed, since 1997, by a New Labour emphasis on stakeholders, citizens and partnerships.

This chapter discusses South African public service organisation and management since 1994, using examples from management development in health and welfare services. What are the distinctive features of public service policy and management in South Africa? What kind of interplay can we observe between these and Western public management concepts? These questions are important in themselves, given the worldwide interest in the dismantling of apartheid in South Africa; they are also important in terms of understanding international developments in public management.

The chapter combines an overview of relevant literature with observations based on experience in health and welfare management development and related qualitative research in South Africa. Public management discourses within these settings are diverse: some reshape Western frameworks, both mainstream and critical; some seek to integrate notions of an African renaissance into aspects of conventional Western management practice; some draw on radical initiatives in public health or community development. Many public management policy initiatives reproduce a consumerist discourse alongside one of community participation and redistribution. There is much evidence of the difficulties obstructing the public service transformation originally envisaged by the ANC; however, much scope does remain for innovation in public service management, however fragmented this may be.

The discussion below draws on work carried out in South Africa between 1997 and 2000: a first phase of consultancy and facilitation of management development programmes, and a second phase (1998–2000) of related research and evaluation. Both phases were funded by the UK Department for International Development as part of a wider programme involving health and welfare departments at provincial and national levels in South Africa.

Management and management development in public services

Three perspectives are relevant here. First, some recent literature combines critical social science perspectives with a concern for organisational change – even potentially for democratic 'transformation' in the sense reflected in ANC policies of the early 1990s (Alvesson and Willmott 1996). These authors note that management schools benefited from recruiting accomplished 'critical scholars', with commitments both to teaching and to research output, when other options for social scientists contracted in the 1980s and 1990s. The resulting body of work includes their own explicitly eclectic, 'theoretically promiscuous' approach to the analysis of management and organisations. This draws on various elements within Critical Theory (CT) – notably a Foucauldian approach to the production of power relations, and a commitment, following Habermas, to analyse and challenge technocratic rationality:

> In sum, the intent of CT is to foster a rational, democratic development of modern institutions in which self-reflective, autonomous and

responsible citizens become progressively less dependent upon received understandings of their needs, and are less entranced by the apparent naturalness or inevitability of the prevailing politico-economic order ... CT encourages the questioning of ends (e.g. growth, profitability, productivity) as well as their preferred means, such as dependence upon expert rule and bureaucratic control, the contrivance of charismatic, corporate leadership, gendered and deskilled work, marketing of lifestyles, etc.

(Alvesson and Willmott 1996: 39)

This approach facilitates critiques of mainstream approaches to management that are framed in terms of instrumental rationality and which present themselves in terms of a set of neutral 'techniques'. Alvesson and Willmott focus instead on management as social practice, embodying choices and contested areas and opening up areas of management and organisational development practice, both for analysis and for dialogue; they focus on patterns of resistance and interpretation in organisations, not just on patterns of managerial or state control. Brewis (1996) provides a related example, with her analysis of management courses in personal effectiveness and of facilitators acting as 'agents provocateurs' rather than as purveyors of orthodoxy. With its emphasis on promoting reflection and critique, CT does offer potential for an awareness of the limitations of Western social theory or management theory in relation to South African contexts. Similarly, there is potential here to explore gendered aspects of policy and management processes, although this is not an explicit priority in the publications cited above.

A second set of themes comes from debates concerning new public management (NPM; Hood 1995; Ferlie *et al.* 1996). Ferlie *et al.* note the contradictory set of characteristics that can be bracketed under 'new public management', comparing it to an empty canvas on to which diverging interpretations can be painted (Ferlie *et al.* 1996: 10). Hood (1995) cautions against assuming a homogeneous, globalising move towards converging public management models, stressing the importance of distinct national contexts. Gibb and Knox (1998) caution against simplistic assumptions about the dominance of managerialist models; their case study of management development in UK local government shows how distinctive public sector values and practices survived sustained managerialist initiatives from Conservative governments in the 1980s and 1990s. However, there is a degree of consensus about some key features of NPM; Ferlie *et al.* (1996: 10–14) present four main models:

Model 1:　Efficiency Drive, aiming to bring private sector notions of efficiency into public services.

Model 2:　Downsizing and Decentralisation, a development across private and public sector organisations, emphasising 'flexibility' and restructuring.

Model 3:　In Search of Excellence, an emphasis on notions of 'organisational culture', motivation and change management, referring back to the 1982 Peters and Waterman text of the same name. A 'bottom-up' version deploys concepts of organisational development and of 'the learning organisation'; a 'top-down' version focuses on charismatic leadership and the promotion of corporate values.

Model 4: Public Service Orientation, an explicit assertion of distinctive public sector values, combined with an emphasis on high-quality services.

The third subsection below comments on how far current public management policies in South Africa fit within this framework. Gender remains a marginal issue at best in this area of work: at an empirical level, Ferlie *et al.* note that changes in NHS trust and health authority boards in the early 1990s led to a drop in the representation both of women and of ethnic minorities; however, these themes are not followed through explicitly in relation to further theoretical or empirical analysis of NPM.

Finally, there is a thread of reflective discussion in public management journals, based on academics' and consultants' analyses of management development work and research in international contexts. Shaw (1998) uses a study of a health service management training initiative in Pakistan to expose 'universalist' assumptions, among donors and consultants, concerning management. Drawing on Hofstede's analysis of four dimensions within the concept of culture (i.e. power distance, uncertainty avoidance, individualism–collectivism and masculinity–femininity), she uses observation and interview data to illustrate conflicts between dominant Western management models and local practices. For instance, local networks of obligation may prevent subordinates speaking frankly during appraisal processes, or may require family and community demands to take precedence over organisational deadlines in a way that would conflict with Western time-management models. Her proposal is to emphasise process consultancy rather than training or instruction: echoing the 'critical action learning' methodology proposed by Alvesson and Willmott, she emphasises:

> developing in managers the capacity to critique a practice and synthesise an appropriate response, ... by recognition of the underlying attitudes and assumptions, not by imposition of alien orthodoxies.
>
> (Shaw 1998: 411)

Bevan (2000) develops a framework of criteria for assessing the appropriateness and the success of consultancy interventions in public service contexts, including a South African example. Although this does not draw explicitly on social theory, Bevan also stresses the need for sensitivity to local factors, and for partnership not instruction. As with the work referred to earlier on Critical Theory, there is scope here to examine gender relations, but this remains marginal or underexplored.

Turning now to the South African context, the sections below will address:

- the general policy background;
- public service policy and management initiatives;
- discourses in recent South African management texts;
- a qualitative study of a UK-funded initiative with new health and welfare managers.

South Africa after 1994: the scale of transformation

When the Government of National Unity was formed in 1994, it embarked on a 'dual transition', described by the Minister for Public Service and Administration as follows:

> South Africa is experiencing a constitutional and political transition ... we are also experiencing a transition at the institutional level of government. Our situation is special in the sense that we are required to change the actual nature of the South African state.
>
> (Skweyiya and Vil-Nkomo 1995: 217)

This meant bringing together organisations and departments that had been fractured along ethnic lines, creating new, unified services in each of the nine provinces and decentralising some management processes to new regional bases. It also meant addressing staggering inequalities:

> To some, South Africa is a country of affluence and luxury, to others a country of dismal poverty and deprivation. Poverty afflicts fewer than two per cent of whites, but more than half the black population. Ten per cent of black children, compared to one per cent of white children, die in infancy. Per capita, whites earn 9.5 times the income of blacks and live, on average, 11.5 years longer ...
>
> (Skweyiya and Vil-Nkomo 1995: 217)

Health care provision was uneven, divided on ethnic lines and biased to secondary and tertiary care; many rural areas were largely excluded from provision. Malnutrition was estimated to underlie a national 'stunting' rate of between 23 and 27 per cent of young children (rising to 38 per cent in the poorest fifth of the population; RSA 1998). As one analyst put it, from the perspective of local government before the 1999 general elections:

> All is supposed to be ready for elections in 1999. But the scope of the changes is vast. Boundary revisions, a new tax regime, a new support grant mechanism, most aspects of the law governing local government *and a new approach to management at all levels* ... In Britain, with a well-established

system, we generally assault ourselves with one of these reforms at a time.

(Curtis 1998: 85; emphasis added)

For the individuals, political parties and community organisations leading these changes, there has also been the transition from opposition to the ambiguities and tensions of government (Adam *et al.* 1997). The 'talisman' wielded by the Government of National Unity, in the face of these challenges, was the Reconstruction and Development Programme (RDP; Lund 1996). The South African Congress of Trade Unions (COSATU) pushed for pre-election commitments to 'fundamental transformation'; this developed into a programme with specific targets to be met within 1 year and within 5 years (Blumenfeld 1997). Guiding principles included width, not depth (more houses rather than better houses); rapid delivery of infrastructure; addressing need in rural areas; targeting vulnerable groups, particularly women and children; and affirmative action (Lund 1996). Alongside this, the Women's Budget Initiative, led by parliamentarians and non-governmental organisations, examined the impact of government spending on gender inequalities (Budlender 1996; Valodia 1998). Crucially, this was not a separate budget 'for women', but an attempt to integrate a focus on gender into the work of *all* government programmes.

The RDP became a unifying focus for the processes of national reconciliation and reconstruction (Blumenfeld 1997: 67); it had a national office, a project fund and a brief to lead the reprioritising of spending across all public services. Yet within 2 years, the RDP office was closed and a new 'Growth, Employment and Redistribution Programme' (GEAR) was in place. Outcomes had been poor in areas such as housing, where budgets remained underspent (Tomlinson, 1998); there was also evidence of fraud and corruption (Blumenfeld 1997: 68). Meanwhile, pressures on the government to address poor economic performance were increasing.

There is much consensus about the uneven achievements of the first ANC-led government, but commentaries polarise when it comes to interpretation. The eventual move to GEAR was variously seen as pragmatic consolidation and continuity (by the ANC leadership) and as capitulation to market forces (Bond *et al.* 1997; Bond 2000). Bond *et al.* (1997) argue that despite continuing policy commitments to reconstruction and participation, the government has adopted a neo-liberal economic agenda, amenable to multinational business interests but marginalising the poor. This is attributed partly to a failure of nerve in the face of currency crises and lack of economic growth and partly to the pursuit of personal interests by emerging black elites (Bond *et al.* 1997: 26; Bond 2000).

Alternative analyses (Blumenfeld 1997) identify an almost paralysing ambiguity within the RDP itself from the start: a 'top-down' programme that nevertheless solicited strong community participation. For example, an emphasis on job creation and public works that steered clear of socialist-style references to planning but lacked any other explicit economic models.

The early achievements of the Government of National Unity deserve recognition: it is only plausible to refer to achievements, such as a free primary health care system for pregnant women and young children and guaranteed reproductive rights, as 'limited' when they are set against such enormous early expectations. These early achievements also have a specific relevance to reducing gender inequality. However, it is clear that policy commitments to land redistribution, new housing and minimum wage levels among others (Bond 2000: 112–18), as well as to improved health care (Wallis 2000) became substantially delayed or diluted again. This can only have undermined the genuine impetus to reduce gender inequality that the Women's Budget Initiative represented.

Discourses in public service policy development: customers, citizens, communities?

The first interim constitution set out the following:

> to promote an efficient public administration broadly representative of the South African community.
>
> (RSA 1993, quoted in Sidloyi 1996: 138)

However, the negotiated settlement included a 'sunset clause': civil servants were guaranteed the right to remain in post for up to 5 years after the election. Public services management was 94 per cent white and male, with considerable over-representation of Afrikaners. Pay increases of up to 20 per cent were awarded to some civil servants in the run-up to the 1994 election (Sidloyi 1996). So the starting point at that time was:

> a bloated public service which was sapping national resources, and not delivering even the existing, racially biased services with anything approaching efficiency.
>
> (Sidloyi 1996: 139–40)

This was a situation that was hard to tackle in the context of a stated government emphasis on transformation *and* reconciliation. A sequence of policy developments initiated the intended public service transformation:

- The 1995 White Paper on the Transformation of the Public Service (WPTPS), proposing 'the creation of a people-centred and people-driven public service' (RSA 1995).
- The 1966 Constitution, similarly framed in terms of professional ethics, fair service provision, effective and efficient use of resources and public participation.
- The designation of 1997 as a 'Year of Delivery', with a national conference on public service delivery and the Batho Pele (People First) White Paper:

Although much has been done in the public sector, there is still much to do, specifically in relation to everyday things that the public service gets wrong, such as having inappropriate office hours, untidy waiting areas, long queues at lunch times caused by staff being on lunch breaks, etc. The Constitution sets out the basic values and principles which should govern public administration and these must not remain words on paper. Batho Pele aims to turn words into reality.

(RSA 1997)

- The Public Service Act, bringing public services under central political control, and the new Public Service Regulations (1998), phrased in terms of improved service standards, quality monitoring, customer focus and performance management. Together, these provided a broad national framework; responsibility for detailed planning and implementation was devolved to provinces and regions.

There are explicit parallels here with the NPM models described earlier, particularly Model 3 (excellence and customer orientation) and Model 4 (a distinctive public sector ethos). South African discourses of public service transformation still combine radical perspectives – participation, people-centredness, equity – with the language of customer focus and performance management. Is this Western managerialism with a rainbow gloss? How are policies like these being interpreted in practice? I will now turn to examples from current management texts, and from research with new health and welfare managers.

Discourses in South African management literature

Libraries and bookshops in South Africa display a range of popular UK and North American management literature: Charles Handy's *Empty Raincoat* sits alongside handbooks about total quality management and neuro-linguistic programming. Searching databases for recent, specific South African perspectives produced fewer items, but suggested five distinct clusters of material. However, to date this remains an overwhelmingly gender-blind body of work.

First, there are post-1994 textbooks, clearly based on 'instrumental rationality' and on the application of rules and techniques but incorporating new aspects of content and emphasis. This sometimes produces interesting incongruities. For example, *Managing for Excellence in the Public Sector* (van der Waldt and du Toit 1997) is based on systems theory, combining overviews of current policy with step-by-step approaches (e.g. for rational planning) and checklists (e.g. for change management). Defining resistance as a problem regarding change management (a view that not all management texts would adopt), the authors comment:

A practical example of such a situation is the programme of affirmative action in the South African public service, which may create resistance, particularly among older white officials.

(van der Waldt and du Toit 1997: 257)

This is a context-free understatement of dizzying proportions about a policy, the implications of which provoked heated debate in the press and among professionals, academics and managers. Was it an essential plank of progressive policy? A tokenistic diversion? A threat to established professional standards? Perhaps the textbook example is simply intended to stimulate debate; however, at a minimum there are missed opportunities here for articulating different interpretations.

Second, there is an emerging body of work that stakes a claim for distinctive South African approaches to management. Several common themes underlie work that ranges from anecdotal accounts of consultancy work to models drawing on and reshaping existing management theory. At the former end of the spectrum, Mbigi (1997) draws on his own teaching and consultancy work in order to explore the scope for a form of African renaissance in business contexts. The concept of *ubuntu* is fundamental to this approach, with many references to the business potential of harnessing the perceived holistic qualities of traditional social relations in parts of Southern Africa:

> Ubuntu ... is a literal translation for collective personhood and collective morality. It is best expressed by the Xhosa proverb ... *I am* because *we are* ... I am only a person through others.
>
> (Mbigi 1997: 2)

Mbigi and others sometimes blend references to *ubuntu* with mainstream management discourses, and the results are instantly recognisable from any recent, popular US or UK management text:

> Ubuntu may help to facilitate the healing process to create the mind-set required to build a rainbow nation. We can also harness our black cultural heritage to create effective performance relationships. This could be a source of competitive advantage ...
>
> (Mbigi 1997: 3)

Other examples are expressed in more sweeping, ahistorical terms:

> Whites primarily have designed exclusive institutions which give primacy to the individual, his development, self-fulfilment, which serve to foster liberal democracy. Blacks, on the other hand, believe that man [*sic*] is very much part of the societal fabric and see the need for each individual to find his place in a societal structure ... In other words, he desires organisations to be *inclusive*.
>
> (Koopman 1993: 41; original emphasis)

These texts are both frustrating and informative: they hint at important questions, for example concerning the ways in which apartheid became embedded in organisational practices or concerning models of leadership or community; however, the approach remains general and anecdotal, and references to 'inclusiveness' do not take any account of gender divisions. Lessem and Nussbaum (1996) explore similar territory, drawing on work associated with the 'South African Management Project', based at the University of the Witwatersrand Business School in Johannesburg. One aspect of this is Lessem's 'four world model': referring to cultures at the national level as well as the organisational, he associates North on this map with rationalism; West with pragmatism; East with holism; and South with humanism. Here, Lessem's work intersects directly with Mbigi's, on the basis of a common appeal to 'African' values of solidarity and community. The second aspect of this work is a set of case study examples, based on a range of private sector companies. Again, what is interesting here is the way in which 'African' values (and a range of national stereotypes) are invoked, rather than examined in any depth. There is no reference, for example, to gendered patterns in family and village life.

Human (1998) also draws on a combination of consultancy and academic links with the University of Cape Town, adapting Checkland's soft systems theory to the South African public service context. This is much more rigorous than the examples discussed above; a good UK parallel might be Charles Handy's *Understanding Organisations*, which the Open University uses as a recommended text on postgraduate management certificate programmes. Human emphasises the scale of the task facing South African public service organisations, pointing out that an average provincial health department employs more people and deals with a more complex range of tasks than most private companies, without the benefit of any consistent investment in management training. Again, this is a gender-blind account; however, Human does raise problems over the key concepts referred to by Mbigi and Lessem, including 'community' in the post-colonial context, seeing this as both a 'tyranny' of mutual obligations, and a necessary survival strategy arising from scarcity of resources (ibid.: 36–7). Human reworks a range of management ideas and techniques into a popularised and explicitly South African approach; this combines 'bottom-up' development principles with soft systems techniques in a hybrid model called 'Yenza': not an abstract notion of 'African values', but the Zulu term for 'do it'. This is linked explicitly to the 'Batho Pele' (People First) public service policy initiative referred to above, emphasising the urgent need to move from policy formulation to the practical implementation of reform.

All these texts combine deeply problematic aspects with informative case study examples and challenging insights: in that sense, they resemble much UK and US popular management literature. They provide a tantalising glimpse of themes that merit much more sustained critical analysis and empirical investigation. With the exception of Human's work, they also tend to focus on the private sector rather than the public sector. And none address the issue of 'gender'. References to African values suggest that *ubuntu* could take on the attributes that 'quality' acquired in the UK in the 1990s, or that 'modernisation' has taken on more recently, terms with potential both for critical exploration and for ritual deployment to support new policies or management orthodoxy – perhaps a variant of the 'culturist' forms of social control discussed by Kunda (cited in Alvesson and Willmott 1996: 32).

The third cluster of relevant work has more in common with Critical Theory. Nuttall and Coetzee (1998), for example, assemble a range of studies related to the South African transition. Eduard Fagan documents the ways in which the new constitution has been framed to keep the importance of past injustice and current transformation in focus, for example by including not only civil rights but also – somewhat ambiguously – socioeconomic rights such as 'access to adequate housing' (Fagan 1998: 259). Eve Bertelsen (1998), in the same collection, considers the role of post-apartheid advertising in reconfiguring black identities in line with consumerism rather than struggle or citizenship – a theme with direct relevance to current public service policies, in which the concepts of 'customer' and 'citizen' coexist uneasily.

Fourth, there are empirical studies directly related to management development. Schutte and Silverman (1996) make the case for participative, problem-centred learning approaches in public service management; however, concepts such as 'effectiveness' or 'leadership' tend to be taken for granted here (Schutte and Silverman 1996: 332). A comprehensive review by Heywood *et al.* (1998) for the Health Systems Trust identifies progress in establishing participative-learning approaches for new managers and emphasises the need for training related to decentralisation and district health and welfare service development and for evaluation.

Finally, there is an emerging literature that raises problems about the management models being incorporated into current policy documents and management development strategies, questioning the aid and consultancy processes through which these are delivered. Jones *et al.* (1996), in a study in Botswana, found that interpretations of leadership practices and other factors differed significantly from Western management models. Curtis, reviewing local government developments, argues that:

> the ... constitutional development process has leaned heavily upon foreign models and the 'latest' management fads ... burdening municipalities with structures and competency requirements in which they will be proved incompetent.
>
> (1998: 85)

For example, he found an overemphasis on formalised performance management systems at the expense of building on well-established local community networks. Taylor (1998) stresses the achievements of non-governmental organisations and the importance of ensuring that development funding builds on community development initiatives, rather than focusing uncritically on government agencies.

Commentaries regarding management, then, remain diverse and fragmented, and most draw heavily on European and North American sources (although they rarely address the issue of gender). However, this does support Hood (1995) in cautioning against hasty assumptions about globalisation in management practices – a point underlined by the qualitative study of new health and welfare managers discussed in the next section.

A UK NHS management development programme in South Africa: from customer chains to stakeholder maps?

The NHS has an established open-learning programme for managers, developed with the Open University: 'Managing Health Services', which was part of the NHS 'Management Education Scheme by Open Learning' (MESOL) and has since been revised as 'Managing Health and Social Care'. The design of the open-learning material invites critical reflection on experience, through structured individual and group activities as well as through assessment options based on analysing practical management problems. The content is based on Management Charter Initiative competencies but also offers examples of contrasting perspectives on management theory and practice. Thus, there is considerable flexibility for interpretation by tutors and students. The version of the programme discussed below pre-dated the 1997 Labour government; course materials therefore reflected the Conservative government health reforms of the 1980s and 1990s, containing case-study examples based on 'quasi-market' structures (Ferlie *et al.* 1996) and customer relations concepts.

Within a consultancy arrangement between the national NHS MESOL office and the South African Department of Health, the UK Department for International Development (DfID) funded a pilot implementation of Managing Health Services in South Africa, from 1996, entitled 'Managing Health and Welfare in South Africa' (MHWinSA). The aim was to assess the appropriateness of the programme for South African health and welfare organisations; the programme's emphasis on developing and applying management skills in the workplace context was seen as particularly appropriate in the light of the 'Batho Pele' focus on service quality and practical reform. This programme was coordinated by the MESOL national office, which recruited a small team of UK tutors. Standard UK course materials were used as the basis, supplemented with additional case studies and external speakers reflecting the South African context.

Three groups of health and welfare managers took part between 1997 and 1999 (forty-seven in total; twenty-five women and twenty-two men) attending seven 2-day workshops over 14 months, and working on the open-learning materials in the intervals. The discussion below draws on data from these three groups. (A further four groups were recruited to complete the programme during 2000–02, again with DfID funding.) Participants were nominated by provincial health and welfare departments, coming from senior and middle management posts; some occupied new roles (e.g. district secretaries in decentralised health structures), while others were hospital superintendents, doctors, ward sisters or social work managers in reforming but more long-established organisations.

Methodology

The discussion below draws on questionnaire and interview data, on written participant evaluations and on an analysis of participants' written course work. Detailed post-course questionnaires were returned by twenty-eight of the thirty-six participants (fifteen women and thirteen men), who had completed their course work by mid-1999, (a further eleven deferred some course work because of work or personal pressures). We carried out both group and individual interviews with thirty-five participants and fifteen line managers or other colleagues. Approximately 80 per cent of the sample was black, with a broadly equal representation of men and women. An external evaluator from the South African Institute for Distance Education carried out one-third of the interviews. Questionnaires focused on participants' appraisal of content and assessment; interviews explored broader themes, concerning public service development and the relevance (or otherwise) of UK-based initiatives.

Findings

Responses from the MHWinSA participants do illustrate some of the current shifts in public management practices in South Africa. Questionnaire and interview responses indicated a high degree of congruence between participants' and line managers' expectations, and the areas of skill, knowledge and competence that they felt the programme helped them to address. There were no distinct differences between responses from men and those from women. Themes singled out for positive comment included:

- change management;
- understanding organisational contexts in health and welfare;
- team building.

In general, 'managing people' was the area valued most consistently, with a particular emphasis on developing the confidence to delegate and to consult. Some aspects of MHWinSA course materials were clearly seen as too specific to the UK and needing revision. Key elements here were information on budget systems, on labour relations legislation and on leadership. In terms of 'process', the participative, open-learning approach was described as unfamiliar but welcome in comparison with the more didactic methods that still prevail in South African training and education contexts: 'the first time I have experienced genuine adult education', as one hospital manager put it.

Do these positive responses simply reflect convergence between public sector discourses in South Africa and those in Europe and North America? Certainly, many comments reflected the public service discourses discussed in the section above, showing strong parallels with aspects of NPM. For example, many managers felt that they were moving from a professional or clinical identity to a managerial one, in precisely the way intended by the UK NHS reforms of the 1980s and 1990s, and which is also reflected in many South African public service policies:

> I find that I'm now able to reflect on my management practice ... and analyse my actions ... Before the course, my confidence depended on my professional expertise; since the course, I have grown in confidence as a manager.
>
> (Hospital superintendent)

However, the UK health system models were not accepted uncritically, as this comment illustrates:

> The model of the British nursing system, for example, which is one towards which we are moving, helped me to see what it entails and what the pitfalls are ... Having case-studies which reflect a different setting can work as a stimulus to develop one's own relevant examples, and this exercise helps to deepen one's own understanding of the underlying principles and the implementation requirements.
>
> (Nursing sister)

UK approaches to public service performance management were welcomed, in a context in which promotion in many health and welfare organisations still depends on time served rather than on merit, harking back to the racialised bureaucracies of the apartheid period, for example:

> Your manager these days is afraid – if a subordinate has completed three years' service, and approaches the manager and says 'I'm supposed to be promoted', there's not much that the manager can do to stop that, even if the manager knows that this is not a productive person ...
>
> (Hospital secretary)

An example from another perspective:

> Where I'm working, the [nurse] tutors don't know what is expected of them, except going into class ... there's no guideline, so you find that there's no review of what you have done from this term to that term ... It's a serious problem, because there are people being paid without producing anything. How do you pin them down ... ?
>
> (Nurse tutor)

More fundamentally, the programme was clearly seen as needing significant adaptation in order to address the South African context fully. Comments were sometimes framed with reference to culture:

> The culture reflected is Western and the whole notion of being career-driven and competitive is especially foreign to people working in small towns and rural areas, where the pace of life is more laid back and relaxed, and people are more driven by community needs.
>
> (Hospital training and development manager)

More frequently, however, participants referred to specific political processes or organisational contexts, underlining the ways in which these differ from European examples:

> Labour is playing a very active and major role in health and welfare ... Not just playing a consultative role and bringing forward suggestions which we should incorporate ... . In many cases labour are even involved in negotiating in management discussions. One could say that unions are 'co-managers' in certain situations. They are often part of the interviewing panel ... Consultative management is not as straightforward as it seems. South African models need to be developed which can show managers what this implies and how to do it effectively.
>
> (Welfare department manager)

The following example emphasises more clearly the South African context for interpreting process re-engineering models:

> Traditionally 'white' and 'black' hospitals are in the process of being restructured. For example, individual hospitals are now being restructured as complexes where various services are grouped together ... Engineering new systems and structures demands an innovative style of management and requires a set of management competences which are different from those needed when managing established systems.
>
> (Regional health department training officer)

Finally, the process of 'transformation' itself was often taken for granted, in routine references to the 'transformation units' and 'task teams' that characterise public service organisations; at the same time, concerns were also expressed about the personal costs involved, and about the difficulties in implementing and sustaining reforms:

> Difficulty in handling change on the ground is a real challenge, as evidenced by the symptoms of stress and inability to cope such as alcoholism, and a desire to want out, which are becoming increasingly frequent [in the public service] ... We need to create some stability within the dynamic process of

change, otherwise people become paralysed, their morale sinks and they are unable to function effectively. We need tools to manage transformation and to persuade people to become involved in the process.

(Hospital training and development manager)

The result of this is:

The common complaint is that there is not time to develop the district [health system], because staff are involved in responding to crises all day long.

(District health secretary)

These sample comments suggest that health and welfare managers actively contested and debated interpretations of public management skills and processes through their work on this UK-funded and -designed programme. This has perhaps been facilitated by the coexistence of contrasting discourses within the programme itself. A participative open-learning approach, emphasising reflection and critique coexists alongside a framework of management competences and theories, which owes more to instrumental rationality than to any radical tradition and which explicitly integrates 'new right' 'mixed economy' models of health and welfare provision. This tension between process and content appears to allow considerable space for the facilitator as 'agent provocateur' (Brewis 1996) or as partner (Shaw 1998) – rather than as expert purveyor of 'foreign models and management fads' (Curtis 1998). This may also explain how easily the programme can be revised. In the new (UK) version, customer chains are less prominent and stakeholder maps loom large: there is an emphasis on partnership and inter-agency working, which is likely to be more explicitly compatible with South African policies than the previous course materials. But the emphasis on analysing and reflecting on experience is still a defining feature.

The MHWinSA programme, then, has offered genuine scope for critical initiatives in public management development among participating tutors, managers and health and welfare organisations. There are parallels with the UK here; as Gibb and Knox (1998) illustrate with reference to local government, many years of sustained 'new right' policies proved unable to eliminate distinctive public sector values and practices, and management development processes remain a domain for contesting managerialist ideas. However, looking at the MHWinSA programme within the longer term, international context of aid relationships and public services, the picture is more disturbing. Over 4 years into the project, costly UK consultants remained central to the programme's delivery. South African MHWinSA graduates have been recruited to co-tutor in its second phase, but key funding and planning decisions are still firmly UK led. An adaptation of written course materials is under way, but still incomplete, in South Africa; there is little clarity about how the programme might be integrated into South African accreditation processes or higher education provision, or what the career opportunities for new South African open-learning tutors might be. If this is representative of the pace and emphasis of other UK-funded initiatives in public service development, it suggests a strong element of fostering dependence rather than autonomy. This raises questions about how closely UK agencies and South African government departments monitor collaboration with local partners in aid-funded projects or look for factors that promote or obstruct local ownership.

Discussion

Neither the new public service policies nor health and welfare managers' own responses reflect an unambiguous 'managerialism' in South Africa. There are managerialist strands: for example in policy references to customers and charters, and in professionals' enthusiasm for a new managerial identity. But managers' comments on performance management emphasise fairness and accountability – an agenda not reducible to state or managerial control. Until very recently, both white and black South African public service bureaucracies exercised power specifically through delays, overt humiliation of individuals and staff access to promotion through time served, not performance. In turn, black communities exercised a degree of power through strikes, boycotts and non-payment campaigns: a legacy of oppositional practices that still creates conflicts with local authorities or universities, when non-payment of rates or fees brings partly reformed services close to collapse (Curtis 1998). In this context, dependable and transparent reward systems, or charters with explicit quality standards, represent a clear rejection of the racialised practices of the past.

New public service policies and practices still show continuity with the post-1994 Reconstruction and Development Programme, prioritising negotiation and a democratic approach to service delivery and planning. Recruitment patterns to senior positions have begun to change: figures up to January 1996 showed 38 per cent of new appointments going to black applicants (and just over 50 per cent of the most senior posts; Sidloyi 1996). In 1999, the Department of Public Service and Administration (DPSA) found that African women were the fastest growing component in public sector recruitment, noting however that women remain under-represented at senior levels (DPSA 1999). Emerging appeals to an African renaissance are not limited to business contexts, moreover, they can be immensely problematic. In 1999, President Mbeki and his health minister both appeared to deny the link between HIV and AIDS, on the basis that such 'inappropriate' Western explanations obscured the greater importance of poverty in the African context. Significantly, COSATU opposed the ANC government on this. It is, however, a mixed picture. For at the same time, the South African government has spearheaded a major challenge to the multinational pharmaceutical companies, the pricing policies of which keep drugs for treating HIV-positive patients (and many others) out of the reach of health services in Africa ('South Africa's sick wait for judgement day', *Guardian*, 5 March 2001: 16).

International journals contain periodic commentaries on public policy and management in South Africa, but there is also a need for more explicit theoretical dialogue. Critical Theory provides a starting point, identifying potential for critique and reflection within management development processes. There is much potential for dialogue between UK and South African managers, professionals and academics here. But competing claims to define 'African' values and 'African' management draw on a different tradition. This suggests considerable potential for both theoretical and empirical exploration of issues of professional and managerial identity, of concepts of citizenship and of models of community involvement. Gender relations and ethnic differences cross-cut all three; to date, very little work has been done to examine any of this ground in any depth.

Ambiguous new developments in UK policy, ranging from community participation in health or education 'action zones' to the Department of Health's references to 'user' and 'community' involvement, represent openings for analysis and exchange on these themes. These options were clearly not readily available during the 'new right' push for privatisation and internal markets. However, these areas require a basis of partnership and dialogue that is very different from the 'aid' agenda.

Conclusion

I began this chapter by referring to an advert featuring former ANC militants, who used their experience to go into business as security guards. Does this represent a process of 'forgetting and erasure', with new historical subjects 'repositioned as consumers' in an aggressive market context, rather than as citizens or activists in a radical democracy (Bertelsen 1998)? If so, then the early public service promises to challenge gendered patterns – as well as those based on ethnicity – will certainly be threatened. However, on a visit to South Africa before the 1999 elections, coinciding with President Mandela's birthday, another advert (this time on TV, for a mobile phone network) made me think. It featured 'Happy Birthday' tapped out in tune on prison bars, with a voiceover acknowledging that twenty-seven of Mandela's previous birthdays had been spent in prison. This may be a reworking of memory and identity that is fraught with contradictions, but it does not –as yet – seem like 'forgetting'.

'Subjects' in community enterprises are also engaging in reconfigurations of their own. Taking an example from the tourist industry (fundamental to economic reconstruction), Imbizo Tours in Soweto offers visitors conducted tours of the township. Tours are advertised in the international airport, prices reflect Western income levels, and a proportion of the earnings supports a community day-care centre. The itinerary starts in the wealthy northern Johannesburg suburbs, with their electric fences and prominent 'Armed Response' alarm systems. Then a drive round the ring road to Soweto leads to Nelson Mandela's original home (now a small museum), almost next door to the jocularly named Mandela Squatter Camp and the Soweto Cappuccino coffee house. But the culmination of the visit is still the Hector Petersen memorial to the young people who died in the 1976 uprisings: a reference point that is not likely to slip from view at the moment.

Acknowledgements

I gratefully acknowledge the help of the very supportive team of colleagues I have worked with since 1997: Jacqui Habana, Charles Magagula, Stan Kahn and Christine Randell in South Africa; Penny Lewis, Jill Sandford, Vicky Davison, Kay Phillips, Alan Watson and Tony Mapplebeck in Britain. The interview and questionnaire data discussed in the chapter were collected and analysed by Jill Sandford, Christine Randell and myself (Owen *et al.* 1998; 2000). Thanks also to Kevin Bellis, in South Africa, for many helpful discussions and exchanges of information.

References

Adam, H., Slabbert, F. Van Zyl and Moodley, K. (1997) *Comrades in Business: Post-liberation Politics in South Africa*, Cape Town: Tafelberg.

Alvesson, M. and Willmott, H. (1996) *Making Sense of Management*, London: Sage.

Bertelsen, E. (1998) 'Ads and amnesia: Black advertising the new South Africa', in Nuttall, S. and Coetzee, C. (eds), *Negotiating the Past: The Making of Memory in South Africa*, Cape Town: Oxford University Press, pp. 221–41.

Bevan, P. (2000) 'The successful use of consultancies in aid-financed public sector management reform: A consultant's eye view of some things which matter', *Public Administration and Development*, 20: 289–304.

Blumenfeld, J. (1997) 'From icon to scapegoat: The experience of South Africa's Reconstruction and Development Programme', *Development Policy Review*, 15: 65–91.

Bond, P. (2000) *Elite Transition*, London: Pluto Press.

Bond, P., Pillay, Y. G. and Sanders, D. (1997) 'The state of neo-liberalism in South Africa: Economic, social and health transformation in question', *International Journal of Health Services*, 27 (1): 25–40.

Brewis, J. (1996) 'The "making" of the "competent" manager: Competency development, personal effectiveness and Foucault', *Management Learning*, 27 (1): 65–86.

Budlender, D. (ed.) (1996) *The Women's Budget*, Cape Town: IDASA.

Curtis, D. (1998) 'Re-inventing South African local government: Opportunities and pitfalls in the process', *Local Governance*, 24 (2): 85–90.

Department of Public Service and Administration (DPSA) (1999) *Annual Report*, www.dpsa.gov.za/docs/reports/annual99-00b.html.

Fagan, E. (1998) 'The constitutional entrenchment of memory', in Nuttall, S. and Coetzee, C. (eds), *Negotiating the Past: The Making of Memory in South Africa*, Cape Town: Oxford University Press, pp. 249–62.

Ferlie, E. Ashburner, L. and Pettigrew, A. (1996) *The New Public Management in Action*, Oxford: Oxford University Press.

Gibb, S. and Knox, L. (1998) 'The evolution of management in UK local government: Reflections on the creation of a competence-based management development programme', *Local Government Studies*, 24 (2): 71–85.

Heywood, A., Schaay, N. and Lehmann, U. (1998) *A Review of Health Management Training in the Public Health Sector in South Africa*. Braamfontein: Health Systems Trust.

Hofstede, G. (1997) *Cultures and Organizations: Software of the Mind*, London: McGraw-Hill.

Hood, C. (1995) 'Contemporary public management: A new global paradigm?', *Public Policy and Administration*, 10 (2): 104–17.

Human, P. (1998) *Yenza: A Blueprint for Transformation*, Cape Town: Oxford University Press.

Jones, M., Blunt, P. and Sharma, K. (1996) 'Managerial perceptions of leadership and management in an African public service organisation', *Public Administration and Development*, 16: 455–67.

Lessem, R. and Nussbaum, B. (1996) *Sawubona Africa: Embracing Four Worlds in South African Management*, Johannesburg: Zebra Press.

Lever, J. and Krafchik, W. (1998) 'Spending on socio-economic services', in James, W. and Levy, M. (eds), *Pulse, Passages in Democracy-Building: Assessing South Africa's Transition*, Cape Town: Idasa, pp. 69–78.

Lund, F. (1996) 'Changing social policy in South Africa', in Baldock, J. and May, M. (eds), *Social Policy Review 7*, London: Social Policy Association, pp. 29–42.

Koopman, A. (1993) 'Transcultural management – in search of pragmatic humanism', in Christie, P., Lessem, R. and Mbigi, L. (eds), *African Management: Philosophies, Concepts and Applications*, Randburg: Knowledge Resources, pp. 41–76.

Mbigi, L. (1997) *Ubuntu: The African Dream in Management*, Randburg: Knowledge Resources (Pty).

Ncholo, P. (2000) 'Reforming the public service in South Africa: A policy framework', *Public Administration and Development*, 20: 87–102.

Nuttall, S. and Coetzee, C. (1998) *Negotiating the Past: the Making of Memory in South Africa*, Cape Town: Oxford University Press.

Owen, J., Sandford, J. and Randell, C. (1998) Managing Health and Welfare in South Africa: Preliminary Evaluation, unpublished report to DfID Pretoria and the national MESOL programme.

Owen, J., Sandford, J. and Randell, C. (2000) Managing Health and Welfare in South Africa: Final Evaluation, unpublished report to DfID Pretoria and the national MESOL programme.

Peters, T. J. and Waterman, R. H. (1982) *In Search of Excellence: Lessons from America's Best-run Companies*, London: Harper & Row.

Robinson, S. (1998) 'Demographics and quality of life', in James, W. and Levy, M. (eds), *Pulse, Passages in Democracy-Building: Assessing South Africa's Transition*, Cape Town: Idasa, pp. 53–9.

Republic of South Africa (RSA) (1993) *Interim Constitution*, Pretoria.

RSA (1994) *White Paper on Reconstruction and Development: Government's Strategy for Fundamental Transformation*, Pretoria.

RSA (1995) *White Paper on the Transformation of the Public Service (WPTPS)*, Pretoria.

RSA (1996) *Growth, Employment and Redistribution: A Macroeconomic Strategy*, Pretoria.

RSA (1997) *Report of the National Conference on Public Service Delivery, 27–28 February 1997, University of Fort Hare, Bisho*, Pretoria: Department of Public Service and Administration.

RSA (1998) *Poverty and Inequality in South Africa*, a report prepared for the Office of the Executive Deputy President and the Inter-Ministerial Group on Poverty and Inequality, Pretoria.

Schutte, L. B. and Silverman, L. (1996) 'Knowing and doing: an integrated approach to education and training in South Africa', *Public Administration and Development* 16: 331–9.

Shaw, J. (1998) 'Cultural variations in management practice: An exploration of the management trainer's dilemma', *Public Administration and Development*, 18: 399–412.

Sidloyi, S. (1996) 'Public service reform: A statistical analysis of the restructuring of the public service', in Maganya, E. and Houghton, R. (eds), *Transformation in South Africa: Policy Debates in the 1990s*, Johannesburg: Institute for African Alternatives, pp. 138–55.

Skweyiya, Z. and Vil-Nkomo, S. (1995) 'Government in transition: A South African perspective', *Public Administration and Development*, 1 (5): 217–23.

Taylor, J. (1998) 'Transformation and development: A South African perspective', *Community Development Journal*, 33 (4): 292–300.

Tomlinson, M. (1998) 'South Africa's new housing policy: An assessment of the first two years, 1994–1996', *International Journal of Urban and Regional Research*, 22 (1): 137–46.

Valodia, I. (1998) 'Engendering the public sector: An example from the Women's Budget Initiative in South Africa', *Journal of International Development*, 10: 943–55.

Van der Westhuizen, J. (1998) 'Public sector transformation and ethics: A view from South Africa', *Public Money and Management*, 18 (1): 15–20.

van der Waldt, G. and du Toit, D. F. P. (1997) *Managing for Excellence in the Public Sector*, Kenwyn: Juta.

Wallis, M. (2000) 'Development planning in South Africa: Legacies and current trends in public health', *Public Administration and Development*, 20: 129–39.

4 Gender, welfare regimes and the medical profession in France and Greece

Clientelism, étatism and the 'Mediterranean rim'

Mike Dent

Introduction

In this chapter I compare the work and organisation of hospital doctors in France and Greece in the broader context of the state and gender. First, this chapter is an exploration of two variants of the 'Beveridge' and 'Bismarckian' systems within Europe: France, because it is, perhaps paradoxically, an étatist variant of a 'Bismarckian' system; Greece, because it is an unusual variant of the Beveridge model. The examination of these two countries' health systems is carried out initially in terms of Esping-Andersen's (1990) welfare state regimes. This provides a useful framework within which to raise questions of the relationship between gender, family and health care provision, in particular the work of the medical profession. Part of the argument here is that professional jurisdiction (Abbott 1988) and autonomy – in the more loosely coupled sense of individual practitioner's discretion – is partly shaped by the officially defined role(s) of women in society (Lewis 1992; O'Connor 1993; 1996; Orloff 1993; Sainsbury 1994; Williams 1994).

The chapter will discuss four sets of issues and examine their inter-relationship:

1   the organisation and funding of the two health care systems and the public/private sector boundaries;
2   gender and welfare state regimes;
3   governmentality and state/profession relations;
4   the family and the issue of co-payments – official and unofficial.

The first, concerning the organisation and funding of the two systems, is largely descriptive and it is the relationship among the remaining three that is the focus of the analysis here.

Health services organisation and funding and public/ private sector boundaries

The funding of the health services in both countries is based on social insurance (sickness funds) with the state taking an active interest.

France

Public health expenditure as a percentage of gross domestic product (GDP) for France was 7.8 per cent in 1996 compared with 4.9 per cent for Greece (OECD 1997). France is middle ranking in terms of gross national product (GNP) per capita but third overall in terms of health expenditure (de Kervasdoué *et al.* 1997: 59), a contributing factor to the general satisfaction the French feel for their health care system (Mossialos 1997; Boseley 2000: 3; WHO 2000). Other factors include the range and choice of services even though this makes it one of the most complex in Europe (OECD 1992: 45). The system is based on a hypothecated system of funding in which virtually everyone is covered by the statutory health insurance – sickness fund – (Assurance-Maladie). The largest scheme, Régime Général, covers 'trade and industry sectors' (Lancry and Sandier 1999: 443), which is 80 per cent of the population, and is financed by payroll contributions by employees and employers. The overall system is under state control and coordinated by the National Sickness Fund (Caisse National d'Assurance Maladie des Travailleurs Salariés) – CNMATS – a public institution (de Pouvourville 1997: 163). There are twenty-two Regional Sickness Funds (Caisses Régionale d'Assurance Maladie) and approximately one hundred Primary Sickness Funds (Caisses Primaires d'Assurance Maladie). These bodies are managed by autonomous boards of trustees comprised of elected union representatives and appointed employer representatives. The sickness funds cover less than three-quarters of patients' costs with the shortfall being made up mostly by voluntary health insurance (*mutualle*) and 'out of pocket' monies.

It was the Jeanneney Ordinances of 1967 that first brought the sickness funds under state control. The CSMF (the medical/doctors' union) had initially proposed a nationwide contract with the CNMATS (Godt 1987: 467), but this had the unintended consequence of building inflationary pressure into the system. By the mid-1970s this had become a major problem for the United Left government, for it was incapable of containing the cost of health care, because the demands of the conservative physicians were, perversely, reinforced by those of the Socialist/Communist alliance. The first group was interested in raising its income, the latter was concerned with improving health provision for the working classes. If the government attempted to defeat the demands of the physicians, it would alienate many of its own supporters. Following the defeat of the United Left in 1978 the new right-wing government conceived a strategy involving the *indirect* control of the sickness funds and *direct* control of the hospitals. It included an increase in patients' co-payments for prescription drugs, and even more fundamentally in 1979 (Godt 1987: 467–8) the health minister introduced the 'global envelope', which linked health expenditure directly to the country's GDP. The government instructed the CNMATS (national sickness fund) to impose a new national contract. Physicians in the independent sector had to choose between accepting the new fee schedule or choosing to charge higher fees, but in either case patients were to be reimbursed at the same (i.e. lower) amount. Very few doctors opted for the second arrangement. The government's success with this strategy was helped by the expansion of the supply of doctors in the post-1968 period (Wilsford 1991: 130 and 145–6) as well as 'traditional' conflicts of interest within the profession (Godt 1987). During the 1980s over 80 per cent of office-based doctors were no longer able to determine their own fees (Godt 1987: 477). At the same time, a growing number of young doctors chose the relative security of salaried hospital appointments.

Meanwhile, acute medicine was costing a disproportionate amount of the health budget. Public sector hospitals were accounting for 50 per cent of all health expenditure (Godt 1987: 468). In part the problem related to the autonomous Chef de Services commitment to *la médecine libérale* and imperviousness to appeals for cost restraint. New reforms introduced in the early 1980s were designed to bring costs under control in part by challenging the privileged 'mandarins' Godt (1987: 468–9). The most important element of these reforms was the 1983 law that introduced the prospective global budget for each hospital, paid in monthly instalments.

Greece

Whereas France is the one of the highest public spenders on health, Greece is one of the lowest at 4.9 per cent of GDP (OECD 1997). If, however, one includes private expenditure on health, the figure, according to the National Statistical Service of Greece, rises substantially. The most recent figure cited in Sissouras *et al.* (1999: 352) is a total of 8.29 per cent total expenditure on health for 1992. This figure cannot be directly compared to the OECD figures as the calculations are based on different assumptions. The OECD (1994: 155) has estimated that just over 40 per cent of health expenditure is for private payments, which cover the costs of the widespread 'underground economy of health' (Colombotos and Fakiolas 1993: 140). Clearly Greek people spend considerable amounts of their income on health. This is despite, unlike France, the Greek Health Service being based on a national health system (ESY), which was created in 1983 by the country's first socialist administration. It is not, however, primarily funded from taxation but through sickness funds (i.e. health insurance). Membership of these is based on occupation and the largest of these is IKA, established in 1937 and covering industrial workers – manual and non-manual (OECD 1994: 149). The system of health insurance coverage was expanded during the 1950s, including the setting up of the 'sickness funds' for public sector employees and self-employed professions. In 1961 the Agricultural Insurance Organisation (OGA) was established for rural workers (over half the population). Today, there are around 40 social health insurance organisations but the three largest cover 80 per cent of the population (OECD 1994: 157). These are IKA, OGA and TEVE, the last of which cover small businesses (Sissouras *et al.* 1999). Services cover varies between these organisations but will normally include all hospital care, primary medical care, diagnostic services and pharmaceutical care. The majority of these social insurance organisations are funded by a combination of employer and employee contributions although the government funds OGA directly from taxation. IKA is also subsidised.

Public hospital income comes mainly from government subsidies. In 1992 the figure stood at 86 per cent (Sissouras *et al.* 1999: 369), while 'sickness funds' covered less than 13 per cent. Since 1993 there have been attempts to rationalise the hospital financing system in order that cost containment could become feasible. But the complications of the budgetary process, lack of communication between hospitals and 'sickness funds', and general arbitrariness of the process makes this unlikely for the moment.

The 1983 ESY legislation was intended to introduce a system of primary health care clinics, in part to take on a gatekeeping role in relation to the specialist services. This never really happened. The specialism of general practice, which was established in 1987 (OECD 1994: 159) has never been popular within the profession. In 1993 only 500 out of a total of nearly 39,000 doctors were GPs. To resolve the problem of staffing the clinics the government insists that newly graduated doctors have to complete one year's compulsory service in one of these primary health care clinics before moving on to their specialist training. Equally, the service has not appealed to the public; it is only those people in the rural areas without transport to the nearest hospital who tend to use these services. Instead patients go directly to the hospital outpatient or emergency units of their choice. Many middle-class patients choose to travel directly to university hospitals in Athens. The outcome is that Athens hospitals experience excess demand, while hospitals in rural areas are underutilised, with patient occupancy rates of around only 60 per cent (OECD 1994: 160). A significant minority of patients, who are unable to find the level or type of medical care they require, can seek treatment elsewhere in Europe funded by IKA social insurance. The trend during the mid-1990s, however, was for IKA not to fund as many of these trips as previously on the grounds that the facilities are available within the country (*Ta Nea* [*The News*], 22 December 1998: 38)

Welfare regimes and gender

Part of the rationale for selecting these particular two countries is to 'look "behind" difference for similarities and [attempt to] explain them' (Pickvance 1999: 355). Neither France nor Greece fits neatly into the ubiquitous Esping-Anderson's (1990) typology of *liberal, corporatist* (conservative), *social democratic* regimes. One of the problems with the model is that it tends to overemphasise the ideal typification of the United States, Germany and Sweden (Bagguley 1994: 78–9).

Turning to the issue of gender, Esping-Andersen analyses the welfare regimes in terms of the '[v]ariations in the de-commodifying potential of social policies … across … nations' (Esping-Andersen 1990: 47). However, as O'Connor (1993: 512), for example, has pointed out:

before de-commodification becomes an issue for individuals a crucial first step is access to the labour market. The de-commodification concept does not take into account the fact that not all demographic groups are equally commodified and that this may be a source of inequality.

Women in particular are most likely to be 'constrained by caring responsibilities' from fully entering the labour market unless there are a range of child care and 'family friendly' policies in place. All welfare regimes are gendered, to a greater or lesser extent, and all are, to some degree, 'male-breadwinner' states (Lewis 1992).

Figure 4.1 appears in an article by Trifiletti (1999: 54). It overlays and extends the Esping-Andersen (1990) typology to include the Mediterranean type, drawing on the distinctions made by Lewis (1989: 595) between those welfare regimes that primarily viewed women as 'wives and mothers' and those that viewed them as 'workers'. To elaborate:

1   The 'breadwinner' (corporatist) regime assumes that women are not principally engaged in the labour market but concerned more with family matters (i.e. social reproduction). The regime is premised on entitlements being tied to occupation and is heavily influenced by the principle of 'subsidiarity', which means that 'the state will only interfere when the family's capacity to service its members is exhausted' (Esping-Andersen 1990: 27). Historically, this has been the policy of the (Catholic) Church, although in its desanctified form it translates as: authority will lie outside

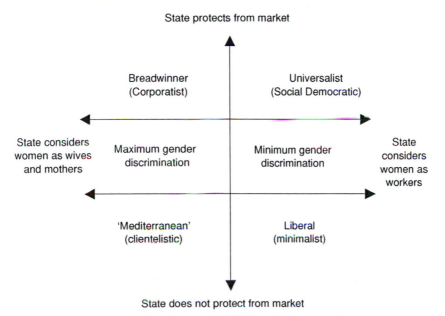

Figure 4.1   Typology of welfare regimes. Source: Trifiletti (1999: 54), with some modifications. Reprinted by permission of Sage Publications.

the state wherever possible and with the smallest functioning unit. Handy (1994: 115) explains subsidiarity as ' "reverse delegation" – the delegation of the parts to the centre'.

2   The 'universalist' regime is one that treats women principally as workers and is designed to deliver social policies that will provide the support necessary for them to fulfil that role in terms of child care, maternity/ paternity leave, care of the elderly and so on. This is the social democratic variety of Scandinavia.

3   The 'liberal' regime model accepts that women are workers but does little to protect them from the labour market. It more or less ignores their family roles expecting them instead to make their own care arrangements. Only in the case of poverty will the system deliver any support. The key example here is the United States although the model can be found, to a greater or lesser extent, in Australia, New Zealand, Canada and the UK.

4   The Mediterranean variant regime assumes that women are defined by their traditional family roles. The state provides little support for child care or care of the elderly nor much protection within the labour market. To a degree this is a consequence of 'late development' (Ferrera 1996; Katrougalos 1996) but it is also related to the phenomenon of 'clientelism', characterised by a networks of loyalty and obligations that underpin political, social and family life in most Mediterranean countries.

This variant on Esping-Andersen's typology is just as much a set of 'ideal-types' as the original. Individual countries will always only approximate to any particular type and may even reflect characteristics of more than one. As both versions of the typology (Esping-Andersen and Trifiletti) clearly indicate, however, the state is a crucial actor in the shaping of welfare regimes. It also plays a significant role in the organisation of the professions that work within the regimes. This brings me to the question of 'governmentality' and the role of the medical profession.

Governmentality, the medical profession and the state

At its most general level, the Foucauldian concept of 'governmentality', as applied to modern liberal democracies, relates to the ensemble of institutions that ensure, more or less, the continuing reproduction of the self-regulating subjects (citizens). It is concerned with the mechanisms by which governments govern in line with 'the personal and collective conduct of subjects' (Johnson 1995: 12). This includes institutions and knowledges, such as the modern professions. Governmentality contrasts to Durkheim's notion of the professions as the *corps intermédiaires*[1] between '*laissez-faire* individualism and state collectivism' (Johnson 1972: 12), for it suggests that the professions are part of the process of governing in the wider sense:

Governmentality is ... all those procedures, techniques, institutionalisations and knowledges that as an ensemble empower ... political programmes. Important here is the notion that expertise [i]s crucial to the development of such an ensemble, and that the modern professions [a]re the institutionalized form [of] such expertise ... .

(Gane and Johnson, 1993: 9; tense changed)

The form of governmentality and the ways in which institutionalised expertise operates within any particular national system will vary according to its history. This is well brought out in a comparison between the French and Greek medical professions, which, moreover, provides for a critical reflection on the term.

Medicine and the state

France

France's medical profession operates within a continental framework within which the state plays a leading role (Burrage *et al.* 1990: 219–20). The health system is a complex mix of public and private provision (Wilsford 1991; de Pouvourville 1997). The French health system is a particular example of the 'Bismarckian'/corporatist model but one in which the state plays a markedly interventionist – étatist – role. French étatism is legitimated by reference to Rousseau's principle that it is the state's duty to protect the 'general will' (*volonté général*). In practice étatism, its definition and defence, is upheld by the country's civil servants – the *grand corps*. These are the people who monopolise the interpretation of the 'general will' (Crozier 1974: 24). They constitute a secular order of functionaries who are trained, educated and socialised by the elite *grandes écoles*.

There is, apparently, no room within the system for interest groups (*groupes d'intérêt*) to have a role, they are as corrosive of the *volonté général*. Professions circumvent this limitation by using a particular vocabulary in which they 'defend their rights' (*défendent leurs droits*) (Wilsford 1991: 34). It is the state that awards the rights (*droits*) and it is the state can take them away. This 'fabulous contradictory formula of anti-corporatism, glorification of the State, and individualism' (Ehrmann 1983: 182ff, cited in Wilsford 1991: 33) presents a complexity of relationships that makes it difficult to easily delineate the boundaries of the state and associations. This is perhaps more readily understood in the terms suggested by Johnson (1995: 8) – drawing on Foucault – 'the state is ... an ensemble of institutions, procedures, tactics, calculations, knowledges and technologies'. Neither Johnson, nor Foucault, are referring solely to France and even less so to the French medical profession but they could easily have been doing so.

The revolutionaries of 1789 believed in the Rousseauian principle of the 'social contract', which tolerated no interest groups. All medical schools were closed and, more or less, anyone could practise or teach medicine (Foucault 1973: 49). Medical schools were later re-established (1803) but the state directly controlled the organisation of the profession, including education, malpractice and professional confidentiality. The new arrangements, however, were 'operated along loosely democratic lines' (Abbott 1988: 158–9).

According to Herzlich (1982: 243–4), the nineteenth century saw the emergence of two – paradoxical – professionalisation projects instigated by doctors:

1   establishment of the conditions for the practice of liberal medicine;
2   entry into the social game.

The first was the concern of the medical elite of independent means who viewed medicine as a liberal art. The second interested more the practitioners who made their living working for the charitable welfare bureaux (*bureaux de bienfaisance*) and the 'mutual benefit societies' (established from 1850), which served the industrial working class. These doctors, while fearful of exploitation were yet aware that the working-class demand for health care represented a major extension of the medical market. They lobbied for the extension of social and health insurance and were prepared to accept state-controlled medical practice so long as they were guaranteed a medical monopoly. This is what Herzlich means by '*entry into the social game*'.[2] By the end of the nineteenth century this had become the dominant strategy of the medical profession.

It was during the last decade of the nineteenth century that the Third Republic introduced social legislation – including health reforms – intended to placate the working classes. In 1893 laws were passed covering medical assistance to indigents (1893) and accidents at work (Herzlich 1982: 244; Immergut 1992: 89) – changes that extended the medical market considerably.

ORGANISED MEDICINE

It was not, however, until 1892 that doctors finally obtained *the law* that rescinded the Chapelier law (Herzlich 1982: 245) and made possible a legitimately organised profession of medicine. Physicians were now legally able to unionise and to negotiate fees. In 1927 doctors' professional autonomy was enshrined within a medical charter (Immergut 1991: 94), which set out four principles of *la médecine libérale*:

1   freedom of physician choice by the patient;
2   freedom of prescription by the physician;
3   fee for service payment;
4   direct payment by the patient to the physician for services rendered.

These changes did not, however, lead to the emergence of a cohesive and integrated medical profession. In 1884 there were approximately 150 departmental unions (*syndicats*) with a total of 3,500 physician members (Wilsford 1991: 105). In that year, forty of them joined together to form the USMF (Union des Syndicats Médicaux Français).

At this time there were two issues that exacerbated the tendency towards fragmentation within the profession. The first concerned the type of health system the doctors 'should' support. This issue became particularly pressing in the period following the 1914–18 war in Europe (Wilsford, 1991: 106). The question was: should France adopt a health system based on the German corporate model? The attraction for the medical profession would have been a system based on collective contracts between physicians and local sickness funds. The model appealed to the dominant USMF as well as to successive governments, but it contradicted the principles of *la médecine libérale*. The argument 'split' the profession, and in 1926 a 'liberal' rival to the USMF was established, the FSMF (Fédération des Sydicats Médicaux de France). It was this *syndicat* that drafted the medical charter (*la médecine libérale*) adopted by the whole profession in 1927. The upshot was the establishment of the CSMF (Confédération des Syndicats Médicaux Français) in 1928, which combined elements of both factions (Immergut 1992: 94).

The second divisive issue concerned ethics and licensing. In the nineteenth and first half of the twentieth century the lack of an independent organisation for dealing with malpractice and administering licensing was a problem. Eventually the Ordre des Médecins was set up by the state, by the Vichy government, in 1940 (amended in 1945) to take on this role (Wilsford 1991: 106).

THE DEBRÉ REFORMS

It was, however, not until 1958 that the organisation of hospital medicine took on its present form. The reforms were the result of a commission chaired by Professor Robert Debré, a controversial figure within the medical elite.[3] The aim was to make the organisation of hospital medicine and medical education more rational and scientific. There were three central principles to the reforms:

1   To improve the planning of the hospital system by reorganising it on a regional basis, with clear distinctions between types of hospitals. Government was to control the growth of the independent hospital sector.
2   To raise the status of public sector hospital specialists by the creation of full-time, senior salaried posts (Chef de Service) to be filled by doctors committed to high-quality clinical work, teaching and medical research. Public sector doctors were no longer to be allowed to work in the independent (private) sector too.
3   To make appointments on the basis of merit, based on competitive examinations, as opposed to the previous practice of patronage.

The Debré reforms were only slowly implemented but have had a long-lasting impact on the French health service.[4]

Greece

The Greek state, too, plays a strong role in hospital organisation and the profession of medicine. The outcome, however, is a little different, in part because Greece has had a very different history from France. Whereas France has a long history of being an independent powerful nation, Greece does not. It shares a common history of being part of the Ottoman Empire with the Balkans (Mouzelis 1986: xiii). It is this that has left a particular clientelistic legacy on the political culture of the country. Greece is unlike other European countries on the Mediterranean in that it does not share their Latin/Catholic traditions, the religion of the country being 'Orthodox'. The differences from other European Mediterranean countries, however, should not be overstated. It shares many social, cultural and political similarities with, for example, Italy and Spain (Katrougalos 1996).

Nevertheless, the impact of the Ottoman Empire and its aftermath has had a major impact in shaping the people's relations to the state. Modern Greece emerged from a struggle for national independence. The kind of state that has emerged in the early twenty-first century has come about after a series of nationalist struggles, civil war and a military dictatorship – all of which adds up to and reflects the complex and ambiguous relationship the Greeks have with their state. Mouzelis (1986: xv) points out that under Ottoman patrimonial rule no *corps intermédiares* were permitted – somewhat similar to the French notion of the general will (*volonté général*) – so there was no 'space' for independent professionals. This intolerance of civil society survived into the country's modern era.

The Greek struggle for independence was heavily influenced by the ideals of the French Revolution, ideals imported by the Greek diaspora, which supported the struggle (Mouzelis 1986: 39 and 41). The war of independence, however, was one in which the British, French and Russians also played a significant role and were influential in imposing change from above (Katrougalos 1996: 44). The consequence was that the Greek people got a monarchy instead of a republic. As a result, the Greek state lacked legitimacy with the people while itself becoming the single most influential dispenser of patronage. However, there is no longer any substantial questioning of state legitimacy, at least not since the dictatorship of the 1970s. Nevertheless, the issue of patronage and political clientelism remains. Appointment to any public sector post – including public hospitals – is affected by it (Samatas 1993). There are, nevertheless, forces within the country bent on trying to eradicate its influence. Current political debate is largely around the question of whether the country needs to be more strongly integrated into the European Union (EU) (Petmesidou 1996: 340–4). This has the implication that party political clientelism would be replaced by greater administrative rationality. In the Panhellenic Socialist

Party (PASOK) party congress of 1999, the premier, Costas Simitis, argued for European monetary union (EMU) remaining the government's primary goal on the grounds that it will change the economic, social and cultural map of Greece (*Athens News*, 19 March 1999: 3). The hope is that the economic and market disciplines, as well as EU regulations, will drive out the older patterns of clientelism.

THE GREEK MEDICAL PROFESSION

Whereas in France the state has fairly direct and effective control over the number of doctors through the regulation of the number of medical students, in Greece this is not the case. Although there are a strictly limited number of places at the seven medical schools within Greece, anyone failing to get a place at a Greek university can enrol at a medical school outside the country (usually in Italy or Eastern Europe). Then, on their return, following a practical examination, they can have a licence to practise. Overall, there is no restriction on the number of doctors. The country now has one of the highest number of doctors in relation to its population in Europe, only Italy and Spain have higher ratios (WHO 1996: 47). According to a newspaper report in December 1998 (*Ta Nea* [*The News*], 23 December 1998: 16), the average doctor–population ratio is 1:201, as compared to 1:336 in France and 1:562 in the UK. Within Greece, however, the figures reflect great inequality between Athens – at 1:170 – and the rest of Greece. The ratio for central Macedonia and Thessolonika is 1:236, which contrasts markedly with 1:630 in central Greece. Athens is the main 'honeypot' of Greek medicine. Fifty-four per cent of all doctors work in the conurbation, while only 3 per cent work in central Greece. Part of the reason for this concentration is that there is far more opportunity to attract private patients in Athens than elsewhere in Greece. Moreover, while public sector doctors are officially prohibited from engaging in private practice, many, and possibly most, do.

As in France and across the continent generally, there are three types of collective medical organisations:

1   official medical societies;
2   specialist medical societies;
3   doctors' unions.

Although they have much in common with their French counterparts, they also have peculiarities of their own:

1   *Official medical societies*. The Pan Hellenic Medical Society (Paenllionios Iatrikos Sillogos – PIS) was established in 1923 and codified in 1939 under the Metaxas dictatorship (Colombotos and Fakiolas 1993). Membership of one of the fifty-eight local societies is mandatory. Its role and function is similar to the Ordre des Médecins in France. The local societies are

responsible on behalf of the state for the detailed administration of the profession at the local level, including disciplinary procedures. The organisation, however, is largely seen as having very limited influence even over such central issues as education, training and professional development.

2   *Specialist medical societies.* There is a wide range of learned societies, although their influence within the profession is very limited because the state pays little attention is paid to the work of these bodies. Their lack of influence, however, can be overstated for they provide a reasonably autonomous organisational space for the profession to discuss clinical developments and medical science. Moreover, they provide an informal network for academic physicians who have an important influence on appointments and on related policy.

3   *Doctors' unions.* These represent the independent voice of doctors. The main union is the Union of Hospital Doctors (EINAP – Enosis Iatron Nosileftirion, Athinon–Piraeus), which was established in 1976 and represents around 8,000 salaried doctors. Another important union is the Society of Professional Health Personnel of IKA-SEIPIKA (Sillogos Epistimonikou Igionomikou Prosopikou, IKA) representing around 6,000 doctors. There are regional counterparts of both organisations throughout Greece. Yet even these organisations cannot escape the imprint of clientelism. Even EINAP has PASOK representatives sitting on its central committees.

The health workers' committee at each hospital formally represents the workers – including doctors and nurses. However, the doctors view this committee as largely irrelevant to their interests and concerns.

The family and co-payments for health care services

France

Sickness funds in France cover only about 72 per cent of health expenditure (de Kervasdoué *et al.* 1997: 65; de Pouvourville 1997: 163), compared with 85 per cent in Europe generally. Typically, ambulatory care includes 30 per cent co-payments, coverage of inpatient care is more comprehensive at about 92 per cent (de Kervasdoué *et al.* 1997: 65), and for private practitioners' fees the reimbursement rate averages around 74 per cent (ibid.: 66). The shortfall, however, is typically not paid in cash by the patient – as is the case in Greece – but from private health insurance. France unusually has an extensive system of cost sharing, which covers the public as well as the private sector. Eighty-four per cent of the population has private insurance (mutualles) (Kutzin 1998). The increase in co-payments was intended by government to inhibit demand from patients and assist in slowing down health care expenditure. French people, however, are accustomed to visiting the doctor of their choice, whether in the private or public sector. In line with the principles of *médecine liberale*, all that has effectively happened is that they have taken out additional health insurance. Co-payments and private insurance, however, tend to further disadvantage the disadvantaged. It is the workers in small firms, the young and the unemployed who tend not to have private insurance.

Greece

Doctors' official salaries are surprisingly low. In 1992 the salary in the ESYwas between US$9,500 and $19,000 and for IKA doctors it was even lower (Colombotos and Fakiolas 1993: 140). The attractiveness of the profession lies less in the official salary than in the opportunity it offers for unofficial and private income. The known presence but hidden existence of an 'underground economy of health' (ibid.: 1993: 140) means that its cost is difficult to estimate accurately. Sissouras *et al.* (1994: 152) cite research that indicates that the informal economy amounts to a little over half of the total health expenditure, while Liaropoulos and Tragakes (1998: 159–60) estimate that it amounted to 3.43 per cent of the country's GDP in 1992. Colombotus and Fakiolas (1993: 139) estimate that 25 per cent of the cost of health care for families is paid for 'out of pocket' in cash. There appears to be a conspiracy in which doctors encourage patient dissatisfaction with the national health system and thereby entice them to visit them in their private offices or even in the hospital. Doctors play on patients' anxieties by accepting the fakelakia (little envelope), a cash payment direct to the doctor for services formally covered by insurance. Receipt of payment is recognition that the doctor has a personal obligation to the patient, but if it is not paid the patient can expect long delays in getting treatment. The simplest way to understand the phenomenon is that it is inversely related to the doctors' salaries (Abel Smith *et al.*, 1994); illicit private practice and fakelakia earnings in 1992 averaged US$30,461 (i.e. approximately £19,000) in 1992. The authorities make little attempt to curb these activities, and middle-class patients would worry even more if they were not able to pay 'out of pocket' to ensure good service. Even so, and unlike the French, Greek citizens are dissatisfied with the health service (Ferrara 1993; Mossialos 1997), including the need to make informal payments (fakelakia). They are also unhappy with the lack of guidance on where to get the best treatment, the lack of continuity of care, and poor facilities in hospitals and clinics (OECD 1994: 152–3). Patients will commonly seek second and more opinions, not infrequently visiting outpatient clinics several times to see different doctors for the same complaint.

In part the patients' suspicions about the quality of the health service may be well grounded. The Greek Consumer Council in 1999 reported fifty-nine hospitals as being of 'third world' quality (*Eleftherotypia*, 13 January 1999: 16). At the same time, patients' own approach to the health care services distorts their perception and exacerbates the inequalities and variations in quality of care. Petmesidou (1996: 325), for instance, points out '[that the] socioeconomic and political structures ... have hardly favoured the development of a universalist culture'.

This is in contrast to France and the culture of 'clientelism' supporting an individualistic and familial culture is deeply rooted. Here, value is placed on particularistic/discretionary health care provision.

Concluding discussion

The French welfare regime has here been characterised as following the *modified male-breadwinner* model. Although there is enough commonality for the country to be identified as *corporate*, according to Esping-Andersen's typology there are also some very distinct differences. These are rooted in the country's distinctive history, which intertwines Catholic traditions of familialism and subsidiarity with the rationalist (and anti-clerical) traditions of the French Revolution. It is the latter that is characterised by the country's étatism and the general belief that the state best represents the common interest. On the other hand, the cultural and domestic traditions of Catholic subsidiarity, which it shares with most countries of the Mediterranean rim and within which 'patriarchal control is vested in husbands more than trade unions, employers or governments' (Lewis 1992: 167), has resulted in a paradoxical outcome, in which French women have benefited from natalist policies to support the family and child care while accepting women's role in the labour market.

Greece fits the Esping-Andersen model even less well. It adopted a national health system approach to health care delivery in 1981, but despite organisational similarities to the UK and Scandinavian versions, the cultural expectations of the citizens – as well as of the professions – are more akin to the 'state corporatism' of France. Katrougalos (1996: 43), for instance, argues that the Mediterranean welfare states – including Greece, are 'merely under-developed species of the Continental [i.e. corporatist] model'. It is, however, more useful to view this group of countries (Italy, Spain, Portugal and Greece) as a distinctive variant within Europe, for just as its nationalised health system approach differs from the UK and Scandinavia, so too, I suspect, would any adoption of a corporatist (i.e. Bismarckian) model.

The modern history of the French and Greek health care systems and the organised professions in both countries also reflects a complex set of relations between the doctors and the state. The apparently Byzantine relations and regulations pertaining to the French and Greek health care systems, the professions and the patients can be usefully explained with reference to Foucault's (1979) concept of governmentality (Gane and Johnson 1993; Johnson 1995). The role of the medical profession in France appears to be more Gramscian than Durkheimian (i.e. the professions are part of the state apparatus), in part because there is not the official 'space' for an autonomous role such as that advocated by Durkheim (Lukes 1975). Members of the organised profession who are sufficiently well connected and organised will be able to influence the regulations government imposes on them, but as individuals not as an organised interest group. To quote one senior manager working within the French health system:

> [W]e use the word 'regulations' in France, which is not 'regulation' in English, but is ... a system [that] auto regulates itself ... but not through prices, through [a doctor's] ... reputation.
>
> (Paris 1998)

It is those doctors with reputations that are most likely to be successful in influencing government policies and getting their ideas embedded in the official regulations. In Greece the situation is similar in some respects. Although government consults with the organised profession, there is no real expectation that the regulations will necessarily be adhered to. The influence of the medical profession depends on particular doctors being enmeshed in a network of clientelistic relationships with the governing party. Nevertheless, the state relies on the medical profession to deliver health care services even if it has to rely on established informal practices. The problem, however, is that the relationship between the public sector health services and the 'underground economy' is not a symbiotic one. The profession provides a site from which to pursue individualistic career and status at the expense of both the wider profession and the national health system (Petmesidou and Tsoulouvis 1994: 508). It is not a case of the doctors playing the *social game* as in France.

More generally, the French version of the 'corporatist' welfare regime has been relatively successful in institutionalising the 'effects' of familialism and subsidiarity through, for example, *la médecine libérale* and the *mutualle* without recourse to clientelism. Within the Greek 'Mediterranean' type this has not been possible for it remains dependent on the operation of clientelistic networks. For families to exercise choices in relation to health care services they have to do so illicitly. But to the extent that the Greek family has the resources to be able to exercise choice, it has the possibility of providing women – so long as they are wives and mothers – with a voice/choice within an otherwise patriarchal system. This apparent 'empowering' of women, however, is highly individualistic, exacerbates economic inequality and is corrosive of policy reforms.

Acknowledgements

I am indebted to the following people: Gérard de Pouvourville (IMAGE, Paris), Aris Sissouras and Nikos Fakiolas (EKKE, Athens), and Minas Samatas (University of Crete) for the help they provided me while carrying out the research on which this chapter is based. The research would not have been possible, either, without the grants provided through the Staffordshire University Research Initiative.

Notes

1 Durkheim was directly critical of the notion that 'the [French] government is the only translator of general wills' (Lukes 1975: 273).
2 'Entry into the social game' has parallels with the notion of responsible autonomy (Friedman 1977; Dent 1993: 249) as well as being consonant with 'governmentality' (Foucault 1979).
3 The hospital elite and urban practitioners opposed the Debré reforms for they had most to lose from the reforms (Immergut 1992: 121–2). Younger doctors, on the other hand, saw the changes as a way of improving their career opportunities. Provincial doctors were also sympathetic because the reforms offered a secure income and career. The intra-professional conflicts led to a major 'split' within the profession and to the establishment of the anti-reform Fédération des Médecins de France (FMF) in 1968 (ibid.: 273, fn. 102).
4 Between 1965 and 1980, full-time posts expanded by 15,000 (Immergut, 1992: 275, fn. 114). The 1970 Hospital Law was based, in part, on the Committee's recommendations. Private beds were not eliminated from public hospitals until 1982.

References

Abbott, A. (1988) *The System of Professions*, Chicago: University of Chicago Press.
Abel Smith, B., Calltorp, J., Dixon, M., Dunning, A., Evans, R. and Holland, W. (1994) *Report on Greek Health Services*, Athens: Ministry of Health and Social Welfare of Greece, Pharmétrica SA.
Athens News (1999) 'Simitis stresses unity, vows to win Euro polls: Combative PM peppers speech with populist rhetoric', 19 March, p. 3.
Bagguley, P. (1994) 'Prisoners of the Beveridge Dream? The political mobilisation of the poor against contemporary welfare regimes', in Burrows, R. and Loader, B. (eds), *Towards a Post-Fordist Welfare State?*, London: Routledge, pp. 79–94.
Boseley, S. (2000) 'Controversial health list ranks Britain 18th in the world', *Guardian*, 21 June, p. 3.
Burrage, M., Jarausch, K. and Siegrist, H. (1990) 'An actor-based framework for the study of the professions', in Burrage, M. and Torstendahl, R. (eds), *Professions in Theory and History*, London: Sage, pp. 203–25.
Colombotos, J. and Fakiolas, N. P. (1993) 'The power of organized medicine in Greece' in Daugherty, F. W. and McKinley, J. B. (eds), *The Changing Medical Profession: An International Perspective*, New York: Oxford University Press, pp. 138–231.
Crozier, M. (1974) *Où Va l'Administration Française?*, Paris: Les Editions d'Organisations.
Dent, M. (1993) 'Professionalism, educated labour and the state: Hospital medicine and the new managerialism', *The Sociological Review*, 41 (2): 244–73.
Ehrmann, H. W. (1983) *Politics in France*, 4th edn, Boston: Little, Brown.
Eleftherotypia [Freepress] (1999) 'Third World situation in 59 major Greek hospitals', 13 January, p. 16.
Esping-Andersen, G. (1990) *Three Worlds of Welfare Capitalism*, Cambridge: Polity Press.
Ferrera, M. (1993) *EC Citizens and Social Protection: Main Results from a Eurobarometer Survey*, Brussels: Commission of the European Communities.

Ferrera, M. (1996) 'The "Southern Model" of welfare in social Europe', *Journal of European Social Policy*, 6 (1): 17–37.

Foucault, M. (1973) *The Birth of the Clinic*. London: Tavistock.

Foucault, M. (1979) 'On governmentality', *Ideology and Consciousness*, 6: 5–22.

Friedman, A.L. (1977) *Industry and Labour*, London: Macmillan.

Gane, M. and Johnson, T. (1993) 'Introduction: The project of Michel Foucault', in Gane, M. and Johnson, T. (eds), *Foucault's New Domains*, London: Routledge, pp. 1–9.

Godt, P. J. (1987) 'Confrontation, consent, and corporatism: State strategies and the medical profession in France, Great Britain, and West Germany', *Journal of Health Politics, Policy and Law*, 12 (3): 459–80.

Handy, C. (1994) *The Empty Raincoat: Making Sense of the Future*, London: Hutchinson.

Herzlich, C. (1982) 'The evolution of relations between French physicians and the state from 1880 to 1980', *Sociology of Health and Illness*, 4 (3): 241–53

Immergut, E. M. (1992) *Health Politics: Interests and Institutions in Western Europe*, Cambridge: Cambridge University Press.

Johnson, T. (1972) *Professions and Power*, London: Macmillan.

Johnson, T. (1995) 'Governmentality and the institutionalization of expertise', in Johnson, T., Larkin, G. and Saks, M. (eds), *Health Professions and the State in Europe*, London: Routledge, pp. 7–24.

Katrougalos, G. S. (1996) 'The south European welfare model: The Greek welfare state, in search of an identity', *Journal of European Social Policy*, 6 (1): 39–60.

de Kervasdoué, J., Meyer, C., Weill, C. and Couffinahl, A. (1997) 'The French health care system: Inconsistent regulation', in Altenstetter, C. and Björkman, S. W. (eds), *Health Policy Reform, National Variations and Globalization*, Basingstoke: Macmillan, pp. 59–78.

Kutzin, J. (1998) 'The appropriate role for patient cost sharing' in Saltman, R. B., Figueras, J. and Sakellarides, C. (eds), *Critical Challenges for Health Care Reform in Europe*, Buckingham: Open University Press, pp. 218–35.

Lancry, P.-J. and Sandier, S. (1999) 'Twenty years of cures for the French health care system', in Mossialos, E. and Le Grand, J. (eds), *Health Care and Cost Containment in the European Union*, Aldershot: Ashgate, pp. 443–70.

Lewis, J. (1989) 'Lone parent families: Politics and economics', *Journal of Social Policy*, 18 (4): 595–600.

Lewis, J. (1992) 'Gender and the development of welfare regimes', *Journal of European Social Policy*, 2 (3): 159–73.

Liaropoulos, L. and Tragakes, E. (1998) 'Public/private financing in the Greek health care system: Implications for equity', *Health Policy*, 43: 153–69.

Lukes, S. (1975) *Émile Durkheim*, London: Penguin.

Mossialos, E. (1997) 'Views on health care systems in the 15 EU member states, *Health Economics*, 6 (2): 109–16.

Mouzelis, N. P. (1986) *Politics in the Semi-Periphery: Early Parliamentarism in the Balkans and Latin America*, Basingstoke: Macmillan.

O'Connor, J. S. (1993) 'Gender, class and citizenship in comparative analysis of welfare state regimes: Theoretical and methodological issues', *British Journal of Sociology*, 44 (3): 501–18.

O'Connor, J. S. (1996) 'Trend report: From women in the welfare state to gendering welfare state regimes', *Current Sociology*, 44 (2): 1–124.

OECD (Organization for Economic Cooperation and Development) (1992) *The Reform of Health Care: A Comparative Analysis of Seven OECD Countries*, Paris: OECD.

OECD (1994) *The Reform of Health Care Systems: A Review of Seventeen OECD Countries*, Paris: OECD.

OECD (1997) *OECD Health Data 1997*, Paris: OECD.

Orloff, A. S. (1993) 'Gender and the social rights of citizenship: The comparative analysis of gender relations and welfare states', *American Sociological Review*, 58: 303–28.

Petmesidou, M. (1996) 'Social protection in Greece: A brief glimpse of a welfare state', *Social Policy and Administration*, 30 (4): 324–47.

Petmesidou, M. and Tsoulouvis, L. (1994) 'Aspects of the changing political economy of Europe: Welfare state, class segmentation and planning in the postmodern era', *Sociology*, 28 (2): 499–519.

Pickvance, C. J. (1999) 'Democratisation and the decline of social movements: The effects of regime change on collective action in Eastern Europe and Latin America', *Sociology*, 33 (2): 353–72.

de Pouvourville, G. (1997) 'Quality of care initiatives in the French context', *International Journal for Quality in Health Care*, 9 (3): 163–70.

Sainsbury, D. (ed.) (1994) *Gendering Welfare States*, London: Sage.

Samatas, M. (1993) 'Debureaucratization failure in post-dictatorial Greece: A socio-political control approach', *Journal of Modern Greek Studies*, 11 (2): 187–217.

Sissouras, A., Karokis, A. and Mossialos, E. (1994) '11. Greece' in OECD', in *The Reform of Health Care Systems: A Review of Seventeen OECD Countries*, Paris: OECD.

Sissouras, A., Karokis, A. and Mossialos, E. (1999) 'Health care and cost containment in Greece', in Mossialos, E. and Le Grand, J. (eds), *Health Care and Cost Containment in the European Union*, Aldershot: Ashgate, pp. 341–400.

Trifiletti, R. (1999) 'Southern European welfare regimes and the worsening position of women', *Journal of European Social Policy*, 9 (1): 49–64.

Williams, F. (1994) 'Social relations, welfare and the post-Fordism debate', in Burrows, R. and Loader, B. (eds), *Towards a Post-Fordist Welfare-State?* London: Routledge, pp. 49–72.

Wilsford, D. (1991) *Doctors and the State*, Durham, NC: Duke University Press.

WHO (World Health Organisation) (1996) *Health Care Systems in Transition – Greece*, Copenhagen, Regional Office for Europe, WHO.

WHO (2000) *World Health Report 2000*, www.who.int/whr/2000/en/report.htm.

Part II
Managing professional work

5   Identifying the professional 'man'ager

Masculinity, professionalism and the search for legitimacy

Stephen Whitehead

Introduction

Critical examinations of professionalism have an intermittent history, usually being adjunctive to ongoing debates concerned with, for example, new managerialism (Busher and Saran 1995; Clarke and Newman, 1996); new work practices (Legge 1995); and the intersections of work and capitalist systems (Thompson 1983). Partly as a consequence of both this relative marginalisation in mainstream organisational analysis and the dominance of 'realist' labour process perspectives (O'Doherty and Willmott 1998), studies of professionalism and professionals have often remained locked in notions of ideological practice (Elliott 1975; Collins 1979; Murphy 1988). Moreover, much of the literature on the professional and professionalism has been presented without reference to gender (Davies 1996). Where critical analysis of women's relationship to professional practice has taken place, it has, as Davies (1996) notes, largely drawn on the notions of closure and exclusion central to realist labour process perspectives (see, for example, Crompton 1987; Witz 1990; Witz 1992). Consequently, while such studies have made important contributions to illuminating the gendered characteristics of professional practices, there has been little subsequent examination of professionalism in relation to gendered subjectivity and identity. This gap in academic knowledge is particularly acute in respect of masculinities and the professional manager. Thus, while feminist studies have exposed the gendered character of professions, giving a critique of the previously unproblematised synonymity of men and professionalism, little attention has been given to the ways in which masculinity and men's subjectivities combine to form and define dominant notions of professionalism within the managerial context (see Davies (1996) and Kerfoot (2001) for discussion).

Recognising that gendered identity work is a central element of occupational and organisational dynamics, this chapter undertakes a re-evaluation of the concept of professionalism. In so doing, the intention is to contribute to a deconstruction of the term professional(ism), away from dualistic accounts of autonomy and regulation, while concurring with those feminist scholars who argue that gender is a key feature of professionals and notions of professional practice (Crompton and Sanderson 1986; Davies 1996). In attempting to develop a more nuanced account of the relationships between men, management and professionalism, this chapter considers the processes of identity work undertaken by masculine/managerial subjects (Kerfoot and Whitehead 1998; Whitehead 2002). In particular, drawing on feminist poststructuralist understandings of the discursive subject, it is suggested that (men) managers' search for professional legitimacy has both organisational and identity dimensions, specifically the alleviation of managerial and ontological insecurities (see also Whitehead 2001). As a project of 'being and becoming' (Deleuze and Guattari 1977) a 'professional manager', this identity work becomes informed by the ideal representations of managerialism and masculinity that are immanent to organisational cultures. Thus, this chapter suggests that notions of professionalism exist as a seductive set of discourses for men managers in terms of enhancing their sense of personal and organisational legitimacy. However, in respect of its gendered ramifications, this identity work is not neutral, for it contributes to both sustaining and reinforcing the symbiotic relationship between masculinity and professions (Davies 1996). Consequently, this desire by men managers for organisational legitimacy can be understood as *identity work with political implications*. In emphasising this relationship between work and identity processes, the aim is to explore professionalism as a fluid and contingent discourse, available for subjective appropriation by discursive subjects, with notions of masculinity symbolically and politically framing labels such as the 'professional manager'.

The chapter is structured in two sections. The first considers several of the key debates which have thus far informed understanding of managerial and professional work. Within this discussion attention is given to poststructuralist perspectives on work and identity processes while highlighting the ambiguities surrounding the managerial/professional self. The second explores the relationships between identity, desire and the masculine subject in managerial and professional work, in so doing drawing on feminist poststructuralist understandings of the gendered discursive subject. The chapter concludes by considering some of the implications of the above debates in respect of understanding the relationship between professionalism and masculine/managerial identity.

Managers as professionals: discussions and debates

Labour process debates

The term 'professional' is ubiquitous within organisational discourse, being endlessly appropriated, like the term 'competent', as a badge of some worth and value for its 'owner'. This apparently innocuous descriptor of the organisational actor is understandably perceived to be a potent symbol of self-worth, for who would wish to be deemed as non-professional? The regulatory and disciplinary overtones of 'professionalism' are, then, quite apparent (see Fournier (1999) for elaboration). Yet to date, much of the discussion surrounding the efficacy of a

distinct professional ideology and the subsequent power of occupational groups
to maintain privilege and advance influence has centred around variations of
labour process theory (see Elliott (1975), Thompson (1983) and also Smith *et
al.* (1996) for discussion). Interlinked with emerging debates concerned with
patriarchy at work (Witz 1990; 1992), women in organisations (Ledwith and
Colgan 1996), and bureaucracy (Clarke and Newman 1996), two distinct and
opposing themes have emerged. First, within the structuralist orthodoxy of
Braverman and the labour theory of value, a 'realist' position can be identified which suggests that professionalism exists as an a priori logical cause
of productive systems of control, surplus value, demarcation (of roles) and
deskilling (Braverman 1974; Friedman 1977; Thompson and Ackroyd 1995).
Concerned to highlight and expose the 'objectivity of capitalist relations,
property interests and any systemic tendencies within capitalism' (Smith
and Thompson 1992: 14), orthodox labour process analysts suggest that
professionalism/professionals can be understood as an ideological formation
of vested interests, with the 'professional class' largely benefiting from transformations in the capitalist system (see Thompson (1983) and Rowlinson and
Hassard (1994) for discussion). The structuralist insights afforded by realist
labour process perspectives have been subsequently utilised and reframed by
those feminist scholars concerned with highlighting the patriarchal paradigm
of occupations and organisations within the capitalist system (see, for example,
Crompton 1987; Witz 1990).

Although recognised to have complex and discontinuous features (Thompson
1983), the realist perspective is based on certain assumptions surrounding
organisational and individual power. Specifically, it rests on a juridico-discursive
model (of power), whereby contesting interests, both individual and group,
are understood to seek and maintain advantage in part through the objective
recognition of common interests and the subsequent rational exercise of power
(see, for example, Elliot 1975). One consequence of the polarisation inherent
in the realist perspective is that notions of professionalism and the professional
quickly become locked into the structure/agency dualism. In particular, the
professional appears as a grounded identity, fraught perhaps with concerns
over autonomy or regulation but nonetheless perceived as a concrete entity,
with some rigidity and structure, (co)existing, albeit not unproblematically,
within a capitalist system.

The second theme can be described as an 'anti-realist' response to the
above debates. Typified by the work of Knights (1992; 1997) and Willmott
(1994), the anti-realist approach draws heavily on poststructuralist analysis
in order to emphasise the role of the subject in the (re)formation of labour
processes, work organisation and divisions of labour. Here, professionalism can
be understood as not simply a form of hegemonic positioning and exploitation, but importantly as a contested set of languages and practices that the
subject draws on as part of a wider agenda concerned with power/resistance
and identity work (Jermier *et al.* 1994). Connected to this approach is the
work of Calas and Smircich (1991), which develops a feminist anthropological

understanding of organisational dynamics (also Wright 1994). For Calas and Smircich, organisations are understood as only reified and reifiable in the intersubjective actions and engagements of organisational subjects. Thus, rather than seek to mark professionalism as a causal factor in a universal system of power and control, (feminist) poststructuralist anthropological understandings stress the importance of discursivity, difference and subjective interpretation to the formation of what Foucault describes as regulatory 'regimes of power' (1980).[1]

In terms of a polarisation of perspectives, the above two themes can be seen to encapsulate the key arguments continuing to circulate critical studies of work and organisations (see O'Doherty and Willmott (1998) for an overview). However, in terms of their contribution to understanding professionalism and professionals, complications arise with the impact of managerialism across both public and private sectors. For it is evident that, despite both its various local manifestations and questions about what counts as 'good' management knowledge, managerialism continues to receive increased legitimacy across most organisational sites (Pollitt 1993). Therefore, as a consequence of the dominance of managerialist discourse, the spaces and opportunities for managers to identify with, and invest in, professional discourses would appear circumscribed. For if managerialism speaks to a performance-oriented, transparent and pragmatic culture, then professionalism can be seen to inhabit the terrain of paternalistic self-regulation (Clarke and Newman 1996).

Yet, might this tidy dichotomised polarisation be problematic? Certainly it can be argued that managerialism challenges the normative power of the 'professions/professional', but how do organisational actors 'manage' this apparently fixed dualism? Specifically, how do they (re)negotiate, (re)invent and (re)present themselves within this power/knowledge nexus? Importantly, what other variables operate here, notably at the intersection of managerial regimes and the wider (inter)subjectivities of the individual? At this point, the discrepancies in a 'realist' approach to understanding occupational power/ influence become evident. For, as Littler and Salaman (1982) suggest, the importance of the professional's 'feelings of identification' with 'the enterprise' of work and organisational processes is paramount. Yet even this reference to the relationship of identity to work practices gives little indication of the ambiguities and contradictions contained in organisational subjectivities. Theories that draw on realist concepts of (professional) collectivism and hegemonic power can be seen, then, to be especially limited. For while possibly useful at a metanarrative level, they remain inadequate in terms of revealing the complexities surrounding managers' motivations, beyond, that is, the instrumental attainment of materialist goals.

Investing in the professional manager – organisational factors

Much of the managerialist rhetoric surrounding (idealised) corporate culture models can be seen to draw heavily on a Weberian pseudo-scientific narrative, sustained moreover by a humanistic belief in the rational self. However, despite this belief in the purposefulness of the human agent, predictable organisational outcomes continue to be elusive. As numerous studies clearly indicate, attempts at reforming organisational work practices and cultural focus can never be predetermined nor made absolute (Anthony 1994; Watson 1994).

One consequence of this search by corporations for solutions to organisational conundrums has been the emergence of more mechanistic and instrumentalist ways of being a manager, increasingly packaged, however, in a softer more 'feminine' way. This repositioning of dominant managerialist discourse is not an attempt to facilitate women into management, but rather an attempt to achieve organisational members' commitment to corporate goals while maintaining an emphasis on performance measurement (Sennett 1998). Thus while organisations now place a heavy reliance on the pseudo-scientific control systems encapsulated in the term 'performativity'[2] (see Dent and Whitehead (2001) for discussion), expressed through, for example, human resource management, performance indicators and total quality management discourses (Legge 1995), these are paradoxically mixed with a counter-rhetoric of cooperation and collaboration. Consequently, managers are frequently required to straddle competing if not largely incompatible discourses of managerialism: in this instance the manager as entrepreneurial individual, as opposed to, or alongside, the manager as paternalistic, trusted team player (Sennet 1998; Misztal 2001).

The sheer fluidity of managerialist discourse, exemplified here in the emergence of a new cooperative rhetoric, presents managers with numerous dilemmas. Not least of these, for many men at least, is the need to negotiate the tension between individualistic, instrumentalist dispositions and the new requirement to present oneself as a collaborative, trusted teamworker (Kerfoot and Knights 1999). A further dilemma is that any negotiations and accommodations must be worked out by a manager already rendered insecure through numerous organisational restructurings. Consequently, the inherently contingent process of organisational positioning in which managers are involved, is played out in an environment – management – already understood as uncertain and anxiety provoking in its lived experience (Anthony 1994).

The extent to which this experience of uncertainty and contingency can be mitigated by the manager is dependent on numerous variables. Among them will be the degree to which she or he can indicate a high level of specialist knowledge and accompanying competencies and managerial skills. For by demonstrating such, so managers might succeed in repositioning themselves as 'professional'; special, valued and committed. Accompanying this association will be important considerations of autonomy, quality and trust (Clarke and Newman 1996; Misztal 2001). There is, then, much for the manager to gain in assuming the mantle of 'professional'; that is, someone deemed worthy – by peers and others – of a larger association with a discrete but privileged body of (managerialist) knowledge. In adopting the mantle 'professional' so the manager can be understood as striving for enhanced status and self-esteem, an understandable quest given the extent to which managers are increasingly exposed and rendered insecure and anxious in rapidly changing organisational environments (Watson 2001).

The notion of a 'professional manager' can be seen, then, to have significant currency when set against the uncertainties of organisational life. Moreover, as Alvesson and Willmott argue, 'professional management' has come to be seen as fundamental to a 'good society' (Alvesson and Willmott 1996: 25); managers being perceived by many as deploying their specialist expertise for the benefit of a society within which the 'objective organisation' is a foundational and pivotal element (Drucker 1977). Yet this association between manager and professional is not without its ambiguities. For in searching for a more 'secure' organisational location as a professional, managers are required to (re)invent themselves vis-à-vis wider organisational codes, the result being that they must constantly perform and regulate their organisational distinction as 'professional managers'. Given the endless shifts in terms of what counts as a 'good manager', this becomes a process that can neither be concluded nor can its consequences be predicted. For despite never being entirely sure what defines this label, the 'professional manager' must, by definition, always be aware of what counts as important, privileged knowledge in the shifting cultures of contemporary organisations. In this respect, in terms of organisational positioning, it matters little whether the manager engages in the collaborative or competitive discourse. What matters more is that she or he is seen to be closely associated with those organisational discourses considered to be most privileged at a particular time. What is apparent, then, is that the position of the 'professional manager', far from being secure in organisational and work environments, is highly fluid, subject as it is to subjective appropriation and interpretation by diverse and numerous organisational actors. Moreover, as will now be discussed, this investment in what is deemed 'professional' has a further dimension, for it connects at a deeper, more profound level for managers – the ontological level of self-identity.

Investing in the professional managers – identity factors

As 'anti-realist' labour process theories suggest, a key characteristic of work dynamics is the very identity of the practitioners themselves (see, for example, Jermier *et al.* 1994; Casey 1995; du Gay 1996; Dent and Whitehead 2001). Yet these identities are not fixed and grounded. Being discursively informed, they remain subject to both external factors and the subjective practices of the self as a contingent subject (Foucault 1988). Recognising this, it is clear that the manager is not 'choosing' appropriate managerial discourses as a rationally selecting agent. While there may be a cognitive element to the manager wishing to be seen as a 'professional', the fact remains that the manager can neither predict nor predetermine the outcomes of his or her actions. In post-structuralist terms there is no self external to discourse (Sarup 1993). Thus there is no individual who can predict and control either the subjectivities of others or, consequently, others' perceptions of him or her.

The means by which the discursive subject achieves what is in effect, then, an elusive sense of self-coherence is in engaging with and being inculcated by those practices of identity signification that circulate the social arena and which are subsequently performed as practices of self (Butler 1990). Thus, it can be argued that, for managerial subjects, the term 'professional' connects directly to issues of *personal legitimacy*. For in taking up those organisational practices that might be invested in the term 'professional', so the discursive subject is also engaged in self-validation. Following this, it becomes apparent that a manager's sense of him- or herself as professional has an important ontological dimension,[3] for it serves to inform, to some degree, that subject's sense of self-identity, while yet remaining highly contingent on the interpretations of others. In recognising the importance of identity work to work practices, it is possible to perceive managers' investment in organisational narratives as simultaneously an investment in the self (as manager) and in corporate discourses – a relationship which serves to reify the self while also regulating and proscribing what it is to be a 'proper' manager (see also Parker 1997).

The 'proper' professional manager can be seen, then, to be a complex label, not only enabling of identity work but, moreover, invested with both regulatory and disciplinary characteristics. However, I would argue that, while significant, this does not imply an ideological causality in the Marxist sense of monolithic power (Clegg 1998). For such an interpretation would assume a prior rational agent/agency or, as Clegg describes it, 'an intentional effect of will' (1998: 30). Rather, following Foucault (1980), it is possible to link the subjective practices of the discursive subject with the disciplinary characteristics invested in discursive regimes of power but without recourse to a simplistic, overarching determinism (see McKinley and Starkey (1998) for discussion; also Hetherington and Munro 1997). For, in Foucauldian terms, disciplinary power is enabled by the very power/resistance indicative of the active discursive subject (Sawicki 1991). Thus, while it offers a means for the subsequent reification of difference and hierarchical positioning within organisations, it cannot be assumed that professional identification directly correlates to the untroubled exercise of power by managerial actors, any more than it can be argued that managerialism has somehow displaced professionalism. Both terms are discursive, fluid, but with disciplinary characteristics. For example, it can be argued that managerialist discourse, as a disciplinary technique within organisations, has problematised if not undermined notions of professional autonomy (Legge 1995; Clarke and Newman 1996). But when attempting to explore the relationships between managerialism and professionalism, it is useful to recognise that despite the impact of marketisation across both the public and the private sectors, notions of professionalism and 'the professional' continue to exert a powerful presence across organisational sites and, importantly, within the subjectivities of individual organisational actors, particularly managements (Dent and Whitehead 2001). In this respect, professionalism remains a core organisational narrative, containing seductive *promises and associations* of power/autonomy for managerial actors, while also performing an ontological service for the ungrounded subject.

The relationship between the manager and notions of 'the professional', while a seductive one, can be seen to be anything but tidy. Indeed, it can be argued that the unresolved contradictions and ambiguities contained in the notion of professional manager are made more acute by the particular economic and social transformations apparent at this juncture in postmodernity (Hassard and Parker 1993; Lemert 1997). As Hassard (1993) suggests, a condition of the postmodern has been to question the myths and orthodoxies of grand (bureaucratic/organisational) narratives, which, it can be argued, have previously sustained any wider professional identification. A similar point is also made by Sennett (1998), who argues that an important consequence of unfettered 'flexible capitalism', has been to disrupt and fragment narratives of organisational identification, subjecting communities of workers, including managers and professionals, to the stark indifference of the corporation. Thus, in the absence of those metanarratives that have previously served to distinguish the professional from other social and economic groups, what it means to be a professional is increasingly open to question, disruption and subjective interpretation. Reinforcing this uncertainty is the question of what counts as professional knowledge, few professional managers being able to claim absolute privileged knowledge in the fast-moving global, high-tech knowledge economy (Handy 1994; Prichard 1998).

These, and the other factors previously discussed, only serve to emphasise the ambiguity of professionalism as a fixed and secure position within an a-priori logical formation of wider capitalist systems. Yet it is also evident that the label 'professional' remains an important resource for many managers in their pursuit of organisational security. For the term 'professional' is clearly a useful and potent adornment of the subject position 'manager' (Mouffe 1995), not least because it presupposes the occupier of this label to have valuable expertise and privileged knowledge.

To summarise, this section has examined the notion of manager as professional. It has been argued that in a constantly shifting and increasingly insecure work environment, such as management, the pressure and urgency for managers to associate with the label of professional manager is apparent. Yet, while managerialist techniques such as cost cutting, appraisal and performance targeting have a clear material actuality, the term 'professional' remains an amorphous one. For the notion of what is a 'professional' is constantly subject to wider appropriation, including shifting fads surrounding 'good' management practice and, not least, subjective interpretation by organisations, their members and user groups. Rather than see, then, the professional manager as simply caught between notions of autonomy and constraint, it is possible to perceive this identification as multiple, fluid and highly contingent.

While it can be readily appreciated why managers would wish to be associated with the term 'professional', this engagement is not merely a cognitive one. Understanding that the subject only comes to 'be' through discourse (Deleuze and Guattari 1990), it can be seen that organisational discourses are potent sources of identity signification, coming to frame and inform the discursive subject's sense of self-coherence. As a 'professional manager' the individual (subject) necessarily inculcates and engages with the dominant discourses that serve to reify this position, in the process subjecting him- or herself to the regulatory and disciplinary facets contained within this discursive subject position (Mouffe 1995). Thus, while the individual's sense of self and sense of organisational well-being is reinforced by this association, one important outcome is to create a frame of regulatory practice that acts as an important measure and reference point for managers in their quest to define themselves as 'professional'. In their search for organisational and ontological legitimacy, the professional manager becomes simultaneously enabled and constrained by those dominant discourses that serve to define his or her self. However, as has been intimated, there is a further important and defining dimension to this identity work, for it is significantly gendered, drawing as it does on wider (ideal) representations of masculinity.

Masculine identity work and the professional manager

Having considered some of the prominent debates in organisational theory concerned with identity, management and professionalism, this section will examine the relationship between gender and notions of the professional manager. Specifically, the aim will be to explore how masculinity and professionalism connect as self-sustaining discourses for masculine/managerial subjects. In so doing, the chapter aligns with those feminist scholars who have been concerned to highlight the gendered character of management, organisations and professionalism. Following Davies's (1996) argument that professionalism is embedded in a masculinist vision, one which 'privileges male characteristics while denigrating and/or suppressing female ones' (Stivers 1993, quoted in Davies 1996: 671), the intention is to develop a critical theoretical perspective on the men, management and professional symbiosis.

Masculine ontology and the desire to be

In undertaking its critical examination of professional practice/identity, this chapter draws on a poststructualist concept of self; that is, one that considers identity to be multiple, unstable and contingent and the self as non-authentic. Yet the sense that subjects have of being concrete and grounded is strong. One way of understanding this apparent contradiction is to see it in terms of identity work. That is, self and identity become manifest through the pursuit of 'ideal representations' by the discursive subject (Lacan 1977). As persons emerge into the social world the desire for ontological purchase is compelling. Deleuze and Guattari (1977; also Bogue 1996) describe this in terms of being and becoming – the quest for and production of self-(identification). Managing and defying ontological insecurity (Giddens 1991) can be understood then, as the most important psychological need of the otherwise amorphous and ungrounded self. The search for ontological security and the subsequent minimisation of existential anxiety that comes with the absence of an a-priori self is a driving force for all subjects as they work at 'going on' in social life. The absence of any biological grounding to self-identity creates the very conditions of dread and anxiety that come with recognition of unpredictability and tenuous existence, conditions that can never be totally removed, only assuaged. Weber describes this existential anxiety in terms of an 'unprecedented inner loneliness' (1930: 104); a lurking, ever-present condition that is immanent to the discursive subject's existence (see also Deleuze and Guattari 1990).

While the desire for being and becoming (an individual) can be understood as inherent to all subjects and consequently non-gendered, the actual exercise, experience and process of this in the social world clearly has gendered implications. Thus, as I have detailed elsewhere (Whitehead 1999; 2002), the search for ontological security and subsequent identity validation can be considered, for men, as engagement with a masculinist ontology by masculine subjects. Concomitant with accepting the notion of a non-authentic self, is the recognition that 'man' (and woman) have no biological base beyond specific re-productive embodiments (Butler 1990; Game 1991). Yet man and woman clearly exist as powerful and fundamental dichotomised, political identities for all individuals. In poststructuralist terms, the reification of these otherwise amorphous labels and identities is only made possible by the discursive subject's quest for identity validation. As Butler (1990) describes it, the individual comes to be through the taking up and inculcation of (prior) gendered practices of identity signfication. These gendered practices can further be identified as 'ideal representations' of masculinity and femininity, which, while historically, spatially and temporally specific, continue to circulate the social web.[1]

The masculine subject then, is that discursive entity which, in the quest for gendered identification, pursues the ideal representations of manliness, which are offered and accessible at a particular time and place. As man is not a foundational entity 'it'/'he' can only be reified through the discursive expressions and ontological quest of the masculine subject. However, it is an identity quest with political implications and consequences, for by reifying 'man', a particular gender is privileged and an accompanying discursive regime of power substantiated. As Sarup puts it, 'discourse is the agency whereby the subject is produced and the existing order sustained' (Sarup 1993: 24).

Once the importance of ideal representations of masculinity are recognised as part of the reificational processes of 'man', then it becomes possible to connect the desire to be with the material actualities of masculinity. For while masculinity can be considered an illusory concept, historically and culturally specific (see, for example, Roper and Tosh 1991), there is a material dimension to the identity work of the masculine subject. This material actuality emerges out of the recognition that discourse is not confined to language but is also manifest in practice. As will now be discussed, the material actuality of discourses of masculinity and managerialism is that, taken in unison, they become self-sustaining and thus powerful in respect of how they serve to form and define the professional 'man'ager.

Ideal representations and the professional 'man'ager

As an increasing number of critical gender theorists note, masculinity is embedded in the dominant cultural and discursive codes of managerial and organisational life (Kerfoot and Knights 1993; Roper 1994; Cheng 1996; Collinson and Hearn 1996; Kerfoot and Whitehead 1998). It is an embeddedness with two fundamental aspects. First, there is the historical and continuing numerical dominance of men in management.[5] Second, there are the distinct masculinist organisational cultures apparent across most public and private sector sites (Ledwith and Colgan 1996; Whitehead and Moodley 1999). As numerous feminist scholars have indicated, organisational culture is both materially and symbolically gendered in favour of a masculine 'ideal' (Gherardi 1995; Marshall 1995; Bruni and Gherardi 2001). However, masculinity should not be understood as a biological characteristic of the male species, nor indeed as simply an aspect of men's socialisation experience. As I have discussed elsewhere (Whitehead 1999; 2002), masculinity is axiomatic to the gender category of men, being both a condition and a consequence of the (masculine) subject's desire for ontological purchase. Following recognition of the symbiotic relationship between men and masculinity, masculinity emerges as immanent to the capitalist system generally (Connell 1995) and indicative of management values specifically (Kerfoot and Knights 1993).

While recognising that discourses of masculinity, as expressed in management, have pre-eminence over discourses of femininity (Davies 1996), the actual form these discourses take can be quite diverse. Kerfoot and Knights (1993), for example, discuss the transitions between the entrepreneurial and the paternalistic in masculine/management discourse in the financial services. Similarly, Roper (1994) charts the rise of the hard-edged technical manager in British business, displacing the 'gentleman amateur' of the post-war period. The variety and extent of masculine/managerial discourses is explored by Collinson and Hearn (2001), who note that the masculinities surrounding management are multiple, diverse and fluid. At the same time, however, masculinity remains a fundamentally illusory concept, spatially and temporally specific, and grounded only in the everyday interactions of the discursive subject.

The illusory multiplicity of masculinity requires, however, that its dominant forms be sustained and expressed in opposition to femininity and thus relational to the 'Other'; the female and 'un-masculine' codes of being (Connell 1995; see also Hollway 1996). For in so doing, this gives the sense of form and substance otherwise absent in what is, in effect, a highly contingent 'definer' of maleness. Consequently, what is understood as appropriate masculine/managerial practice invariably connects to broader social and cultural representations of male behaviour. In this way the relationship between the competitive, aggressive, non-emotional and instrumental concerns of organisations and of masculinity is strengthened (Kerfoot and Knights 1993; Whitehead and Moodley 1999), as is the association between men, management and mastery (of self and other;

see Kerfoot 2001). Moreover, it can be argued that the prevailing managerial discourse of performativity only serves to reinforce these connections. For performativity has come to privilege the (pseudo)scientific (Lyotard 1984), in the process displacing or rendering as marginal and unimportant more subjective, intimate and emotional narratives that might otherwise surface in the organisational environment. As discussed, the relationship between performativity and the rhetoric surrounding teamworking and collaboration is that the latter can be used to garner the commitment of those managers and employees made 'untrusting' of organisations, in part through the effects of performativity itself.

For men/managers the discourse of performativity is, then, particularly seductive, for it privileges, and is exemplified by, instrumental engagement, endless competition, control mechanisms, and the functionality of performance measurement (see also Usher and Edwards (1994) for discussion). In short, performativity, while not apparently gendered, connects to wider social and cultural representations of 'ideal' or typical male behaviour. In this respect, the performativities that new managerialism embraces can be seen to be axiomatic to, and synonymous with, dominant discourses of masculinity – and thus, men.

The cultural associations between men and management also feature in ideal representations of the professional, with professionalism coming to be framed around a masculine vision of control, rationality, personal agency/ accomplishment, and distant instrumentality (Davies 1996; Kerfoot 2001). Thus, if one takes these three aspects of organisational culture in unison, that is management, masculinity and professionalism, then a triumvirate of power-ful discourses emerges. Together, this triumvirate not only serves to reinforce men's organisational location, it constitutes important and, for men, acces-sible, self-sustaining elements in the masculine/managerial subject's desire for personal identification. The material actuality of this discursive symbiosis is, of course, further grounded in the historicity of the men/professional association. Thus, while professionalism and masculinity can be described as illusory, they contribute to the gendered material actuality of organisational and social conditions. They suggest men managers to be 'naturally' invested with certain traits and characteristics, which are further common-sensically understood to speak to a professional discourse of non-emotional, rational, exclusive and technical organisational knowledge and practice (Glazer and Slater 1987; Witz 1990; see also Weber 1930).

While masculinity, management and professionalism can be seen as sym-biotic and elementary to males/men, these terms can, paradoxically, also be understood as vulnerable and contested. For none of masculinity, managerial-ism or professionalism are given and secure. Each is understood within wider social and cultural codes and, thus, dependent on subjective interpretations. Moreover, in respect of men's sense of being a man and professional manager, this can only be sustained in the moment – through the gendered practices of signification in which the masculine/managerial subject engages. The sense of being a professional manager (and that is all there is) is, then, fraught with uncertainty and contingency. There can never be a final 'knowing' of oneself as a professional manager, nor indeed as masculine. Like all subject positions (Mouffe 1995), these identities are achievable only in the moment of self-interpretation of the elusive gaze of the 'Other' (Lacan 1977). There is no rational unitary subject who is male/man/manager/professional, only the component parts of a composite subject.

In seeking to displace both masculinity and professionalism from the structure/agency and regulatory/autonomy dualism, this chapter argues that an inherent myth of both masculinity and professionalism is that they are absolute, fixed and constant entities. Rather than understanding these terms as grounded, I suggest that both masculinity and professionalism are multiple discourses and, as such, highly amenable to subjective interpretation. Consequently, the very elusiveness yet cultural potency of masculinity and professionalism signals their power. For as defining facets of organisational life (Collinson and Hearn 1996), each speaks to a particular constituency – the gender category of men. In this respect masculinity and professionalism, while being quite distinct terms, can be understood as mutually reinforcing. As such, they are useful and accessible tools for the masculine/managerial subject in its desire for individualisation. Moreover, taken in unison, both discourses serve to sustain the sense of legitimacy of men as 'natural' professional managers.

Conclusion

In contributing to a re-evaluation of professionalism, this chapter has sought to draw connections between men, masculinity and those competing discourses that serve to reify the 'professional manager'. In so doing, the concern has been to highlight the fluidity and contingency of the term 'professional' while also emphasising its importance in respect of men managers' search for both organisational and personal (gender) legitimacy.

Rather than simply perceive professional and managerial identity in terms of a fixed location within a binary divide of 'old' and 'new' forms of expression and definition, I have stressed the gendered multiplicity and contingency of professional identification, and its relationship to privileged meanings of masculinity (Davies 1996; Kerfoot 2001) and management (Bruni and Gherardi 2001). In so doing, the intention has been to contribute to a deconstruction of the term 'professionalism', away from notions of structure and agency, most notably expressed in the literature as regulatory or autonomy discourse (Busher and Saran 1995; Clarke and Newman 1996; Gleeson and Shain, 1999). Thus, this paper considers that professionalism should not be understood as an entity that people have and hold, but rather as a pliable, multiple concept, one that is amenable to subjective interpretation and reification by different organisational subjects. While these subjects are understood to occupy different subject positions across various spatial and temporal settings, in the final analysis they hold a largely fixed identification, that of gender.

In recognising the centrality of gender to formations of identity, the chapter has drawn on feminist poststructuralist perspectives, in particular the concept of the masculine subject (Kerfoot and Whitehead 1998; Whitehead 2002). In so doing, it is taken as given that organisations are gendered both in terms of the numerical dominance of men, particularly at a managerial level, and in terms of the managerialist expressions of particular masculinist discourses (Gherardi 1995; Collinson and Hearn 1996; Bruni and Gherardi 2001). Also, that professional is itself not a gender-neutral term, but one invested with wider 'maleist' meanings in respect of competency, trust, accountability, autonomy and rationality.

Recognising such, this chapter aligns with that feminist scholarship that has sought to explicate the masculinities in professional discourse, in particular, the work of Davies (1996), which has drawn attention to the 'masculinist vision of professional work' (see also Kerfoot 2001). Thus, in respect of women managers' relationship to the 'professional manager' label, this chapter suggests that women's inclusion within this term, marginal as it currently is, is likely to remain defined by dominant masculine/managerial codes; the triumvirate of masculinity/management/professional discourses being not only powerful but self-sustaining and, crucially for women, self-defining and self-legitimising. Following the work of Bruni and Gherardi (2001), further research could usefully explore the problematics of professional identity that ensue for those women in search of a legitimacy as 'professional managers'.

Given that the term professional is not gender neutral, having long been associated with the constituency of men, the relationship between men and professionalism would appear to be secure. For this reason, professionalism would seem to be a particularly attractive discourse for men managers to associate with – embellishing and thus reinforcing their sense of organisational legitimacy. Moreover, the notion of being a professional manager contributes to the masculine subject's desire for ontological security. Thus as a discourse, 'the professional' offers the (masculine) amorphous subject two interconnected forms of legitimacy – that of male self-identity and organisational status. Far from being problematised by new managerialist discourse, the notion of professionalism and the professional can be seen to be both reinforced and reified by its association with the masculine subjectivities of men/managers.

However, while professionalism can be an undoubtedly seductive discourse for those managers facing the insecurities of organisational life, the notion of 'the professional' is not without its contradictions and ambiguities. Not least of these is the very contingency of the term itself. For in the dominant performative, but insecure culture that defines contemporary management, that which is considered 'professional' increasingly resides in the latest management fad or fashion. Thus, there is no grounded orthodoxy that defines the professional manager. There is only the subjective interpretation of the other, whether that 'other' be one's peers, employers or the 'customer'. Moreover, in so much as 'professionalism' presents itself as based in a privileged knowledge, that which is considered privileged knowledge is increasingly difficult to pin down in the new global knowledge economy. Consequently, the professional manager can never relax in the protection suggested by this descriptor. On the contrary, what is required is a constant policing of one's language, practices and intersubjective moments, always the aim being to be seen as 'professional'. The cognitive and emotional element of this endless organisational (re)positioning must be fraught in itself. Yet in respect of men managers' identity work, further dilemmas abound through the very illusory character of masculinity and from the recognition that individuals do not occupy an extra-discursive position. Consequently, as conflicting discourses of 'good management' circulate management spaces, there is the constant tension faced by men managers in respect of 'managing' the ambiguities of various masculine identifications. For many men managers, their well-honed individualistic dispositions do not sit comfortably with the emergent managerial rhetoric of collaboration and cooperation.

It can be seen, then, that despite management continuing to be a primary fulcrum from which organisational practices proliferate and are replicated, the threats to managerial knowledge and self-identity are multiple. The 'professional' identification may go some way to mitigating the anxieties inherent in managerial life, but it can not completely remove them. Indeed, as has been discussed, the 'professional manager' finds him or herself further burdened with often contradictory expectations, which, once assumed, cannot easily be dispensed with. For the threat of the 'non-professional' label exercises a regulatory and disciplinary condition on the managerial subject. Thus, while managers may consider themselves to be 'in control' of their relationship to 'the organisation', the disciplinary power invested in dominant professional manager discourses suggests otherwise. In anthropological terms, the professional manager, through his or her presence and actions, constitutes the organisation; he/she is not external to it. There being no cognitive agent that exists prior to discourse, the managerial/masculine subject can be seen to be both a condition and a consequence of the particular configuration of discourses that serve to inform organisational dynamics, reinforce gender difference, and frame the conditions or terms of women's and 'others' inclusion/exclusion. Recognising this alerts us to the complex interplay of powers/resistances in organisational life, which exist in a symbiotic relationship to the proscribed and creative identification practices of the professional 'man'ager in search of legitimacy.

Notes

1   The notion of power being utilised in the term 'power regimes' is a Foucauldian one, in which power is in a 'capillary form', engrained in individuals; 'a regime of its exercise **within** the social body, rather than **from above it**' (Foucault 1980: 39, original emphasis). The emphasis here is on the instability of power, rather than a juridico-discursive understanding, which would perceive power as monolithic, fixed and always oppressive.

2 Lyotard describes 'performativity' as the endless search for efficiency in contemporary, 'post-modern' society. He goes on to argue that 'narrative knowledge', has been marginalised, if not displaced, by (pseudo)scientific knowledge. Consequently, through the application of technical criteria, instrumental mechanisms and scientific 'verifiability', the dominant questions are 'is it efficient?' and 'what use is it?'. See Usher and Edwards (1994) for a discussion of Lyotard's work in respect of educational issues, also Whitehead (1998).

3 See Giddens (1991) for discussion and elaboration of the concept of ontological security in respect of risk, security, trust and identities in high modernity; see also Misztal (1996).

4 See Bell (1999) for extended discussion of Judith Butler's work, in particular her notion of 'performativity' as a legitimising practice of the discursive self.

5 A recent survey undertaken by the Institute of Management reveals no change in the gendered constitution of key private sector positions; only 3.6 per cent of company directors are women (Institute of Management 1998).

References

Alvesson, M. and Willmott, H. (1996) *Making Sense of Management*, London: Sage.

Anthony, P. (1994) *Managing Culture*, Buckingham: Open University Press.

Bell, V. (ed) (1999) 'Performativity and belonging', *Theory, Culture and Society* (Special Issue), 16: 2.

Bogue, R. (1996) *Deleuze and Guattari*, London: Routledge.

Braverman, H. (1974) *Labour and Monopoly Capital*, London: Monthly Review Press.

Bruni, A. and Gherardi, S. (2001) 'Omega's Story: The heterogeneous engineering of a gendered professional self', in Dent, M. and Whitehead, S. (eds), *Managing Professional Identities: Knowledge, Performativity and the 'New' Professional*, London: Routledge.

Busher, H. and Saran, R. (eds) (1995) *Managing Teachers as Professionals in Schools*, London: Kogan Page.

Butler, J. (1990) *Gender Trouble*, London: Routledge.

Calas, M. and Smircich, L. (1991) 'Voicing seduction to silence leadership', *Organization Studies*, 4: 567–602.

Casey, C. (1995) *Work, Self and Society*, London: Routledge.

Cheng, C. (ed.) (1996) *Masculinities in Organizations*, New York: Sage.

Clarke, J. and Newman, J. (1996) *The Managerial State*, London: Sage.

Clegg, S. (1998) 'Foucault, power and organizations', in McKinley, A. and Starkey, K. (eds), *Foucault, Management and Organization Theory*, London: Sage.

Collins, R. (1979) *The Credential Society*, Orlando, FL: Academic Press.

Collinson, D. L. and Hearn, J. (eds) (1996) *Men as Managers, Managers as Men*, London: Sage.

Collinson, D. L. and Hearn, J. (2001) 'Naming men as men: Implications for work, organization and management', in Whitehead, S. M. and Barratt F. J. (eds), *The Sociology of Masculinity: A Reader*, Cambridge: Polity Press.

Crompton, R. (1987) 'Gender, status and professionalism', *Sociology*, 21: 413–28.

Crompton, R. and Sanderson, K. (1986) 'Credentials and careers: Some implications of the increase in professional qualifications amongst women', *Sociology*, 20: 25–41.

Connell, R. W. (1995) *Masculinities*, Cambridge: Polity Press.

Davies, C. (1996) 'The sociology of professions and the profession of gender', in *Sociology*, 30: 661–78.

Deleuze, G. (1990) *Expressionism in Philosophy: Spinoza* (trans. M. Joughin), New York: Zone.

Deleuze, G. and Guattari, F. (1977) *Anti-Oedipus*, Minneapolis: University of Minnesota Press.

Dent, M. and Whitehead, S. (eds) (2001) *Managing Professional Identities: Knowledge, Performativity and the 'New' Professional*, London: Routledge.

Drucker, P. (1977) *Management*, London: Pan.

Elliott, P. (1975) 'Professional ideology and social situation', in Esland, S., Salaman, G. and Speakman, M. (eds), *People and Work*, Buckingham: Open University Press.

Foucault, M. (1980) *Power/Knowledge* (ed. C. Gordon), New York: Pantheon Books.

Foucault, M. (1988) 'The ethic of care for the self as a practice of freedom', in Bernauer, J. and Rasmussen, D. (eds), *The Final Foucault*, Cambridge, MA: MIT Press.

Fournier, V. (1999) 'The appeal to 'Professionalism' as a disciplinary mechanism', *The Sociological Review*, 47 (2): 280–307.

Friedman, A. (1977) *Industry and Labour: Class Struggle at Work and Monopoly Capitalism*, London: Macmillan.

Game, A. (1991) *Undoing the Social*, Milton Keynes: Open University Press.

du Gay, P. (1996) *Consumption and Identity at Work*, London: Sage.

Gherardi, S. (1995) *Gender, Symbolism and Organizational Cultures*, London: Sage.

Giddens, A. (1991) *Modernity and Self-Identity*, Cambridge: Polity Press.

Glazer, P. and Slater, M. (1987) *Unequal Colleagues: The Entrance of Women into the Professions, 1890–1940*, New Brunswick, NJ: Rutgers University Press.

Gleeson, D. and Shain, F. (1999) 'Under new management: Changing conceptions of teacher professionalism and policy in the further education sector', *Journal of Education Policy*, 14 (4): 445–62.

Handy, C. (1994) *The Empty Raincoat*, London: Hutchinson.

Hassard, J. (1993) 'Postmodernism and organizational analysis: An overview', in Hassard, J. and Parker, M. (eds,) *Postmodernism and Organizations*, London: Sage.

Hassard, J. and Parker, M. (eds) (1993) *Postmodernism and Organizations*, London: Sage.

Hetherington, K. and Munro, R. (eds) (1997) *Ideas of Difference*, Oxford: Blackwell.

Hollway, W. (1996) 'Masters and men in the transition from factory hands to sentimental workers', in Collinson, D. and Hearn, J. (eds), *Men as Managers, Managers as Men*, London: Sage.

Institute of Management (1998) *National Management Salary Survey*, Kingston upon Thames: Institute of Management.

Jermier, J., Knights, D. and Nord, W. (eds) (1994) *Resistance and Power in Organizations*, London: Routledge.

Kerfoot, D. (1999) 'The organization of intimacy: Managerialism, masculinity and the masculine subject', in Whitehead, S. and Moodley, R. (eds), *Transforming Managers: Gendering Change in the Public Sector*, London: UCL Press.

Kerfoot, D. (2001) 'Managing the professional man', in Dent, M. and Whitehead, S. (eds), *Managing Professional Identities: Knowledge, Performativity and the 'New' Professional*, London: Routledge.

Kerfoot, D. and Knights, D. (1993) 'Management, masculinity and manipulation', *Journal of Management Studies*, 30 (4): 659–79.

Kerfoot, D. and Knights, D. (1999) 'Man management: Ironies of modern management in an "old" university', in Whitehead, S. and Moodley, R. (eds), *Transforming Managers: Gendering Change in the Public Sector*, London: UCL Press.

Kerfoot, D. and Whitehead, S. (1998) ' "Boys Own" stuff: Masculinity and the management of further education', *The Sociological Review*, 46 (3): 436–547.

Knights, D. (1992) 'Changing spaces: The disruptive power of epistemological location for management and organizational sciences', *Academy of Management Review*, 17 (3): 514–36.

Knights, D. (1995) 'Hanging out the dirty washing: Labour process theory in the age of deconstruction', paper presented to the *13th International Labour Process Conference*, Blackpool, April 1995.

Knights, D. (1997) 'Organization and theory in the age of deconstruction: Dualism, gender and postmodernism revisited', *Organization Studies*, 18: 1–19.

Lacan, J. (1977) *Ecrits: A Selection*, London: Tavistock.

Ledwith, S. and Colgan, F. (eds) (1996) *Women in Organisations*, London: Macmillan Business.

Legge, K. (1995) *Human Resource Management: Rhetorics and Realities*, London: Macmillan Business.

Lemert, C. (1997) *Postmodernism Is Not What You Think*, Oxford: Blackwell.

Littler, C. and Salaman, G. (1982) 'Bravermania and beyond – recent theories of the labour process', *Sociology*, 16 (2): 251–69.

Lyotard, J. F. (1984) *The Post-Modern Condition*, Manchester: Manchester University Press.

Marshall, J. (1995) *Women Managers Moving On*, London: Routledge.

McKinley, A. and Starkey, K. (eds) (1998) *Foucault, Management and Organization Theory*, London: Sage.

Misztal, B. A. (1996) *Trust in Modern Societies*, Cambridge: Polity Press.

Misztal, B. A. (2001) *Trusting the Professional: A Managerial Discourse for Uncertain Times*, in Dent, M. and Whitehead, S. (eds), *Managing Professional Identities: Knowledge, Performativity and the 'New' Professional*, London: Routledge.

Mouffe, C. (1995) 'Democratic politics and the question of identity', in Rajchman, J. (ed.), *The Identity in Question*, London: Routledge.

Murphy, R. (1988) *Social Closure: The Theory of Monopolization and Exclusion*, Oxford: Clarendon Press.

O'Doherty, D. and Willmott, H. (1998) 'Recent contributions to the development of labour process analysis', paper presented to the *16th Annual Labour Process Conference*, University of Manchester, April 1998.

Parker, M. (1997) 'Dividing organizations and multiplying identities', in Hetherington, K. and Munro, R. (eds), *Ideas of Difference*, Oxford: Blackwell.

Pollitt, C. (1993) *Managerialism and the Public Services*, Oxford: Blackwell.

Prichard, C. (1998) " 'It's intelligent life, Jim, but not as we know it': Re-wording and re-working tertiary education in the age of the global knowledge economy', paper presented to the *Annual Conference of the New Zealand Association for Research in Education*, University of Otago, Dunedin, December 1998.

Roper, M. (1994) *Masculinity and the British Organization Man since 1945*, Oxford: Oxford University Press.

Roper, M. and Tosh, J. (eds) (1991) *Manful Assertions: Masculinities in Britain since 1800*, London: Routledge.

Rowlinson, M. and Hassard, J. (1994) 'Economics, politics and labour process theory', *Capital and Class*, 53: 965–97.

Sarup, M. (1993) *Post-structuralism and Postmodernism*, London: Harvester Wheatsheaf.

Sawicki, J. (1991) *Disciplining Foucault*, London: Routledge.

Sennett, R. (1998) *The Corrosion of Character*, New York: W.W. Norton.

Smith, C. and Thompson, P. (1992) 'When Harry met Sally … and Hugh and David and Andy: A reflection of ten years of the labour process conference', *10th International Labour Process Conference*, Aston University, Birmingham, April 1992.

Smith, C., Knights, D. and Willmott, H. (eds) (1996) *White-Collar Work*, London: Macmillan.

Stivers, C. (1993) *Gender Images in Public Administration*, London: Sage.

Thompson, P. (1983) *The Nature of Work*, London: Macmillan.

Thompson, P. and Ackroyd, S. (1995) 'All quiet on the workplace front? A critique of recent trends in British industrial sociology', *Sociology*, 29: 615–33.

Usher, R. and Edwards, R. (1994) *Postmodernism and Education*, London: Routledge.

Watson, T. J. (1994) *In Search of Management*, London: Routledge.

Watson, T. J. (2001) 'Speaking professionally – occupational anxiety and discursive ingenuity amongst human resources professionals', in Dent, M. and Whitehead, S. (eds), *Managing Professional Identities: Knowledge, Performativity and the 'New' Professional*, London: Routledge.

Weber, M. (1930) *The Protestant Ethic and the Spirit of Capitalism*, London: Allen and Unwin.

Whitehead, S. (1998) 'Disrupted selves: Resistance and identity work in the managerial arena', *Gender and Education*, 10 (2): 199–215.

Whitehead, S. (1999) 'A desire to be: The pursuit of ideal representations by the masculine subject', paper presented at the *'Voices 99' 2nd International Gender and Education Conference*, University of Warwick, 29–31 March 1999.

Whitehead, S. (2001) 'Woman as manager: A seductive ontology', *Gender, Work and Organization*, 8: 1.

Whitehead, S. (2002) *Men and Masculinities: Key Themes and New Directions in the Sociology of Masculinity*, Cambridge: Polity Press.

Whitehead, S. and Moodley, R. (eds) (1999) *Transforming Managers: Gendering Change in the Public Sector*, London: UCL Press.

Willmott, H. (1994) 'Bringing agency (back) into organizational analysis', in Hassard, J. and Parker, M. (eds), *Towards a New Theory of Organizations*, London: Routledge.

Witz, A. (1990) 'Patriarchy and professions: The gendered politics of occupational closure', *Sociology*, 24: 675–90.

Witz, A. (1992) *Professions and Patriarchy*, London: Routledge.

Wright, S. (eds) (1994) *Anthropology of Organizations*, London: Routledge.

6 Women's positioning in a bureaucratic environment

Combining employment and mothering

Elisabeth Berg

Introduction

This study examines middle managers' career opportunities in public administration and identifies factors that encourage women to remain in management positions. It is argued that concepts such as 'habitus', 'gender' and 'positioning' are useful in considering the situation of women and men in the public sector. This analysis identifies a power structure within the social welfare service in Sweden that results in the prioritisation of a certain type of competence. The research shows that women and men have different strategies when they apply for higher level appointments and that women keep their children at the centre of their concerns, even when they follow traditional career paths. Despite women outnumbering men in this sector, it is contended that public administration is structured according to a traditional model that benefits men.

The Swedish labour market is strongly gender segregated both in terms of vocational sectors and in terms of the levels at which women are appointed in the public and private sectors. For example, in local authorities, women account for 79 per cent of all health and social care employees. The greatest gender divide is in the field of nursing and care, in which women dominate, and in technical fields such as engineering, in which men outnumber women (SCB 1993). Women make up 66 per cent of the workforce in the public sector (Dahlström 1962; Wikander 1992) but men are more frequently found in senior positions (SCB 1993).

This study analyses female-dominated vocational fields – using the home help service as an example – and seeks to illuminate women's (and a few men's) 'positioning'. The concept of positioning used in this chapter draws on the work of Linda Alcoff (1988), who sought to develop a Foucauldian approach to subjectivity, which incorporated a measure of agency in the reflexive (re)construction of gender. Here, subjectivity is conceptualised not simply through particular sets of attributes but also through particular positions with the context helping to determine a person's position relative to others 'just as the position of a pawn on a chessboard is considered safe or dangerous, powerful or weak, according to its relation to other chess pieces' (Alcoff 1988: 433).

From this perspective the meaning of gender is created and recreated through interaction, with the terms 'woman' and 'man' conceptualised as existing in a context that is constantly shifting (Alcoff 1988: 434). For this reason it is interesting to examine the understanding that women have of their work and families and to see how men in similar situations, in a typical women's profession, view their own relationship to work and families. The investigation thus takes as its starting point a conversational analysis of middle managers within the context of the organisational structure of the home help service. This analysis offers an interesting challenge to distinguish the dominating discourse in the 'social field' of the home help service, and can serve to show how our identities as women and men are generated and constituted.

I am also concerned with how women and men describe the discourse about the phenomenon 'career' in a typical female-dominated work environment such as the home help service. To help explore this the analysis is organised around four sets of related issues: social background; work; the relation of women and men in the workplace; and their relation to their families. It will be helpful to ask what opportunities exist for the women to make a career in the home help service? What strategies are established? And how do the senior managers (directors) treat both the women and the men in middle management posts?

In the development of any professional career, ascent depends not only on the opportunities that are available within the profession but also on the chances available to the particular individual. Factors such as gender, social class, ethnicity, age, education and civil status influence career opportunities. Many women and men will not, or do not, have the interest, chances or opportunities to advance to higher posts within their vocational branch. Reasons for this include, on the one hand, the fact that the profession may not offer any opportunities for advancement to higher positions and higher salary while, on the other hand, there may be a number of personal reasons why many do not take these opportunities and remain where they are. Some choose to develop in their profession by specialising in new fields, while others view a career as simply having a professional job.

In some professions, for example the caring ones, specialist education is regulated in a way that excludes advancement. A person trained as an assistant nurse can only secure one type of employment, as an assistant nurse, and any advancement requires a different type of further education – nursing or medical training. Other vocational branches are organised according to specialised professional skills and middle managers working in these fields can advance only by applying for higher posts. The structure of the organisation is also important for the individual's career. A hierarchical organisation has one kind of system for promotion whereas a network-structured organisation offers another.[1]

The central concern of this study is to explore women and men's experiences in developing careers in the home help service. These experiences occur in a social and organisational context. It is not the work organisation, or work itself, that creates what is called female- or male-dominated discourses. Work, the organisation and the family constitute a social arena in which men and women generate gender identities.

Methodological considerations

I have chosen discourse as a way of exploring these issues because I want to show how people are trapped by and in discourses that reproduce social practices. The aim is to examine the 'will to truth', but also to show the character of the events within the discourse and attempt to visualise what is central for power to emerge.

What we perceive as 'truth' is created in relation to others in a power relationship. According to Foucault (1993a), we take certain measures and actively struggle in our relationships with others, using different techniques and tactical moves through which power is exercised. Knowledge and power are intimately connected and can only be understood in relation to each other. These relations are not equal but are highly dependent on which positions different groups such as professions hold and the ways in which they are able to exercise influence. Foucault shows that it is not always the case that the people who exercise power confirm its importance; those who contest power but do not gain it do so to an equal degree. The question concerns what it is that takes place in this relationship between groups that fight for their right to define the dominant culture. How and by what means do people act? It is in this sense that the term genealogy is helpful, as it is used to describe social practice as something coincident rather than deterministic (Foucault 1993b). Genealogy involves exploring the inter-relationships between power and knowledge by examining how it is that power/knowledge moulds us – and how the two are intertwined. Power is coercive, productive and enabling. We live power rather than have or do not have it. My assumption is that through language people construct social reality and its representations.

The project from which this study developed started in the mid-1990s with an investigation of the formal administrative organisation of the social welfare services in sixty-five municipalities in Sweden. The contributors participated in a questionnaire survey concerning the formal administration and distribution – according to sex, education and year of experience – of higher posts within the municipal home help service. The questionnaire was followed by telephone interviews with senior managers and middle managers in eight local authorities in Sweden. The interviews were with seven directors (the senior managers), three men and four women, and twenty-seven middle managers, three men and twenty-four women, in the late 1990s. They all worked in the social welfare services and had different educational backgrounds, including training in social care, social work and nursing.

In order to contextualise the study an analysis has been undertaken using data from the empirical investigation of two different cultures that were associated with different divisions located within the same administration

– the 'division of individual and family care' and the 'division of elderly and the handicapped'. Details of the interviews with directors and middle managers are given followed by a discussion of how they understand their careers and their work in relation to their families. A number of concepts are central to the analysis. These are: positioning, profession, gender and habitus. This is followed by a discussion of the strategies used by the women when they combine a professional career with care for their children and consideration of the ways in which men establish themselves in this social field.

Two cultures in the same administration

Different groups of salaried employees are established within the social welfare services, each with its own concepts, terms and types of competence, related to its specific field of activities. This is important because one of my assumptions is that the social background of a person is significant in the choice of education, and that this has implications for organisational analysis. Social background and education generates a habitus, that is, a system of dispositions that is adapted to the game (in the field; Bourdieu 1982). This system involves a specific way of thinking, behaving and expressing oneself, and practical experience (ibid.). Within the social welfare services a 'care habitus' exists both at a structural and at an individual level. There is a determined cultural order and a conversational order in the social field, which men and women step into. They enter a social field in which there are different habitus, out of which some (habitus or the individuals?) are accorded higher value than others.

Boklund (1995) has shown that the division of individual and family care and the division of elderly and the handicapped have different cultures even though they are located within the same administration. Moreover, Boklund has demonstrated that attempts to integrate the activities of the two divisions have failed because their activities are fundamentally different. The individual and family care division is concerned with the treatment of individuals, whereas care of the elderly and the handicapped is concerned with the provision of services. The middle managers have different educational backgrounds and have also been recruited from different social contexts. The majority of those that work as social welfare secretaries are of a lower middle-class or working-class background, whereas the middle managers in the division for the care of the elderly and handicapped are often recruited from the working class, or from an environment that does not encourage academic studies (Boklund 1995). Middle managers in the division for individual and family care have a larger educational capital, that is, a broader and more comprehensive education, in contrast to the more profession-oriented nurses' training and training in social care. The fact that the former type of education is longer and more oriented towards general knowledge is likely to be of some significance. The social workers' training is also closely related to research in their own vocational branch. The middle managers in the two divisions accordingly develop different types of habitus because of their differing social backgrounds and education.

The majority of the middle managers in this study who work with medical care and home help services have a working-class or lower middle-class background. The interviews show that the directors of the social welfare services have a common view on the distribution of appointments. One director (male) pointed out that the educational background of the personnel differs greatly: 'Those that are trained social workers have a more general and comprehensive education with an emphasis on investigation, in contrast to those who are trained nurses or trained in social care and specialists in those particular fields." For this reason social workers are seen as better suited for administrative appointments at top and middle management level, whereas nurses and those trained in social care are thought to be better suited for providing social services and for supervision of such work.

Another director (female) suggested that those who are trained social workers have a problem-directed method of working, whereas those who are trained in social care have a tendency to want to 'put things right' and 'attend to things'. She felt that there are fundamental differences in the attitudes of the occupational groups.

All municipal activities are structured according to bureaucratic principles and men are in the majority in all top positions. Bureaucracy, in its turn, is based on a hierarchical structure (Berg 1994). Inside this classical organisational structure there is the home help service in which women work and have created what can be called a 'care habitus'. Women mainly form this care habitus in private and public work and above all in the nurses' training and training in social care. The municipal home help service, however, is a field in which men dominate in the higher posts and the majority are trained social workers.

In the last 20 years changes have taken (and are taking) place within the social welfare services that have increased the workload of the home help service. The municipalities have taken over some of the responsibility from the county councils for the medical care of the elderly and the handicapped, primarily by taking charge of the care of the elderly in the nursing homes. The size of the staff has for this reason increased both in the number of personnel and in the number of personnel categories. The result has been that the home help service has higher expenses and a larger staff than the individual and family care division; the distribution between these units varies between 65–80 per cent of the social welfare services budget for the care of the elderly and the handicapped and 20–35 per cent for the individual and family care. In some rural districts, the care of the elderly and the handicapped may even account for up to 90 per cent of the total budget. It is not that the individual and family care division has reduced its activities but that the home help services have assumed new areas of responsibility.

The changes that have taken place in the municipalities, including the introduction of economy measures to counter high expenditure, have caused many municipalities to reorganise their activities. The policy of austerity has created uncertainty, especially among the directors of social services, who may feel the need to reassemble their 'troops'. There still exists a tendency to connect the activities of the social welfare services primarily with social allowances and social services – the activities for which the individual and family care division are responsible. In this organisation the nurses and the trained social carers are disciplined, through the dominant culture, to accept a low status in relation to the social workers.

In a similar way Latimer (2000) analyses the work of nurses as a professional group in relation to that of doctors in Sweden. She shows how a great deal of nurses' work is made invisible and their professional status in relation to doctors rendered inferior as a result. She points out that nursing has to change continually and metamorphose to fit into spaces that are often shaped by forces other than its own (Latimer 2000: 3). In my study the nurses and the trained social carers are also defined by those with a senior status to theirs, the senior managers, who see them as closer to the clients and better suited for providing social care. These two professionals groups are accordingly assigned a lower place in the administrative hierarchy in contrast to the social workers, who are seen as more competent, as having more knowledge about public administration, and as better suited to assume managerial positions.

Gender-biased organisation theory

Since this study is focused on women as managers in a women-dominated organisations, the analysis is inextricably connected with the question of the significance of gender in an organisational context. However, traditional organisational theory is what may be called gender biased in the sense that the aspect of gender is generally ignored in descriptions or analyses of organisations. This is a problem in organisation studies that has been brought to the fore by a number of women researchers (Kanter 1977; Acker 1990; Wahl 1992). The fact that there are both men and women in organisations, and the fact that there is distinct job segregation between the sexes in the labour market are circumstances that ought not to be ignored. For this reason a women-dominated organisation such as a municipal home help service should be given all the more attention.

The administrative work of the service is organised according to a classical bureaucratic Weberian model that has gained a firm foothold in the Swedish municipalities (Berg 1994). Middle managers and nursing staff are members of the same organisation and have the same employer, the municipality. This gives them both benefits and obligations and also involves them being under joint control.

It is mainly women, usually trained as nurses or trained in social care, who carry out the practical work in homes and institutions. These women have daily contact with (mainly) female middle managers and investigate and make decisions about the kind of aid needed by clients. In this daily interaction care-oriented work encounters a bureaucratic attitude. Cooperation takes place between an administrative unit, the so-called management, which has to consult with the social political board when difficult cases are involved, and nurses and home-care assistants, who work in private homes or institutions with the elderly and the handicapped. In other words, there is a daily encounter between private and public life in the municipal home help service. There are thus two separate teams in the home help service that work closely together and have different types of competence. The middle managers – nurses and those who are trained in social care – are those who coordinate the work and the nursing and home care assistants are those who carry it out.

That which might be termed a female attitude is reflected in concepts such as rationality of care, rationality of responsibility or rationality of values (Waerness 1983; Aarseth and Holter 1994). Aarseth and Holter (1994) argue that care is not a neutral concept, it can be seen as a female word in the same way as closeness. All these concepts are connected to feelings and consideration towards others. There are also concepts that express different emotional states such as grief, anxiety, fear, loneliness and jealousy. It is the nursing staff that encounter these types of emotion in their everyday work. Their work is characterised by closeness to people who are in need of help.

The middle managers also frequently encounter the same type of emotional manifestations but not as often. Unlike the assistant nurses they do not encounter individuals who are in need on a daily basis. Their task is to investigate the need of social services and to distribute work to the nursing staff. Their work is characterised by distance from the clients. Their social practices have a different language and other issues are discussed. Relations are at the centre, with the conversation involving social and psychological aspects, contrary to technical administration in which technology is the focus.

A formal/normative framework exists in the organisation alongside an informal/descriptive body of laws, rules and regulations that are not always possible to apply (Berg 1994). Both middle managers and nursing staff are forced to try and strike a balance between the formal and informal aspects of the bureaucratic framework. In this social field, a care habitus and care discourse is developed that relates to and reflects a so-called female attitude. It is this social and cultural environment that men enter when they establish themselves in the field of home help service.

To be a manager in a women-dominated vocational field

A number of studies have explored the career development of women (Due Billing 1991; Alvesson and Due Billing 1994; Roman 1994). These studies analyse women's chances of developing a career in male-dominated professions.

However, only a few investigations focus on middle management careers in municipal administrations. Björkdahl Ordell (1990), for example, examines the question of why a person would choose to become a social worker, but she does not extend this to other occupational groups such as nurses and care managers in the municipal administration. Nevertheless, she shows that the men in her research feel a conflict in respect of their children because they work too much, whereas the women feel that they do not have enough time for their children. So what are the implications for the study reported here?

I mentioned earlier that the focus in this study is the career of female middle managers and their career experiences and that I am also concerned with how women and men describe the discourse about the phenomenon 'career' in a typical female-dominated work environment such as the home help service. I explained that in order to help us to explore this we would organise the analysis around four sets of related issues: social background; work; the relation of women and men in the workplace; and their relation to their families. And that this would raise questions concerning opportunities for the women to make a career in the home help service, strategies by which they might achieve this, and the treatment of both female and male managers by the directors. So, what does the analysis reveal?

Examination of the interview data indicates that particular features can be distinguished. While contradictory and ambiguous, certain patterns do emerge. One common discernible feature is that the women have not made a conscious decision to develop a career. For them, it just happened. To make a career is to these women synonymous with being a careerist, whose goal is not another type of work in itself but the advantages that are attached to a higher appointment. When they describe their own careers they simply tell their history of employment. Middle managers who are trained in social care share their experiences of the practical work and tell their educational story by relating how they took courses to advance from nursing assistant to departmental manager. Or they refer to other academic courses taken. The women who were trained nurses or trained in social care when they began their working life had all worked in supervisory positions. This work had in turn led to higher appointments, but not because of conscious choices: the women explain their advancement in terms such as 'it just happened', or 'I was asked if I wanted to work as a divisional manager'. A small number of women describe themselves as capable and competent and express a desire to apply for other and higher appointments, but they are few indeed and reflect a non-traditional attitude.

Björkdahl Ordell (1990) shows that men identify with the profession in a more distinct way, they are work oriented, whether they have children or not, whereas women are family oriented to a higher degree. It is women, not men, who express ambivalence towards their work. This ambivalence is explained partly by the fact that women find their work, and especially the responsibility for personnel, burdensome. It is also explained by the fact that many of them have children, and because of this most of them have worked part-time or night shifts or in some cases changed jobs to accommodate care of their children.

The women conclude that the opportunities to apply for other appointments are limited within a 'flat' organisational structure that offers few career opportunities. A flat structure of organisation puts high demands on middle managers, in the sense that they must be multi-skilled and able to work with many different tasks. This is a work situation that is experienced as demanding. The women conclude that their work involves everything from practical supervision to preparation of the budget. They find the work full of variety, but they also feel that it dissipates their energies. There are very few higher appointments that they can apply for and those that do exist often require some kind of specialisation. The middle managers, who are trained in social care, do not regard themselves as candidates for the post of head of social welfare services. This position is explicitly reserved for those who are trained social workers or academics. Women describe themselves as the kind of people who apply for the jobs they believe they can do well. They apply for a job they believe they can cope with in relation to their knowledge, their children, their husbands and other relatives.

Different strategies for women and men

There are, as may be expected, aspects that unite women in their capacity as women. Nonetheless, educational background affects women's as well as men's positioning.

Their thoughts on positioning, however, are expressed in different ways. Two men and one woman, who are all trained social workers, asked the following questions: 'How do we want things to be in the care of the elderly?'; 'How can we make it possible for citizens to influence the activities?'; 'Which priorities should be made in the existing situation of a shrinking municipal budget?' These three questions also express the opinion that middle managers sometimes must point out that the municipal economy is such that it is not possible to give everybody the help they feel that they need. The woman who is a trained social worker describes her position with the words: 'I don't have that much contact with the nursing assistants since they have a divisional manager above them.' The men and the woman all emphasise the nearness of management and express a loyalty to it.

Despite the fact that they all have the same type of appointment it is not gender that first or finally determines positioning in the last group. For them it is educational background that is the determining factor creating a joint attitude. This is a very small and limited group but, complemented by other studies and the interviews with directors of social welfare services, a conclusion can still be drawn, namely that educational background influences knowledge of the work and also the direction of loyalties. As for whether education overtakes gender aspects, we can see a mutual struggle between different meanings in which different aspects become dominant in different choices. This does not mean, however, that the aspect of gender lacks significance within each educational group.

The factor that unites women collectively, regardless of educational background, is their relation to their husbands and children. The common denominator is the situation of carrying on a job while simultaneously having a home and children to look after. It is significant that the women speak about their work and their family, whereas the men speak about their work and that they have a family. There are differences, nonetheless, between the women in how they relate to work and to their families. These differences can, on the one hand, be explained in terms of generational differences and, on the other, by the degree to which husbands and relatives support the women in their careers.

Even so the emphasis in descriptions of the relation between spouses is on the children. The women all share the experience of conflict in attempting to combine a professional career with care for their children. Different solutions were preferred, for instance, 'I started to work half time when our first child was born.' Another woman said, 'I have constantly to avoid work, which intrudes too much on my time for the family and the children.' A third woman commented, 'My husband and I often argued about who should stay at home with the children, but we had also grandmother and grandfather who helped us.' These women's views on reproduction govern the way in which they organise their housework and salaried work. Our habitus of gender in this sense governs our social lives. The gender field is thus a general social field, a field that is the base for and structures other fields.

In the analysis of the interviews the women elaborate three types of positioning: one is represented by those women who gain an education and then stop working when they have children in order to take care of their family. This is a type of relationship between spouses that is connected to the 1950s image of a 'housewife' (Ihrlinger 1990; Conradsson and Rundqvist 1997). It is a kind of metaphor for the relation between husbands and wives who follow socially and culturally accepted goals. In a society dominated by a housewife ideology, as was the case in 1950s, women as social agents will voluntarily choose the social fate that they cannot in any case escape.

The second positioning is the traditional 'double-working' woman, who implicitly has the main responsibility for the home and the children. These are women who work part-time and/or night shifts and simultaneously have assumed the main responsibility for their children. They are between 35 and 50 years of age. It is not until after their children have passed the pre-school age and begun school that they become more active in the workplace and apply for higher appointments. They are married to men belonging to different occupational groups. They have been accepted as gainfully employed but are relatively subordinate to their husbands. It is still male dominance that constitutes the paradigm for all dominance. A majority of the women have worked part-time, during weekends or at nights so that they could be fully responsible for the children.

The third positioning, 'the professional woman' or 'the revolutionary', is the one that deviates most from social expectation. Here the relationship between the spouses is one in which the tables are turned. The woman works full-time, has a higher salary than her husband and has a management position, while her husband works full-time or part-time and does not have a position of equal status. Yet, despite the fact that the woman's work is of great importance, and prioritised, the family still emerges clearly. The husband is very active in his leisure hours and his main interest is in his family and leisure activities rather than in his work. The viewpoint of these couples is that the one who earns the most should be able to work more, since it is more beneficial to the family's overall finances.

A common denominator for the women who have made a traditional career in the caring services from the beginning of their working lives is that they feel that they are on an equal footing with their husbands. These women also describe their work situation as privileged; they feel that they have been allowed to prioritise their work. Expressions such as 'we have shared most things' and 'I have a husband who has always been there for me' show that these women are dependent on support and encouragement from their family environment in the management positions they are in. Both the men and the women are of the opinion that there is more psychological pressure on a woman who works as a manager than on a man in the same position. Equality between the sexes is not a reality in the context in which these women make their careers, even in organisations such as these in which women are in the majority.

An important factor contributing to men's sanctioning of their partner's decisions to apply for higher posts would appear to be that the men perceive the appointment primarily as a source of income. One of the women says that her husband had expressed explicitly that she should stay in her post because her salary was good for the family. The man regarded his wife's managerial post as good for the family from a material point of view. The men that have had objections to their wives' career object principally to them bringing work home with them. The interviews show that the women in the study have friends or relatives outside the immediate family that they talk to. From this perspective private life and working life can be separated. It is important to point out that these women work at a management level within a traditional woman's profession. The question therefore is not whether this fact might have some bearing on the men's view of their wives' higher position as a threat or an asset to the family. Rather, it is whether the sanctioning is made possible because of the fact that the women make careers in a traditional woman's profession. Many of these men are themselves in traditionally male professions and, in addition, their leisure activities, such as fishing, hunting and sports, cannot be described as anything but typically masculine.

While the family, then, is at the centre for both women and men it is the men who have made a career in a traditional way. By contrast the women have 'been allowed' or 'helped' to make a career. The men describe their wives as always supportive and as not sharing their ambition to make a career. The women describe their husbands as capable and competent in their fields. They are on an equal footing in their relationship and each spouse has his and her own competence and sphere of authority. The principle of keeping things apart is still applied in these relationships, facilitating the positioning of gendered subjectivity.

Men breaking into women-dominated organisations

The analysis has so far been concerned with different types of culture, which reveals that women in general, and women who are trained in social care in particular, do not have the same opportunities to assert themselves in the social practice of the home help service. The interviews with the male middle managers, however, indicate that when men establish themselves in this social field they create a different work procedure than the traditional one that the women describe.[2] What the interviews reveal is that the men in the study seek to reconstruct the prevailing conversational system by showing that their work is clearly separated from the concrete social work carried out in the homes. In other words men who work in this women-dominated organisation seek to change the character of their work by emphasising fields of assignment such as economy, personnel administration and development work. The men thereby become visible in this type of organisation: the so-called female attitude is placed in the background and that which can be called male and masculine is brought to the fore. Men in lower positions simply do not remain in the organisation; they either turn to another vocational branch or are offered a different kind of employment by the municipality. In short, women and men develop different techniques, techniques that ensure the relative subordinate position of women in the organisation.

These expectations and their fulfilment, to which both women and men appear to contribute, are expressions of sexism. Men who behave differently, that is behave differently from the way that women in a women-dominated profession are expected to behave – which means having social competence and ability to work with many different things at the same time – are described as different in a positive way, as 'special' persons (the individual is emphasised). Men that behave according to a typical male mode of procedure, for instance working with one thing at a time and having difficulties with handling conflicts, are yet accepted because they are men (the gender aspect is emphasised). A woman who could be said to behave according to a male rather than a female mode of procedure, for example by being well structured in her manner of speaking and not so emotional, is described in a positive way, but with the addition that she is of a special kind (the individual is emphasised). Both women and men regard it as unusual that a woman (emphasis on the gender) acts in a structured way. The use of stereotypes occurs both between and within the sexes.

Gender differences are, in other words, emphasised and in some cases reinforced in women-dominated places of work. Gender differences are described as if there really are differences between the attitudes and modes of procedure of women and men. However, experiences of difference can be either felt or real: men may be perceived as less emotional and more concerned about providing objective facts because the myth of the man as a rational and sensible being still lives. Both the men and the women hold that there are very few significant differences between the sexes. Nor do they think that it is very important how people behave.

Yet the interviews reveal that both the men and the women are of the view that men have a tendency to be more abstract and goal oriented. Men talk less about what they feel and more about what they think. It is not possible, as one of the men expressed it, to talk exclusively of how you perceive and feel about things while you are having a group discussion. One of the women pointed out that she brings up other issues, in contrast to the men in the administrative group. Her experience was that the men begin the meeting by informing everyone of the latest events in their administration, while she always begins by telling everyone how she is feeling and whether things have been tough lately. The men talk about factual matters and do not mention whether their work situation makes them feel good or bad.

The men are described in terms of plainness, clarity, precision, discretion and continuity. The women are described as talkative, unorganised, emotional, but yet competent in this type of work. They are considered to have the ability to do many different things at the same time. Men are not considered to have this ability, but are believed to be able only to do one thing at a time. A man who is able to do many things at the same time is considered to have a so-called female characteristic. These descriptions of female and male qualities are a reflection of the prevailing norms in society. Both women and men describe men as 'men' and as having a male attitude even if they have chosen to work in a women-dominated profession. If they deviate from the norm, they are considered special because of their ability to also take on a female attitude. It appears to be important not only for the men but also for the women to mark differences between the sexes according to the principle of separation (Hirdman 1990).

When the men describe their relation to the women they speak of them as competent professional people. When women describe their relation to the men's work they emphasise the importance of administrative work and that this determines what is being discussed. It is the content of the work that dominates the conversation. The fact that the conversation is between a woman and a man is of no significance.

These men establish relationships with their families that are not compatible with existing beliefs about men who work in male-dominated vocational branches. The differences are mainly found in their relation to their children. When the men describe their part in the housework they reveal a traditional male attitude. These men are making traditional careers but they feel that they differ from other men in the sense that they have taken a bigger responsibility for their children, usually one that is thought to be equal to their partners with their employers encouraging rather than hindering them to take paternity leave.

The interviews also reveal that the men in their social life have come across prejudice concerning their work in a women-dominated vocational branch, prejudice that in other words exists in society and among the general public. It is not considered quite proper for men to do this type of work. Technology is for men and home help service is for women. This view is expressed in statements such as: 'It is good and well, after all, that there are a few men who want to have that kind of a job, even if it isn't a dream of a profession for every man.' or in questions such as: 'What's wrong with you?', addressed to a man who works in the home help service. The men need courage to face these expectations and attitudes.

The strategy that the men use to counter this prejudice is to point out that the home help service turns over a large amount of funding. They use abstract terms, such as economy, development, personnel and reorganisation to describe their work. The concrete work they do in the homes is not mentioned. Another strategy is to describe the changes that the home help service is undergoing, to describe it as a field that is developing and emphasise that extraordinary efforts will be needed if the social welfare service is to weather the economic crises that the municipalities are facing. In other words, the home help service is portrayed as facing a situation that calls for men in management positions. The question is whether there are any other possible ways for the men to respond to the prejudice? Despite the fact that they work in a field that is dominated by a care habitus, it appears that the only possibility they have to assert themselves is to bring the abstract rather than the concrete to the fore.

Conclusion

The aim is to examine the 'will to truth', but also to show the character of the events within the discourse, and attempt to visualise what is central for power to emerge. According to Foucault (1993a) we take certain measures and actively struggle in our relationships with others, using different techniques and tactical moves through which power is exercised. The aim is also to examining how it is that power/knowledge moulds us – and how the two are intertwined. Power is coercive, productive and enabling. We live power rather than have or do not have it. Positioning has been used in this study to analyse how women and men relate discursively to their work and family. In this study positioning is shown in women's and men's presentation of their relation to others and in their description of career, work and family. In the women's and men's descriptions of their career, the ways which education can separate the genders from each other is made clear. Yet education provides an identity that can both unite and divide gender. Education gives us the right to speak but also excludes those who cannot; it is a sorting out of the speaking subject, according to Foucault. The entrance ticket to this system is the ability to control a specialised technological vocabulary. And as they travel through education and training subjects learn not just to 'master' this language but also to acquire the basic dispositions – not just to acquire the right and ability to express themselves about special things but also the right and ability to use this competence as an instrument for action and power.

These women's positioning in their work is related to their responsibility for children as well as to their collective identity. In addition to the strategies these women have established during their work life, children have been central to their planning of work and career. The women speak about their work, children and their family, the men speak about their work and that they have a family. In their choice of expression men separate the private from the public to a higher degree than the women.

In this study the men become tokens; they are marginalized and kept separate but receive a positive special treatment in their work (Kanter 1975). This is evidenced, for instance, by the fact that the men concerned are provided with special appointments as top and middle managers, economists or investigators. The men are given, or make sure that they get, demarcated and specialised tasks, with their competence defined as special. The men have not moved over to a general 'women's space' but have made their way to, and been allotted, a specific place in the social field.

The prerequisite of a critical discourse is that it can break the prevailing norms and question the indisputable. A number of the women interviewed have gone through divorces, one example of a crisis that changes the relations between women and men both in private and public. Another type of crisis is that in which the local authority has economic problems, which lead them to restructure their activities. Perhaps this initiates a sense of crisis from which openings are created between the given subjective and objective structures, which offend against that which is taken for granted. In such a situation there is also a possibility to break the dominance of masculinity but this is likely to happen only when more women are appointed to higher levels.

Notes

1 A hierarchical organisation is one in which orders are given to people from the top down; a network structure is a much flatter organisational structure, based on individual's specialised knowledge and in which each person has responsibility for their own work.
2 Stephen Whitehead further considers the relationship between professionalism, masculinity and managerial identity in this volume.

References

Aarseth, H. and Holter, Ö. G. (1994) *Män's livssammanhang*, Stockholm: Bonniers.
Acker, J. (1990) 'Hierarchies, jobs, bodies. A theory of gendered organizations', *Gender and Society*, 4 (2): 139–58.
Alcoff, L. (1988) 'Cultural feminism versus poststructuralism: The identity crisis in feminist theory', *Journal of Women in Culture and Society*, 13 (3): 405–36.
Alvesson, M. and Due Billing, Y. (1994) *Gender, Managers and Organisations*, Berlin: De Gruyter.
Berg, E. (1994) 'Det ojämlika mötet. En studie av samverkan i hemtjänsten mellan primärkommunens hemtjänst och landstingets primärvård', *Högskolan i Luleå*, 1994: 148 D.
Björkdahl Ordell, S. (1990) *Socialarbetare. Bakgrund, utbildning och yrkesliv*, Göteborg: Acta Universitatis.
Boklund A. (1995) *Olikheter som berikar? Möjligheter och hinder i samarbetet mellan socialtjänstens*

äldre – och handikappomsorg, barnomsorg samt individ – och familjeomsorg, Rapport nr 71, Institutionen för socialt arbete, Stockholms universitet.

Bourdieu, P. (1982) *Kultursociologiska texter,* Stockholm: Symposium.

Bourdieu, P. (1984) *Homo Academicus,* Paris: Ed. de Minuit.

Conradson B. and Rundqvist A. (1997) *Karriärkvinnan. Myt och verklighet ur etnologiskt perspektiv,* Stockholm: Carlssons.

Dahlström, G. (1962) 'Kvinnorna på arbetsmarknaden i Sverige', in Dahlström, E. (ed.), *Kvinnors liv och arbete,* Stockholm: Norstedt.

Due Billing, Y. (1991) *Kön, karriär, familie,* Köbenhavn: Jurist-og ekonomförb.

Foucault, M. (1986) *Sexualitetens historia,* 2, *Njutningarnas bruk,* Södertälje: Gidlunds förlag.

—— (1993a) *Övervakning och straff,* Lund: Arkiv förlag.

—— (1993b) *Diskursens ordning,* Stockholm: Symposion.

Fowler, B. (1997) *Pierre Bourdieu and Culture Theory,* London: Sage Publications.

Hirdman, Y. (1990) 'Genussystemet. Demokrati och makt i Sverige', *SOU* 1990: 44.

Ihrlinger, I. (1990) *TCO och Kvinnorna, Tidsperioden 1944–1974,* Göteborg: Graphic Systems AB.

Kanter, R. M. (1977) *Men and Women of the Corporation,* New York: Basic Books.

Kvande, E. and Rasmussen, B. (1995) 'Women's careers in static and dynamic organizations,' *Acta Sociologica,* 38: 115–30.

Latimer, J. (2000) *The Conduct of Care. Understanding Nursing Practice,* Oxford: Blackwell Science.

Roman, C. (1994) *Lika på olika villkor. Könsegregering i kunskapsföretag,* Stockholm: Symposium Graduale.

SCB (1993) Löner och sysselsättning inom offentlig sektor. [Salary and employment in public sector.]

Waerness, K. (1982) *Kvinnor och omsorgsarbete,* Oslo: Universitetsförlaget.

Wahl, A. (1992) *Könstrukturer i organisationer. Kvinnliga civilekonomers och civilingenjörers karriärutveckling,* Stockholm: Graphic Systems AB.

Wikander, U. (1992) 'Delat arbete, delad makt – Om kvinnors underordning i och genom arbete', in Åström, G. and Hirdman, Y. (eds), *Kontrakt i kris,* Stockholm: Carlssons.

7 Plural frames of work in public sector organisations

Hans Hasselbladh and Martin Selander

Introduction

This chapter presents a study of the contested status of elderly people and professional work at two nursing homes in Gothenburg. Within Swedish health care, nursing homes have arrived at a crossroads and are confronted with conflicting frames of organisation. The status of professional work and of the elderly has become questioned – a consequence of the recent introduction of new public management (NPM) ideas, especially those relating to customer responsiveness. In 1992 a government reform was implemented, which explicitly defines the elderly living in nursing homes as 'customers', i.e. as consumers of a particular kind of housing and complementary services.

Our chapter raises three aspects of plural frames on the nursing homes. First, the identity of these sites is in flux, as a result of the government reform. Are nursing homes a kind of hospital, or sites for providing care for the very old, or a special kind of housing? Second, the status of the elderly is in a state of redefinition. Are they sick, and to be cured, or are they in a special stage of life with a special need for care, or are they tenants with unusual needs? Finally, the status of professional work is also in a state of change – is it nursing or medical work, or care of elderly people, or service for a particular type of customer? Work in nursing homes is also extremely gendered, as all employees are female. A complex pattern of relations between medicine, care and service as frames of action is presented in this chapter. The competing frames are restricted by an economic frame, which does not intervene in the practices as such but affects them indirectly. The pressure to cut the costs of running nursing homes – which has been very prevalent in the council of Gothenburg – has had an important influence on the emergence of a new balance between the frames of action at the nursing homes.

The chapter is organised as follows. The first section discusses how professions become involved in what we call plural framing – a redundancy of signification of professional work. The second section discusses the framing of professional identity and work and how rationalisation and NPM reforms may influence that. After that follows a background to our case, the reforms of the care for elderly people in Sweden. The frames identified in the case are then presented. In the last empirical section four examples of plural framing are presented. Finally, the concluding section summarises the analysis of the case and connects to the broader issue of NPM in health care.

Public sector reforms as a form of institutional change

Public sector administrative reforms in the Western world in the last few decades has become a central issue in public debate as well as in social science (Klein 1989; Schwarz 1994; Naschold 1996). Most accounts of these reforms include decentralisation, tighter financial control, outsourcing of services, introduction of quasi-markets within the public sector – often summarised under the label of managerialism or NPM (see Hood 1995). It is difficult to pin-point a core of these reforms, but the triplet market–customer–manager seems to appear simultaneously (Hood 1995; Olson *et al.* 1998). Proponents, such as the Public Management Programme (PUMA) group within the Organization for Economic Cooperation and Development (OECD) and Naschold (1996) see this relatively recent development in Western public sectors as historical necessities being realised, late but at last. Critics, on the other hand, consider the reforms as politically induced attacks on basically sound institutions and organisations – in essence an attack on the welfare state.

Management, as many point out, is a way of knowing a domain *in a certain way* (Townley 1994; Yakhlef 1998). Managing is that 'something' that intervenes in reality, shaping it by means of mobilising seemingly neutral devices of categorising, inscription, ordering and measuring (Miller and Rose 1990). Techniques, knowledge and patterns of meaning sometimes become amalgamated and shape organised action in a larger part of society. Such a frame may provide a covering, excluding frame for organising and performing work, defining what is relevant and true, legitimate aims, recognised techniques of work (Kallinikos 1996). The framing, including/excluding effect stabilises and makes non-incremental change less likely. Thus, as many from other points of departure have also concluded, ambitious plans to change organisations are bound to meet open or covert resistance. Organisational change is thus often a process whereby questioning of the existing is intertwined with reform plans as such (see Brunsson and Olsen 1993; Miller and O'Leary 1993). In other words, problematising the existent is a part of change as much as implementing new aims, structures, etc. Following Miller and O'Leary (1987; 1993; 1995), the NPM movement can be seen as a programme, which both problematises a sphere of society and simultaneously advances solutions. The NPM programme is an agenda for institutional change as it goes far beyond everyday tinkering and piecemeal engineering of routines and procedures.

But this conception of change does not necessarily imply that organisations follow an unbroken chain of unfreezing–change–stabilising. To some extent, there have always been competing frames, at least in some organisations. For instance, professional and managerial frames have coexisted in many organisations, especially in the public sector. As will be discussed later, the recent reforms in public sector organisations have aimed at changing the previous patterns of separation and influence of these frames. Further, there are alternative frames of both professional work and the organising of professional work. The NPM reforms can in some cases thus be added to a pattern of partly coexisting, partly conflicting, frames for professional groups in health care. As our case will show, such a plurality of frames shapes how groups see themselves and work, and how they take a position in relation to other groups (Deetz 1992; Parker and Dent 1996).

Framing professional work

In one sense, professional work in organisations is very 'hands on' and situated. You interact with colleagues, supervisors, customers, clients and patients on a daily basis, enmeshed in local practices and knowledge shared by a collective of professionals. On the other hand, one of modernity's distinctive features is generalisation of knowledge and the development of practices less tied to particular social contexts (Giddens 1991). Perhaps the most recognised instance of this is the case of the modern professions. A profession is constituted when the claims of a body of people to hold a generalised type of knowledge are officially validated and sanctioned (Abbott 1988; Freidson 1994). Professions exist as a linkage between such a body of knowledge and a domain of social life, in which this knowledge is at least *one* of the central frames of work. That professions connect actors and bodies of knowledge also illustrates the double nature of work mentioned before. The work of professions is often, on the one hand, deeply rooted in situated interaction, for example human service work (Hasenfeld 1983), but, on the other hand, framed by patterns of meaning and standardised practices belonging to a professional sphere with no time–space boundaries (Meyer 1994; Reed 1996). Professional norms, ideologies and practices can be sanctioned and practised all over the world but at the same time be contested within a national or international professional community. The development of professional groups is thus both a situated process and dependent upon and part of professional processes without boundaries – i.e. in becoming global and national professions as well as local actor groups.

The structuring of professional actor groups and professions has never been an autonomous intra-professional process. Professionals are often and have long been employees in formal organisations, which is largely why their status is of such great interest in organisational research. The autonomy of professionals and public bureaucracies as a tool for economic and political goals has generated compromises as well as conflicts. In health care, there has been a tradition of separating the spheres of influence between principals and administrators, on the one hand, and the organising and execution of health care work in hospitals and other sites of health care organisation on the other (Turner 1987; Preston 1992; Melander 1999). This truce seems to have been challenged in many countries by the NPM movement during the 1980s and 1990s (Dent 1995; Walsh 1995). It is no longer self-evident that professional guidelines and priorities should have the upper hand in how medical work is organised or evaluated in hospitals, clinical departments, wards, or, as in our case, nursing homes for elderly people.

This creates a much more complicated situation for professional work in the public sector. Problematising is no longer simply a pendulum between local reflection and professional debate, as other modes of framing work and identity are at hand and sometimes even made mandatory by politicians and managers. Professional work in health care is no longer set only in professional frames, since some of the barriers between medical work, on the one side, and politics and administration, on the other, have been eroded. Doctors and nurses are no longer unequivocally tied to their previously exclusive professional frames, i.e. doctors and nurses can be divided into different camps according to their stance vis-à-vis how to frame medical work. For instance, the doctor manager and nurse manager become new, possible positions from which to act (Coombs 1987; Dent and Burtney 1996). But it is not the 'old' administration that makes an inroad into the professional sphere. When NPM reforms gain a foothold, administration itself becomes transformed into a blend of classical bureaucratic techniques of control and a new managerialist doctrine. We seem to have a case of what Fairclough (1992) refers to as interdiscourse, a process of constant restructuring of the boundaries and relations between different frames of work in which the NPM programme takes hold.

The fate of NPM reforms in institutionally contested arenas

There seem to be two different interpretations of the effects of NPM reforms among non-managerialist researchers, but neither of them pays any attention to the possibility of plural frames. The first theme is separation or decoupling, inspired by the early work of John Meyer (see Brunsson and Olsen 1993). This explanation refers to the endurance of established practices, something considered to be testified if visible practices are left untouched by change. If teachers teach, doctors meet patients and politicians make decisions, nothing has changed. This neglects the fact that activities are framed by modes of thinking not manifestly present in the running of daily affairs and that resignifying is as important as manifest activities in organisational change. The other theme is a reversal of the former. Managerialism as a frame of organising is considered to replace established ones, a view represented by critics of managerialism (Willmott 1993; du Gay *et al.* 1996). A good example from this tradition highlights the case of managerialism undermining professional values and practices by the use of symbolic violence (Oakes *et al.* 1998).

We would like to suggest that public sector organisations are likely to be institutionally contested arenas – the rules of the game are always open to criticism and change. To rephrase what Power (1997) pointed out, change seldom produces one of the two extremes – colonisation or decoupling. Public sector organisations have been problematised since, with regard to their responsiveness to citizens – a critique that has attacked paternalism, authoritarianism and red tape (Salskov-Iversen 1998). This critique seems often to transcend the former debate, and is not possible to equalise with the party political questioning. The nexus between professional bodies and the sites of professional work has been one further source of ongoing problematisation. For instance, a large part of the critique against medicalisation in Swedish health care had its roots in the debate within the nursing profession, often difficult to separate from the professionalisation process (see Blomgren and Lindholm 1999). Managerialism does not always enter calm and unitary settings, as our following case will demonstrate.

Nursing homes in Sweden

Health care in Sweden has undergone some major changes in recent years and long established structures have been questioned. A major part of these changes followed a government reform (the Ädel reform) launched in 1992, which comprised three main components. First, the responsibilities for non-medical care of the elderly were transferred from the regional councils to the local municipal councils. Because of this, the nursing homes have gone from being an integral part of the health care organisation (organisationally tied to a geriatric clinic) to being more independent units in the municipal organisation. As a result, nurses have replaced doctors as the medically responsible personnel at the nursing homes. Second, a new way of classifying elderly patients in hospitals was introduced by the National Board of Health and Welfare (Fagerberg 1998). The category 'no further medical treatment appropriate' was introduced and defined as when a patient has received all possible and relevant medical treatment and thus is no longer in need of the medical care offered in hospitals. Such patients should immediately be transferred to alternative forms of care, which for elderly patients often is a nursing home, permanently or for a shorter period before going back home. The municipalities had to cover the costs incurred for the patients that were defined as being in this category. This is closely linked to the third aspect of the reform: the redefinition of care for elderly people from a medically oriented to a social service-oriented activity. One motive for the reform was that many old people stayed in hospital because of a lack of better alternatives, thereby causing a shortage of places for other patients. To solve this problem a very clear division was established between hospitals, and their acute medical care, and what is outside that, i.e. the nursing homes were given a new definition of their role and more or less excluded from the entire health care sector.

The nursing homes are interesting because, despite the previously described change, they are still in a borderline zone between health care and social services. The reform has been, and remains, very controversial within Swedish public debate. It has been caught up in a maelstrom of various conflicts, such as the quality of care in nursing homes, the suitability of private entrepreneurs for this type of public service and what type of activity this really is – service, care or medical treatment? There is one further aspect of nursing homes particularly pertinent to this chapter. Women wholly dominate them. The heads of nursing homes, ward managers, the nurses and the assistant nurses are all women. In that sense, we could to some extent regard these almost as laboratories of change of feminised workplaces. The role of gender in bureaucracies has only fairly recently been given serious attention in research (Witz and Savage 1992; Billing 1994). Some commentators (for example Ferguson 1984) have suggested that women, given the opportunity, will choose to organise work according to a non-hierarchic, non-formalist logic, because of differences in the lived experience between men and women. This would seem to have particular relevance in the case of Swedish nursing homes. Such work is to a large extent emotional labour and can lead to a dissolving of the boundaries between work and lifeworld experiences. The changes we studied were, in some part, directed by the state and the local council's bureaucracy but others were not. Are there any signs of a feminine way of organising and working in these settings?

The case study

The empirical study was derived from a larger research project investigating the processes of change in a local health care district. One finding of the larger study was the identification of different frames that constituted professional identity and work, as well as the aims of the organisation. With the empirical material as a starting point much work was devoted to categorising and structuring the material into four different frames. These were medicine, care, service and economy. The empirical study reported here was conducted in two nursing homes in which three different personnel categories were interviewed (head nurses, nurses and assistant nurses). In total, thirty interviews were conducted, each averaging 1 hour in length. In addition, various documents and other studies have been used as complementary sources of evidence. The main empirical sources, however, are the individual statements of the respondents, which explicate their own sense of professional identity and work situation. We draw on these interviews to investigate and account for how people frame and constitute their identity and work under conditions of plural frames.

Before continuing, however, it is necessary to make a key distinction relating to the interviews. On the one hand, modes of knowledge and proposed ways of acting frame professional work, on the other, daily work is not an ongoing active articulation of these frames. Therefore, we distinguish between, first, professional work on a daily basis and, second, episodes of collective, semi-official problematising of this work. The nurses, individually and collectively, take selective parts in 'framing' as a reproduction process as well as reframing that changes their identity and their relation to work. The interviews reflect aspects of this ongoing collective process.

Frames of identity, professional work and elderly people at nursing homes

The identified frames define work, identity and elderly people in different ways. The frames are carried and articulated through different practices and interpretations and by different actors. The local consequences are dependent on the actors and their interpretations as well as how the frames connect, join or conflict with each other during the process. Each frame has a potential to be transformed by the nurses to a directing scheme for defining responsibility and prioritisation in work, but it is not self-evident how that will turn out when there are competing frames at hand.

First, the medical frame has a long history within nursing homes. They have been an integral part of the geriatric clinics at the hospitals and, consequently, have long been dominated by the medical framing. The nurses have tended to be the carriers of this frame. They have been the ones most clearly articulating a medical frame of their work and identity. Their superiors, the head nurses, have been less involved in the daily medical work and assigned a much broader administrative responsibility, and thus have mixed medicine with economy. The assistant nurses, as we might expect, are more concerned with practical care duties even though they sometimes have been delegated more medically skilled tasks. The medical framing of identity begins early on, during nurses' education. Being a professional nurse implies the possession of medical competencies and serves as some kind of assurance for the maintenance of a high-quality medical care. There are many medical routines and rules that make up the medical framing of work (Sebrant 1998; Smith *et al.* 1998). It implies a focus on the patient in terms of medical categories. In addition, besides the frequent use of medical language in interaction, there is also a more formal articulation in the various rules. These regulate how medical work should be done, procedures for contacting doctors, distributing medicine, delegating various tasks, planning for the patients and documentation of all medical measures. In these various ways the medical frame has structured the work and identities of the nurses and other care home personnel.

From the beginning (and in the spirit of Florence Nightingale), care has meant that there has been a moral dimension to nurses' work, implying sacrifice and hard work for the good of the patients. Today it has become a more formalised part of the nursing profession, a knowledge of lifeworld qualities, mediated and performed by communication, responsiveness and empathy (Fagerberg 1998; Smith *et al.* 1998). The care frame (the second in the sequence) defines the professional as more relationally oriented and less distanced. It is often emphasised in the literature that it is important to be holistic and see the patient as a human being without the dividing and distancing that tends to follow medical categorisation. The care competence is now a fundamental part of nurse education and provides a specific knowledge base for the profession. The care and the medical frames have long been the primary and competing components of the nurses' work and professional identity.

The third, the service-oriented frame, is a newcomer in the nursing homes and, as has been already mentioned, its roots lie in the Ädel reform and the related state regulations. The particular professional emphasis contained within the medical and care frames is challenged by a redefinition into a service-oriented frame. A logical effect of this is the redefinition of patients to customers. This attempt to reframe the nursing homes is an antithesis of the medical framing, and an explicit attempt to put forth an alternative frame enhancing customer choice and freedom. The attempt to reframe the identity of the personnel at the nursing home emphasises the socially and customer-oriented content of the work and at the same time undermines the medically and health care-oriented aspects. The nursing home is now defined as a form of institutional living, and not health care; likewise the definition of patient is changed to customer – a tenant paying rent. This is followed by the establishment of a renting contract that gives the elderly the same legal rights as any other tenant, which makes it impossible to move the elderly around as is common in hospitals. The service-oriented frame is far more articulated by formal regulations than the other pre-existing frames.

The last of the four is the economic frame. As mentioned earlier, economic measures have been used in health care in general for quite some time but have regained strength in the wake of the NPM programme and other related reforms. The economic frame works in a different manner to the three previously described in that it does not define work and identity explicitly. It sets restrictions and imposes limits but supports some ways of acting over others. It shapes the identity of the head nurse as more of an administrator, perhaps more managerial, as it involves increasingly working with documentation and control, and so forth. The influence of the economic frame within the nursing homes has been a consequence of the policy of the decentralisation of cost accounting. This is most clearly symbolised by the budget that provides the basis of accountability to the municipal authorities. The budgetary control practices are mainly aimed at employee hours, which indirectly affects what it is possible for the nurses to do. The budget is externally imposed by the municipalities and is the responsibility of particular politicians and local council managers. The economic frame is not embedded in the same manner as the others. Rather, it has materialised in the local setting by other means. First, and foremost, this concerns the head nurse, whose role has become more of ward manager with formal economic responsibility rather than one of professional leadership (Brooks 1999). But, to some extent, it has also involved the nurses (who may, from time to time, act as assistant head nurses) and to a lesser degree the assistant nurses. The effects are, however, of a different kind to the other frames.

The different frames of professional identity, work and elderly people also relate to each other in a variety of ways. The medical and care frames make up what traditionally has been the 'main frame' of the nurses' profession and its activities. The medical frame has a more formal standing, while the care frame, within this Swedish context, is still mostly represented in more informal and relational-based activities between nurses and patient. The service-oriented frame has become regarded as an intruder as it redefines both the identity and work orientation of the nurses (and even makes way for the disposal of nurses in favour of assistant nurses at nursing homes). The effects of the economic frame are less direct, as it shapes the possibilities of acting according to the other frames rather than being a frame of work in itself.

Plural frames in situ

We will illustrate the tension and ambiguity generated in a context of plural frames by analysing four situations. These are situations characterised by contradictory and ambiguous practices and meanings – by plural frames. The situations visualised and questioned establish notions of professional work and identity within the nursing home as an organisation.

The daily distribution of medicine to the patients

Traditionally, the distribution of medicine has been one of the basic medical routines in the work of nurses at nursing homes. Nurses organise the distribution of the prescriptions made by the doctor, choose the appropriate medicine and dosage from the medical supply at the ward and check the patients while distributing the medicines. By this the nurses maintain an ongoing professional communication with the doctors, they monitor the patients and stay updated on pharmaceuticals. On the other hand the service-oriented framing fundamentally alters this set of relations between nurses their patients and the doctors. Here the medicines (prescriptions) are fully prepared and packaged in advance by the pharmacy and then distributed by assistant nurses, delegated to do so by the nurses. The nurses' control of medicines is reduced and medicine distribution becomes a service activity that can be done by less skilled personnel. The medical frame has lost one of its basic pillars and routines within the nursing homes. It has undermined these nurses' sense of medical competence. The nurses are now denied access to the medicine cabinet and thereby access to consult the doctors about medicines and as a consequence any medical knowledge of the patients. The nurses' relation to the patients, in any case, has become so routine that most of the contact is centred on the daily distribution of medicine. While this is seen as a simple change in routines from a service-oriented perspective, as well as a way to improve safety, the nurses' interpretation is very different. It cuts to the heart of the medical frame for the nurses and makes them feel redundant. It has invoked a strong and coherent claim for medical framing of work from the nursing home nurses as a collective. The pharmacy-dosage routine implies that the patients more or less should be able to take their own medicine, which is usually the case for old people living at home with the support of the social services. But the harsh reality is that this is not the case for patients living in nursing homes, the nurses argue, as they are often too old and sick.

To work with reduced personnel

Within the nursing homes the head nurse on the ward quite often uses the concept 'of working short on staff'. It means that when personnel are absent from work it has become common practice to work understaffed. Personnel being absent, because of sickness etc., is a big problem from the viewpoint of the medical and care frames. It increases the stress and workload of the staff, reduces the time available for various care activities and leads to situations in which staff need to give priority to the most important activities. From the viewpoint of the economic frame, on the other hand, the situation of absent personnel is an opportunity rather than a problem. Instead of calling in a substitute it is treated as a way of saving money. The head nurse on the ward (who is mainly responsible for recruitment and the budget) expects the personnel to be able to cover the lack of staff by working harder and by giving priority to the most important activities. It is quite common for the head nurse to cover for the shortage of nurses by working on the ward and leaving the administration aside. The priority of the so-called most important activities might change the balance between the medical and care frames in so far that the medical frame has an easier task of specifying which activities are the most important, while the care activities suffer in comparison. The medical frame, by its formalisation, makes it easier to formulate certain activities in terms of differing priorities. To be able to handle the work with reduced personnel is something that is encouraged at the nursing home (by the nursing home manager and in turn the head nurses). This is manifested at the nursing home meetings at which the different wards are compared on their success in saving money and where those who succeed in that are encouraged, as well as the opposite. One conclusion of this is that the economic frame changes the balance between care and medicine in favour of the latter, making nursing activities even more oriented towards medicine than before.

Leasing contracts

The Ädel reform states that patients should be treated as tenants at the nursing home and they are billed accordingly. The patient is reframed as a particular type of customer. However, this has not been accompanied by any changes in the living conditions, since many patients still share a room with three other persons. It does, however, itemise the costs for the patients since everything has to be specified on the bill (e.g. doctor's visit, use of different hygienic materials, and so forth). This has affected expectations among relatives and, to some extent, patients. The personnel have come under criticism both from the relatives and the municipalities for lacking in service orientation and instead overemphasising the medical and physical aspects. Further, the redefinition of patients into renting tenants means that they cannot be moved between different rooms according to different medical needs, as was possible before, which sets limits on the medical practices. The different frames generate different and contradicting definitions of the elderly. It seems to be a situation in which everybody involved perceives themselves to be worse off than before. The relatives are disappointed because the environment at the nursing home does not live up to the expectations created by the service-oriented framing of the patient. The municipalities, in turn, believe the nursing homes are still dominated by medical thinking with consequently a lack of service orientation. Finally, the people working at the nursing home have experienced the service-oriented framing as contradictory, since they find themselves working with more medically demanding patients but less economic resources. The economic frames impose limits on the possibilities for creating smaller rooms with a more home-like environment and it also implies cutbacks in the personnel working at the nursing homes. It hence becomes difficult to realise the expectations created by the service-oriented frame but also to pursue activities within the medical and care frames.

Individual care planning

As mentioned before, a key event is when patients are referred to as: 'no further medical treatment appropriate'. This means that the patient is defined as no longer in need of hospital care and is to be transferred to an alternative care form such as a nursing home. What is important is how the demarcation is done. In a way, it is a medical categorisation, which serves as a basis for reallocating the patient to the service frame. The very old patients are, on the one hand, defined as in no further need of the acute medical care offered in hospital but, on the other hand, in need of more medical attention than could be provided at home or in service apartments. The definition of the elderly man or woman is floating between different frameworks, patient–not patient, tenant–not tenant, subject–object, etc. When an elderly person has been defined as no longer in need of medical treatment, a more precise, activity-oriented plan is made – which follows the service-oriented one. The responsibility for this planning falls on the social service workers of the municipalities (previously medical personnel at the geriatric clinics at the hospital did the patient planning). They have largely been unprepared to do so, as the diagnosis 'no further medical treatment appropriate' was intended to ensure that the medical needs had been taken care of and that other concerns would have more influence in the future treatment of the patients. But the elderly are often still sick, even though not in need of acute care, and this causes a lot of problems for social workers in their mediating role between hospitals and various forms of housing for the elderly. In some cases the municipalities have had to bring in medical personnel (from the nursing homes or similar) to assist with these patient-planning procedures.

Conclusions

The introduction of more or less competing frames of work has been a cause of conflicts and paradoxes. But it can also lead to a strengthening of previously dominating definitions of work and identity. Even though each frame taken as a separate entity is to be regarded as quite logical and rational, frame interdependence brings about a process of floating and ambiguous definitions of professional work and identity. The Ädel reform, which launched much of the service-oriented argument, meant that the patients were discharged earlier from the hospitals. The patients were, after that, in more need of medical care when they arrived at the nursing home than previously. The service-oriented reform turned out to have paradoxical consequences, as it increased the emphasis on the medical orientation within the nursing homes. This was, in large part, a consequence of the economic framing of the work, which resulted in fewer personnel and less time available for the care of the patients and led to the prioritisation of medical activities over others.

The reform put an end to an ongoing process. The nursing homes had, mainly because of an intra-professional process, been 'demedicalised' over the last 10 years and the care frame guided action more strongly than ever before. The nurses and assistant nurses mobilised the arguments from the care frame to attack the new service frame, but the economic frame, which had brought new forms of cost accounting to the nursing homes, affected both of these when the funding was reduced and new patients were in more need of medical care, a consequence of the earlier discharge of older patients and therefore the 'unblocking' of hospital beds. At the same time, the economic frame defined employee hours as a prime target for cost reductions, rather than a resource for improving care or service. This dilemma increased the domain of the medical frame and decreased that of both the care and service-oriented frames in the everyday work of the nurses. The biggest threat to the care frame, therefore, came from its eternal cohabitant, and the medical frame could now regain its previously predominant position. The paradox is that the nursing homes have become remedicalised (rather than service oriented) as a consequence of the NPM-inspired reforms.

But there are also other effects, ones that seem to have more direct links to the work and identity of the nurses. Their work and that of the assistant nurses became divided into qualified vs. unqualified tasks, with the nurses doing the former. This was a central goal in the explicit professional strategies articulated by Swedish nurses over the last decade. At the same time they also opted for the medical frame, which is highly formalised and distant from lifeworld experiences. This contradiction could be interpreted in different ways. Professional strategies, proposing a 'we–them' view of the world, could be said to be a male frame, colonising the female nurses' consciousness. Another interpretation could be that ideological/professional identities carry the same weight for women as for men, sometimes over-riding or giving a new perspective on lived experience. Gender-specific experiences can cohabit with a more vertical division of work and a more formalised frame of work. It would appear from this study that, as laboratories of change, the nursing homes have shown how economic (masculine) logic can drive out non-hierarchic, non-formalist (feminine) organisational arrangements. Moreover, the strategies of the nurses also strengthened the initiatives from the local council towards bureaucratisation instead of enhancing relational engagement, further undermining the care frame.

Our study points to the need for a better understanding of the possible 'spectre' between plural frames and gendered social closure around one frame. A few tentative conclusions in that direction are proposed here. Increasing pressure towards cost efficiency, cast in an economic frame that measures activities on the lowest level in organisations, is likely to have effects on other frames but be mediated by gender. This is exemplified by how the medical frame has gained in importance. Medical activities are easier to both defend as necessary and organise according to economic criteria of accountability. The documentation of medical activities makes that possible, which also may explain the tendency among nurses to create similar routines in care activities. The nurses may also prefer to work within a 'medical' frame for it provides them with a professionalised work identity, whereas the alternative, the 'service' frame, does not.

The entrance of a new frame appears to make the professional actor groups prone to articulate the previously dominating frames in a more explicit, coherent manner (Baumann 1996). That could, to some extent, be expected. But our case indicates that if new frames are perceived as threats to professionals' identity and work, they will find that the most formalised frame is easier to defend.

A further issue is the question: what makes professions and professional actor groups prone to resist and contradict new frames of organising work? The sudden shifts of how problems and solutions are defined at national and public policy levels, could appear to be imprinted unmediated on local settings, close to that often suggested in neo-institutional research,[1] without regard, for instance, to the particular gendered character of nursing. There are several theoretical arguments against that (Power 1997) and there seem to be, at least, some circumstances that make professional resistance possible, if not certain. If new frames are aimed at professional work itself, i.e. a new definition of professional work, professionals are likely to mobilise a previously established frame if it is:

1   a coherent, covering frame for defining work;
2   available to local actor groups as a shared knowledge;
3   considered as valid in society as a way of signifying work in this particular area;
4   not made impossible to articulate by an oppressive mode of control.

Our case study points to the importance of understanding NPM reforms in the context of historically embedded conflicts within organisations. NPM reforms did not enter a stable, uncontested arena of organisational action in the case of Swedish nursing homes.

Many NPM reforms, however, are unlikely to induce professional resistance

– contracting and new forms of management accounting are not alternative ways of defining professional work as such (Osborne 1993). However, in connection to our case – changes that *indirectly* frame professional work, as techniques of economic control, are both perceived as less obvious threats to, and fairly compatible with, the medical frame. Thus, it is hard to contradict cost accounting by mobilising the care or medical frame. But, as our case demonstrates, acceptance of an economic frame can still produce outcomes neither expected nor desired by any of the stakeholders involved.

Note

1 According to neo-institutional research, rationalised environments in the shape of wider instrumental beliefs and practices constitute organisations as social entities. Instead of the realist–materialist conception that views organisations as adaptive to environmental threats and opportunities, the neo-institutional theory claims that organisations are embedded in complex cultural schemes and rationalised patterns that influence their practices. This is illustrated in the so-called structural isomorphism whereby similar organisational forms are spread throughout the organisational populations (Meyer and Rowan 1977/1991; Tolbert and Zucker 1983; Boli 1987; Jeppersen and Meyer 1991; Meyer 1994; Thornton 1995).

References

Abbott, A. (1988) *The Systems of Professions – An Essay on the Division of Expert Labour*, Chicago: The University of Chicago Press.

Baumann, Z. (1996) 'Morality in an age of contingency', in Heelas, P., Lash, S. and Morris, P. (eds), *Detraditionalization*, London: Blackwell.

Boli, J. (1987) 'World polity sources of expanding state authority and organization, 1870–1970', in Thomas, G. M., Meyer, J. W., Ramizez, F. O. and Boli, J. (eds), *Institutional Structure: Constituting State, Society and the Individual*, Newbury Park, Ca: Sage.

Blomgren, M. and Lindholm, C. (1999) 'To care or not to care? Swedish nurses meet new economic models', in Dent, M. O'Neill, M. and Bagley, C. (eds), *Professions, New Public Management and the European Welfare*, Stoke-on-Trent: Staffordshire University Press.

Brooks, I. (1999) 'Managerialist professionalism: The destruction of a non-conforming subculture', *British Journal of Management*, 10: 41–52.

Brunsson, N. and Olsen, J. P. (eds) (1993) *The Reforming Organization*, London: Routledge.

Clarke, J. and Newman, J. (1997), *The Managerial State*, London: Sage Publications.

Coombs, R. W. (1987) 'Accounting for the control of doctors: Management information systems in hospitals', *Accounting, Organizations and Society*, 12: 389–404.

Deetz, S. (1992) 'Disciplinary power in the modern corporation', in Alvesson, M. and Willmott, H. (eds), *Critical Management Studies*, London: Sage, pp. 21–45.

Dent, M. (1995) 'The National Health Service: A case of postmodernism?', *Organization Studies*, 16: 875–99.

Dent, M. and Burtney, E. (1996) 'Managerialism and professionalism in general practice: Teamwork and the art of pulling together', *Health Manpower Management*, 22: 13–23.

Due Billing, Y. (1994) 'Gender and bureaucracies', *Gender, Work and Organizations*, 1: 179–93.

Fagerberg, I. (1998) *Nursing Students' Narrated, Lived Experiences of Caring, Education and the Transition into Nursing, Focusing on Care of the Elderly*, PhD dissertation, Karolinska Institutet, Stockholm.

Fairclough, N. (1992) *Disclosure and Social Change*, Cambridge, Polity Press.

Ferguson, K. N. (1984) *The Feminist Case against Bureaucracy*, Philadelphia: Temple University Press.

Freidson, E. (1994) *Professionalism Reborn – Theory, Prophecy and Policy*, Cambridge: Polity Press.

du Gay, P., Salaman, G. and Rees, B. (1996) 'The conduct of management and management of conduct: Contemporary managerial discourse and the constitution of the "competent" manager', *Journal of Management Studies*, 33: 263–82.

Giddens, A. (1991) *Modernity and Self Identity: Self and Society in the Late Modern Age*, Cambridge: Polity Press.

Hasenfeld, Y. (1983) *Human Service Organizations*, Englewood Cliffs, NJ: Prentice-Hall.

Hood, C. (1995) 'The 'new public management' in the 1980s: Variations on a theme', *Accounting, Organizations and Society*, 20: 93–109.

Kallinikos, J. (1996) *Technology and Society: Interdisciplinary Studies in Formal Organization*, Munich: Accedo.

Klein, R. (1989) *The Politics of NHS*, White Plains, NY: Longman.

Melander, P. (1999) 'Okonomistyrning og organisatorisk skizofreni – om fattige sprog, lose koblinger og onde cirkler', in Zeuthen, E. Borum, F., Erlingsdottir, G. and Sahlin-Andersson, K. (eds), *Når styringsambitioner möder praksis*, Köpenhamn: Handelshojskolens forlag [Copenhagen: Copenhagen Business School Press], pp. 265–93.

Meyer, J. W. (1994) 'Rationalized environments', in Scott, W. R. and Meyer, J. W. (eds), *Institutional Environments and Organizations*, Thousands Oaks, CA: Sage, pp. 28–54.

Meyer, J. W. and rowan, B. (1977/1991) 'Institutionalized organizations: Formal structure as myth and ceremony', in Powell, W. W. and DiMaggio, P. J. (eds), *The New Institutionalism in Organizational Analysis*, Chicago: University of Chicago Press.

Miller, P. and O'Leary, T. (1987) 'Accounting and the construction of the governable person', *Accounting, Organization and Society*, 12: 235–65.

Miller, P. and O'Leary, T. (1993) 'Accounting expertise and the politics of the product: Economic citizenship and modes of corporate governance', *Accounting, Organization and Society*, 18: 187–206.

Miller, P. and O'Leary, T. (1995) 'The factory as laboratory', in Power, M. (ed.), *Accounting and Science – Natural Inquiry and Commercial Reason*, Cambridge: Cambridge University Press.

Miller, P. and Rose, N. (1990) 'Governing economic life', *Economy and Society*, 19: 1–31.

Naschold, F. (1996) *New Frontiers in Public Sector Management. Trends and Issues in State and Local Government in Europe*, Berlin: Walter de Gruyter.

Oakes, L. S., Townley, B. and Cooper, D. J (1998) 'Business planning as pedagogy: Language and control in a changing institutional field', *Administrative Science Quarterly*, 43: 257–92.

Olson, O., Guthrie, J. and Humphrey, C. (1998) *Global Warning! Debating International Developments in New Public Financial Management*, Oslo: Cappelen.

Osborne, T. (1993) 'On liberalism, neoliberalism and the 'liberal profession' of medicine', *Economy and Society*, 22: 345–56.

Parker, M. and Dent, M. (1996) Managers, doctors, and culture: Changing an English Health District', *Administration and Society*, 28: 335–61.

Power, M. (1997) *The Audit Society*, Oxford: Oxford University Press.

Preston, A. M. (1992) 'The birth of clinical accounting: A study of the emergence and transformations of discourses on cost practices of accounting in US Hospitals', *Accounting, Organizations and Society*, 7: 63–100.

Reed, M. I. (1996) 'Expert power and control in late modernity: An empirical review and theoretical synthesis', *Organization Studies*, 17: 573–597.

Salskov-Iversen, D. (1998) 'New public management speaks the public: The discursive construction of a hegemonic organizational paradigm', paper presented at the *3rd International Conference on Organizational Discourse*, The Management Centre King's College London, 29–31 July 1998.

Schwarz, H. (1994) 'Small states in big trouble. State reorganization in Australia, Denmark, New Zealand and Sweden in the 1980s', *World Politics*, 46: 527–555.

Sebrant, U. (1998) Negotiating professional identity and managerial discourse in a health care unit, paper presented at the *3rd International Conference on Organizational Discourse*, The Management Centre King's College London, 29–31 July 1998.

Smith, P., Masterson, M. and Lloyd Smith, S. (1998) 'Competing discourses in nursing – disease-fighting, care and health-promotion', paper presented at the *3rd International Conference on Organizational Discourse*, The Management Centre King's College London, 29–31 July 1998.

Thornton, P. H. 91995) Accounting for acquisition waves: Evidence from the U.S. college publishing industry', in Scott, R. W. and Christensen, S. (eds), *The Institutional Construction of Organizations*, Thousand Oaks, CA: Sage.

Tolbert, P. S. and Zucker, L. G. (19830 'Institutional sources of change in the formal structure of organizations: The diffusion of the civil service reform', *Administrative Science Quarterly*, 28, 22–39.

Townley, B. (1994) *Reframing Human Resource Management – Power, Ethics and the Subject at Work*, London: Sage.

Turner, B. (1987) *Medical Power and Social Knowledge*, London: Sage.

Walsh, K. (1995) 'Quality through markets – the new public service management', in Wilkinson, A. and Willmott, H. (eds), *Making Quality Critical – New Perspectives on Organizational Change*, London: Routledge, pp. 82–104.

Willmott, H. (1993) 'Strength is ignorance; slavery is freedom: Managing culture in modern organizations', *Journal of Management Studies*, 30: 515–52.

Witz, A. and Savage, M. (1992) 'The gender of organizations' in Savage, M. and Witz, A. (eds), *Gender and Bureaucracy*, Oxford: Blackwell, pp. 3–62.

Yakhlef, A. (1998) 'IT-outsourcing: The construction of accountable worlds', *Organization*, 5: 425–46.

8 On the front line

Women's experiences of managing the new public services

Joanna Brewis

As is now well established, the role of the public sector manager in the UK has changed significantly over the last two decades, shifting from traditional 'public administration' towards private sector 'management' (Morris 1998), and producing what has become known as the 'new public management' (NPM). Underpinned by 'the seldom-tested assumption that better management will prove an effective solvent for a wide range of economic and social ills' (Pollitt 1993: 1), these developments have revolved around improving performance in a sector which, so Conservative logic ran, had historically been badly managed (Pollitt 1993; Flynn 1997; Lawton 1998; Farnham and Horton 1999).

With the above in mind, this chapter focuses on experiences of NPM. It is based on qualitative interviews with twelve public services managers, all women, and all employed in the social services, the National Health Service (NHS), higher education, the probation service and local government. Not all of these respondents are managers in the strictest sense – their job descriptions do not consist entirely of 'getting things done through other people'. However, they each have some experience of managing in the public sector, as the appendix shows. Moreover, although the interviews took place during summer 1997, and the chapter therefore does not cover New Labour public sector policy, the data are still relevant in terms of the twelve women's experiences of NPM, given that it was the Conservative regimes of 1979–97 that effected the key changes to the public services. Moreover, there seems to be 'a great deal of continuity' between Conservative and Labour policy on the public sector, despite 'a different tone in government' and some variations in 'basic values and ... priorities' (Horton and Farnham 1999a: 6 and 19).

But it is not just the emergence of NPM that inspires discussion here. The public sector is still very important in our lives, two decades of reform notwithstanding. For example, public organisations provide goods and services that have a direct impact on our standard of living, and for which we pay through taxation of various kinds (Farnham and Horton 1999: 35). They also employ workers numbering in the millions. So we should arguably be especially concerned with what happens in the public services, and in particular whether it is good, bad or indifferent.

Specifically, the chapter addresses the respondents' accounts of the changes within the public services post 1979, their interpretation of the impact on the role of the public service manager, and their feelings about how these changes have affected quality of provision to the public as well as working lives within the sector. Importantly, these women – despite being employed in different services, having differing career histories, differing political standpoints and differing reasons for choosing to work in the public sector – were in general agreement on all three subjects. This is significant, not least because those involved in public organisations more usually bring varying sets of values to bear on their work (Pratchett 2000). So, the respondents here might be unusual in their consensus on what the public sector stands for. It is also worth noting that these women are not viewed as representative of female (or indeed male) managers in the British public services. Instead, the chapter aims to examine their working lives in detail in order to provide at least some impressions of the realities of managing in this sector.

The most interesting (if not altogether surprising) finding from the data is the suggestion that the changes implemented during the 1980s and 1990s have not necessarily made the public sector more effective in achieving what the respondents see to be its two priorities: service to the public and a duty of care to staff. While none of these women remember the old public sector with fondness, describing it as both inefficient and resource intensive, and also pointing out that there are advantages to the new ways of doing things, they argue that neither is the new public sector actually fulfilling its 'bottom line'. For these managers, the correct balance has not yet been achieved in the management and provision of public services. This conclusion is examined using the concepts of means rationality and ends rationality, as first developed by Max Weber (1968). As far as the respondents are concerned, means rationality continues to prevail in the public services, to the detriment of ends rationality. However, they also suggest that there is now an emphasis on a different type of means in that doing things cheaply is apparently seen as more important than doing things in the prescribed way. The gendered dimensions of this finding are also discussed. In other words, the putative connection between means rationality and (one version of) masculinity and between ends rationality and (the corresponding version of) femininity is analysed to present the contemporary public sector as excessively masculine – at least by the respondents' lights.

We begin with the changes themselves, and an assessment of these changes in terms of their impact on public services managers. Although not all the respondents felt that the changes had dramatically affected their own jobs, they tended to agree that senior public sector managers in particular now need to manage in a different way, as well as to develop new skills.

What has happened to the public sector? What has happened to public sector managers?

Commercialisation and Americanisation

To provide a context for the remodelling of the public sector, several respondents talked about the Conservative intention to 'make it over' along the lines of the private sector. Brenda stated that:

> [I] suppose that the assumption was that, um, this happened in the private sector, um, what happened in the private sector was inherently good and therefore the public sector could be improved by taking on the mantle ... of the private sector practices.

Rachel pointed out the personal irony of the incursion of private sector ideology into the public sector. She quit secretarial work in the former because she wanted to do socially worthwhile work and also felt she was being exploited by her private sector employers. In relation to this, other respondents – notably Meg and Belinda in the NHS – identified the US model of minimal state provision as the Conservative blueprint.

Academic commentators echo these descriptions of a move within the public sector towards a more commercial philosophy. Lawton (1998: 54) suggests the Conservative ideology was very much private sector good, public sector bad, and Wright (1997: 9) argues that the UK government has been the most eager in Europe to import private sector practices into the public sector arena. The two key initiatives here are privatisation and the introduction of the market mechanism where full privatisation was not feasible. Indeed privatisation has ensured that the public services are, broadly speaking, all that is left of the post-war public sector – and the introduction of the market mechanism, among other initiatives, has changed the face of what remains.

In terms of how this overall shift has affected managers in the public services, many of the respondents discussed a growing demand for broader managerial skills. They also noted that there has been a marked, if slow, response to this on the part of the organisations in which they work. Marie argues that management training has become central in that public sector managers now need certain 'basics' such as 'marketing, finance, personnel management'. She says that her university has finally begun to acknowledge this, having recently started to explore management development courses. Rachel, in social services, makes a similar point:

> [social services managers have] always been underskilled because ... they've come through a social work route which, um, is about, um, working with families ... and suddenly there's a job in management but nobody actually tells you what that's [about], how to manage, how to supervise even ... I think I went on my first supervision course, um, about five years ago, after I'd been doing supervision for a long time [laughs].

Public services managers therefore, noted respondents, now need to blend their professional expertise with more generic management skills. However, these women also emphasised that this balance should not tilt in favour of a pure 'management' focus. Belinda argued that:

> If you've got ... administrators running an organisation which is about clinical care, um, making statements that just leave you thinking 'My *God*, you know ... what is this about? ... That's frightening', but if you've got people who've got the [clinical] skills as well, you're basing managerial decisions on clinical issues and you can never get away from that ...

Hilary raises the same issue in identifying tensions in situations in which non-nursing managers sometimes do not listen to nurses' comments about patients' needs, lack of equipment and so on because they have no health care experience.

The importance of a mix of management skills and professional knowledge is also noted in the literature on the changing public services. Pratchett (2000: 119–20) argues that ethical dilemmas in public organisations require that public servants possess 'both the moral and intellectual capacity, and the operational ability, to balance competing imperatives in order to reach ethical decisions'. Wright (1997: 11) likewise, suggests that professionals need to remain at least partly in control of public services because they possess greater legitimacy – for example in the allocation of scarce resources – than do generalist, non-professional managers.

Use of resources

Another common theme identified by the respondents regarding public sector changes centred on the use of resources: the 'three E's' of economy (buying inputs as cheaply as possible); efficiency (turning inputs into outputs as cheaply as possible/doing things right); and effectiveness (producing the right outputs/doing the right things). Simultaneously achieved, these can be considered to equate to value for money (Rouse 1999: 77). Related issues were funding cuts, being expected to do more with less, and increasing demands for accountability and performance monitoring.

This topic appeared by far the most frequently in respondents' accounts of how the public sector has changed. Tracey commented that value for money is now paramount, as well as there being a new emphasis on transparency of procedures. Harriet suggested that monitoring spending has always been an important issue in the public sector, but that it now predominates, as does an emphasis on performance and quality of service provision. She also felt that the general trend in higher education is towards resource cuts and staff having to accommodate these while at the same time maintaining quality. Brenda, likewise, described a 'creaking' funding situation in higher education.

Similarly, Hilary referred several times to there no longer being a 'bottomless pit' of Health Service funding and suggested that staff now have to be more financially accountable and more conscious of the use of resources and of waste, as well as of the costs of equipment. Melissa also pointed to account-ability as the main change in local government. She suggests that it covers a range of issues, including 'value for money ... quality services ... [and] giving power to the local people that use the services'.

Again these comments about the increasing pressure to be resource con-scious and accountable for the use of resources are reflected in the literature on public services reforms. Pollitt (1993: 44) argues that two main objectives of the Conservative project were to cut the public sector borrowing requirement (PSBR) and to eliminate public sector waste. As Peters (2000: 129–30) points out, there has also been something of a sea change in the sector such that the narrow conceptualisations of accountability (to parliament) and responsibility (abiding by ethical and legal principles) have expanded into the ideology of responsiveness – not just to those in political power but also to the public at large. Indeed Rouse (1999: 76) emphasises that performance and service under NPM are not only more important, but also that standards in these areas are now 'judged essentially from the perspective of the customer'.

How has this had an impact on the public service manager? According to the respondents, it has produced a requirement for this individual to be prag-matic, to be able to handle information and to possess quantitative abilities. Olivia stressed 'budgetary skills' and the production of business plans by local government managers, especially in terms of assessing tenders for contracts. Similarly, Belinda stated that the key objective for all NHS trusts is to 'keep within stringent financial controls', which requires data processing skills to ensure that resource decisions stay within budget and that savings are made where possible. This for her is the most important way in which the role of public services managers has changed. Indeed, Belinda has found her own role developing as a result – she now has to work to secure funding for her team as well as to ensure that they conform to resource constraints (e.g. regarding methadone prescriptions). This also underlines the respondents' general point about the growing need for generalist managerial skills in public services.

Such arguments are again present in the relevant literature. Keeling (1972: 91–2) suggests that one key difference between a focus on public *administration* and a focus on public *management* is that the careful use of resources becomes the primary task under the latter approach. Farnham and Horton (1999: 43) also note that public managers are expected to pay much greater attention to the 'three E's', and remark elsewhere that managers now need to have the 'necessary financial and budgetary skills to ensure the financial survival of their organisations' (Horton and Farnham 1999b: 257).

Still on the theme of resource consciousness, respondents also argued that public managers now need to be more effective in terms of ensuring outcomes as well as more efficient in terms of reviewing processes. As Rachel points out about her own area:

outcome was never a word that social workers had to [be concerned with] ... People used to work with families for years and nobody ever questioned why, why these families were, were doing this ... [Managers] just wanted to know how many cases you've got and whether there were any court cases going on. So, so the skills have had to change. You've had to be much more focused on, on where social workers are going ...

Helen also identifies an increasing pressure to meet targets in a confusing and complex environment. She says she has to be able to keep an eye on where she is going and what she is achieving, especially given that her post is fixed term.

Keeling's (1972: 91–2) analysis reflects Rachel and Helen's thinking. Public *management*, he says, is much more to do with the achievement of specific targets within given timeframes, and the continual review of these targets. Similarly, Farnham and Horton (1999: 43) note that public managers are now required to identify costs, watch over the way monies are spent and justify their teams' financial performance by operating precise measurement criteria. Rouse (1999: 78), moreover, argues that performance management is especially fraught with difficulties in the public services because of their wide variety of stakeholders, including present and future users, professionals and other workers, board members and members of parliament (MPs), and consequent variations in definitions of aims, objectives and satisfactory performance. After all, 'those on probation may see the probation service as an intrusion, magistrates may see it as preventing re-offending and the Home Secretary [may see it] as punishment.'

Consumerism, responsiveness and marketisation

Our next set of points concerns Conservative thinking about individualism, choice and freedom. The Conservatives wanted to reduce central government control over individual citizens' lives so as to enable the British populace to become 'self-reliant, self-directing and responsible' and to encourage greater 'national prosperity and international competitiveness' (Morris 1998: 62). The introduction of individual choice and autonomy in the consumption of public services was critical to this initiative, as also recognised by the respondents. Brenda identified 'citizenship and customer needs ... putting the customer first ... [and] the individual being pre-eminent' as key elements of Conservative ideology.

Still, where service users are vulnerable, or are deterred from expressing their real needs, lest it affects how they are dealt with, or are not used to being listened to (e.g. Belinda's drug users and Holly's probation service clients –see also Peters (2000: 134)), where they have little choice whether to use the services provided (e.g. Rachel's families – see also Rouse (1999: 79) and Painter (2000: 179)), and where the implementation of citizens' charters has been paid lip service only (as Hilary claims about the NHS – also see Taylor and Waghorne 1998: 145), respondents argued that consumer responsiveness and consumerism are *not* taking hold in the public services. Instead, the individualist, consumerist rhetoric has, they claim, had most impact among those participating in higher education and those using local government services.

The women working in universities suggested that attitudes across the board have changed, because both students and academic staff now subscribe to the student-as-consumer ideology. Helen commented that:

> the number of students who now come [to see me] as a result of having their results at the end of an examination board, I think ... symbolises this sort of mindset in people about expecting, I suppose it's rights, expecting certain rights and, you know, not having necessarily the obligations tagged on and that's just sort of changed the way in which they see, not a service any more, um, but actually I suppose a product that they're buying ...

She also feels that academic staff at her institution enable and attempt to satisfy such demands by, for example, producing 'a white folder *full, stocked full* of stuff' for Master of Business Administration (MBA) students. This consolidates, Helen implies, the idea of education as a product.

Melissa, in local government, thinks that users are no longer reluctant to speak out about what they need, and that this has been encouraged by policies such as the citizens' charters and the publication of league tables ranking authorities' performance. Olivia, similarly, suggests that she has noted increasing efforts on the part of her authority to be more customer focused – for example her own department's pledge that all housing benefit claims will be assessed within 10 days.[1]

As Peters (2000: 130–1) points out, the 'attempt to enable the public affected by government action to have greater influence over the policies that impact them' can be understood in at least two ways: first, an emphasis on allowing consumers a voice in what the public sector offers them; and, second, an emphasis on rectifying 'maladministration' in the delivery of public services. In the higher education and local government respondents' comments we can see both – examples of the former include students questioning their examination results, and instances of the latter encompass references to the various citizens' charters. However, whether increased consumerism and market responsiveness have come about across the board is another matter, at least as far as our social services, NHS and probation services managers are concerned.

In a related set of comments, respondents identified the injection of competition and a market ideology into the public sector. Brenda pointed to the 'purchaser–provider split, the creation of the internal market, um, this attempt to make it open to competition and compete with other [providers], with private sector providers, those sorts of things'. Likewise, Hilary talked at length about the internal market in the NHS, and Belinda noted that her own service now competes with similar services in other NHS Trusts, as well as with local voluntary sector services.

The introduction of the market as a mechanism for the distribution of resources and a shift towards contracts between public organisations and their suppliers are also well documented in the literature (e.g. Horton and Farnham 1999a: 3; Painter 2000: 166). Marketisation, whether internal (purchaser–provider split) or external (competition for contracts), was apparently intended to make public bodies more efficient, more innovative, more entrepreneurial, more responsive, more attuned to quality, less complacent and less collusive (Lawton 1998: 54; Rouse 1999: 85; Painter 2000: 169–70).

In terms of how all of this has translated into demands on the public service manager, respondents noted that managers now have to pay much more attention to demand from users, supply from funding agencies and/or the activities of competitors. Brenda remarked that, while she personally felt relatively cushioned from the changes that had taken place, she was 'very aware' that her part-time public sector students were increasingly 'asked to be competitive'. She says that her own discipline, marketing, is something these students are 'very hungry to know' about because they increasingly have to work to satisfy the needs of different customer groups. Belinda agreed:

> [I]t's very much a political environment that we work in, um, so that [managers are] juggling all the time, between ... advocating for the clients and ensuring that adequate health care is being provided, while carrying the budget and making very very difficult decisions ...

The requirement that public sector managers become more conscious of their environments in terms of customers, funding bodies and competitors is also noted by academic commentators. Keeling (1972: 91–2) suggests that seeking new opportunities and taking the initiative are important components of the public sector *management* role. Flynn (1997) asserts that coping with competition is a specific challenge for contemporary public sector managers, but also emphasises some of the associated difficulties. For example, he argues that creating a customer-facing culture in the public sector does not mean attracting *all* potential users – instead the requirement is to attract only those that *need* what is being provided. Rouse (1999: 79) concurs, suggesting that in free-at-the-point-of-delivery services, such as the NHS, the issue is often one of rationing demand, such that (in contrast to the private sector) declining demand might be cause for optimism. Controlling demand may also be especially difficult in public services where need is less easy to define – for example in higher education.

It is also true to say that the prevailing sense among the respondents was that public sector reform has made it no easier to deliver bottom line objectives. Although they accepted that certain things had changed for the better, and demonstrated little nostalgia for the old public sector, they also expressed significant reservations about the project described above: they were in the main critical of the contemporary public sector just as they were of its 1970s equivalent.

What has happened to levels of service in the public sector? What has happened to staff?

The respondents here, as we have seen, agree that the core objectives of the public services are service to the public and taking care of staff. They also suggest, however, that the impact of the changes has largely been to the detriment of the service provided and also the well-being of the staff in this sector, although they gave a cautious welcome to elements of the Conservative project. Talking of the rolling back of public services as well as the new emphasis on cost cutting, Marie feels that:

> they *probably went too far* and we've ended up with, you know, a deterioration in services in many ways because they've not actually bought in the right private provider. And of course there's implications for wages and salaries … there's horrendous problems in making people redundant, bringing them back on lower salaries … (emphasis added)

Nonetheless, Marie also applauded the fact that her university has had to become more responsive and strategically minded rather than ploughing its own academic furrow regardless of the outside world.

Tracey argues that local government service provision has been negatively affected by cost cutting as a result of competitive activity, and that authority staff may now face job insecurity because of downsizing, again with the aim of cutting costs. Olivia, on the other hand, feels this last is potentially a good thing inasmuch as staff are no longer complacent about their tenure, and therefore pay more attention to their performance, development and progression. But she also echoes Marie's concerns in her comment that public sector remuneration, as she perceives it, is no longer competitive when compared with remuneration in the private sector. Melissa, also in local government, remarked that 'cutting councils dry' in terms of resources and introducing 'compulsory competition' were not necessarily the most desirable strategies for ensuring 'value for money and quality services'. Although she appreciates the new emphasis on accountability and the empowering of users to ask more of providers, she feels there is a danger of raising public expectations too high, given limited resources, as well as creating extra pressure on staff.

With the NHS internal market now well established, Hilary referred to the fact that certain areas of medicine – such as intensive care and paediatrics – tend to be more competitive in attracting contracts from purchasers, as opposed to areas such as psychiatry and elderly care. She also suggests that these variations in funding generate knock-on effects for quality of care. Hilary went on to argue that NHS budget cuts create immediate savings but necessitate heavier use of resources in the long run – for example, diminished levels of care resulting from understaffing mean that patients discharged from intensive care to the general wards (often before they should be) 'continually' end up coming back because they have not been given enough to drink or enough physiotherapy. But Hilary does approve of the greater emphasis on accountability and attention to the cost of resources, especially in a situation of tightening funding.

Likewise, Rachel feels there has been too much cost cutting in terms of prevention (in her area, attempting to stop future mistreatment of children), while protection (firefighting at the time when mistreatment of a child emerges) has not been as significantly affected. But she also highlighted wastefulness in the 1970s social services:

> with hindsight [I] see a lot of money being wasted then. Um, people [had] a very jolly time as social workers and a lot of money was being poured down the drains really ... I do actually think we need to look at value for money. This is public money we're using ... I want a balance. I don't want it going back to, to, to the '70s.

Nonetheless, Rachel continued to stress the dangers of a budget-led service in terms of standards of provision.

Holly is also worried that budget cuts make it more difficult for the probation service to do 'a good, proper job' as well as arguing that quality of working life has been degraded by the Conservative reforms. The specific problem, she says, is that more people go to prison, but less rehabilitation work is done there, so increasing numbers now rely on the probation service for such support. However, Holly does approve of increased emphasis on accountability, because probation officers now have to examine what they are doing and whether it works instead of simply setting up projects on a whim.

In higher education, Brenda argues that a focus on student needs is being affected by a growing preoccupation with 'money and income', for example the drive to attract foreign students to the UK. This last, she says, is happening regardless of the fact that, because of a lack of command of English, these students may struggle. But Brenda does feel that closer attention to the use of resources is positive, because lax systems tend to lead to abuse. Helen, similarly, worries that students are currently not getting a sufficiently rich experience. She attributes this to burgeoning consumerism:

> I get terribly depressed about it because it's, it's absolutely the opposite of what I think education and development is all about ... [L]earning isn't, isn't something that you can take off the shelf ... [The students] have got to put so much into it ... I mean to go along on a superficial level you gain experience but not in the way that one would hope in terms of the educational aims of what we're doing.

Helen is also concerned about the growing numbers of higher education students and the consequent decline in personal contact with staff. Furthermore, like Rachel, she feels that those at the centre of public service organisations often have little idea of what is happening at the user–provider interface. On the other hand, Helen echoed Brenda in identifying the more proactive approach to resource usage as sensible. Harriet agreed that the reforms had brought benefits – she said her university had become more open, and talked of students 'rightly' demanding of staff that they justify the educational activities and assessments required. However, Harriet also suggested that university staff are suffering because they are striving to provide a consistent level of service to students using reduced funds, and having to 'look cheerful about it' at the same time.

Belinda was probably the most impassioned critic of the changes in the public sector. She feels that, at the highest level, the NHS is extremely badly managed, and describes current levels of service as 'appalling' and 'terrible'. For Belinda the internal market, in particular, has led to a damaging emphasis on quantity as opposed to quality because of the way in which tendering for contracts has been managed by health authorities. Belinda also suggests that, although NHS staff are often resistant to budget cuts, to make a complaint may be to jeopardise one's job. Nonetheless, even she admitted that she approves of some of the developments, recalling very high levels of wastage in hospitals in the past and telling a personal anecdote about spilling an ampoule of an expensive drug, thinking, 'Oh dear', and throwing it away.

In summary, these respondents identify positive aspects of the Conservative reshaping of the public sector. They approve, in particular, of public organisations becoming more user responsive, and of the fact that staff now have to carefully consider the most effective use of their equipment, money and time, and be able to justify it. These changes they feel have improved the public sector in comparison with its wasteful and somewhat arrogant 1970s equivalent. Indeed, their own commentary identifies the unconscious but systemic abuses produced by such a culture – Belinda unworriedly throwing away an expensive drug, Rachel's reference to social services money 'being poured down the drains' and Holly's allusion to probation service projects being set up on a whim. Horton and Farnham (1999b: 250–1) and Peters (2000: 135) also emphasise accountability and responsiveness, as well as improved cost-effectiveness, as benefits of NPM.

Nonetheless, the respondents also view the changes as having highly problematic implications for users and staff. They suggest that wholesale budget cuts and an insistence on competition with other providers, in some cases combined with increasing demand, have produced an obsession with quantity as opposed to quality and made the provision of high levels of service very difficult. They also feel that growing consumerism may create unrealistic expectations and a sense on the part of users that they have many rights but few obligations; that increasing managerialism may mean that those at the top do not understand what goes on at the 'coalface'; and that public service workers are having to 'grin and bear it' in the face of declining resources, uncompetitive salaries, growing job insecurity and rising standards of service delivery. Indeed several respondents were explicit that the changes had been too far reaching and that 'fine tuning' of the public services, in Holly's words, was all that was required, not the massive programme of reform that actually took place.

Public sector commentators tend to agree. Painter (2000: 169) suggests that, while competitive tendering works well where tasks are routine and static and where many providers represent genuine competition, such as in refuse collection or cleaning, it has actually been implemented indiscriminately (and therefore problematically) across the public services. Rouse (1999: 85) notes that contractual relationships in the new public services are also problematic in that judgements are often made on commercial criteria, such that cost reduction dominates standards of service provision when contracts are being drawn up. He is, moreover, concerned that many relationships of this kind in the UK are low trust and characterised by zero-sum beliefs, a point also made by Painter (2000: 170).

There is, then, a measure of ambivalence in the women's evaluations of these initiatives and ideologies. However, they are generally in agreement that the changes have come about for the worse – in terms of both service delivery and quality of working life, their twofold understanding of the public sector's remit. We therefore turn to a theoretical contextualisation of the respondents' accounts of the reforms effected after 1979.

Rationality, gender and the public sector

The UK in the 30 years following 1945 was, it appears, characterised by a widespread belief in direct provision of state services, an emphasis on public ownership and a conviction regarding the need for a government-funded welfare state (Pollitt 1993; Morris 1998: 59–60). The development of the public sector was a direct result of this consensus, following wartime experience of highly centralised government, as well as the war having generated a heightened sense of collectivism and consequent demands for greater equality (Flynn 1997; Horton and Farnham 1999a). The creation of the public sector in the first instance was therefore premised on the 'three E's' of economy, efficiency and effectiveness. Put another way, its architects were motivated to achieve both means rationality (economy and efficiency) and ends rationality (effectiveness) in the provision of key goods and services.

Means rationality, according to Max Weber, focuses on the best way to achieve specified ends, such that the extent to which activities can be said to be means rational is 'the extent of quantitative calculation and accounting which is technically possible and which is actually applied' (Weber 1968: 85). This form of rationality emphasises the implementation of the most economic and efficient means of assuring the achievement of existing goals. As defined by Weber, it involves the examination of various activities in terms of their costs and/or likely generation of income, in order to select one over the others. The idea is to identify the best way to achieve a given set of ends, not to examine the ends themselves to assess whether they are appropriate. There is, it seems, a certain indifference to ends from the perspective of means rationality (Weber 1968: 108).

Furthermore, if we understand organising as gendered, and organisations as fostering, encouraging and reproducing gendered ways of being and managing, as 'characterised by gender-related practices, values, goals, logics, languages, etc.' (Alvesson and Billing 1997: 9), means rationality can also be understood as masculine, or at least as conforming to a powerful version of masculinity. It revolves around masculine values such as control (of procedures), quantification and reductionism (in assessing which procedures best 'fit the bill'), objectivity (in judging those procedures), linear logic (if we manage procedures correctly, we will achieve our goals), decisiveness (distinguishing between various procedures) and competitiveness (in seeking to arrive at the best procedures).

Ends rationality, by way of contrast, turns on

> the degree to which the provisioning of given groups of persons ... with goods is shaped by economically oriented social action under some criterion (past, present, or potential) of ultimate values (*wertende Postulate*) regardless of the nature of these ends.
>
> (Weber 1968: 85)

Ends-rational activity is not based on goal-oriented calculation and the subsequent selection of the most technically apposite means to an end. Instead it turns on criteria based on ends, such that the choice of an action will depend on how well its outcomes measure up against particular values. Considerations based on means, especially if these take the form of calculating how much they will cost, are seen as secondary or even inimical to the achievement of ends in so far as such calculations ignore the actual *use* of the money (Weber 1968: 86). As Weber tells us, therefore,

> the formal rationality of money accounting does not reveal anything about the actual distribution of goods ... formal rationality itself does not tell us anything about real want satisfaction unless it is combined with an analysis of the distribution of income.
>
> (Weber 1968: 108–9)

We can therefore identify ends rationality as more feminine: more reflective (in giving careful consideration to whether means lead to *desired* ends), dialogic (listening to the needs of those whom we are trying to serve), caring (being concerned about the impact of ends on various publics), non-materialistic (costs are less important than whether we are doing the right things), holistic and centred on community (deciding whether the needs of all possible publics are met).

In terms of the public sector in the UK, the 1970s saw the emergence of several trends that cast significant doubt on the ability of this collection of industries and services to deliver in terms of ends rationality. Changing demographics meant that higher taxation was needed to pay for services for growing numbers of the young, elderly and single parent families, as well as to meet the rising expectations of an increasingly literate population. Global recession, triggered by the oil shock of 1973, also meant rising unemployment, price instability, a slowdown in economic growth – and a concomitant reluctance on the part of British citizens to tolerate higher taxes. Finally, liberalist academic critiques of the public sector, and the welfare state in particular, based on the notion that the values of individualism, freedom and inequality were to be preferred over those of collectivism, social rights and equality, began to emerge (Pollitt 1993; Flynn 1997; Morris 1998; Horton and Farnham 1999a; Rouse 1999). As a result, the tide of public opinion turned dramatically during this period to produce a radical revision of beliefs regarding the state's role in the UK and a growing problematisation of public sector activities. Centralisation of certain activities under state jurisdiction had apparently led to too much attention being paid to means rationality: the emphasis on the means of service delivery in the public sector, it was argued at the time, had begun to obscure the achievement of substantively rational ends. This translated into wastefulness, overstaffing, impersonality and a lack of accountability in public sector processes, and a neglect of the satisfactory provision of 'public' goods and services. The public sector had, so the case against it ran, become overly means oriented, overly bureaucratic, insufficiently customer focused and self-legitimating. This is a possibility identified by both Weber (1994: 231), in his argument that a focus on means rationality may result in means superseding ends and becoming ends in themselves, and Merton (1957: 202–3), who identifies the tension between the specific needs of the individual clients of a bureaucracy and the requirement for the bureaucrat to behave consistently at all times. Ironically, moreover, excessive bureaucratisation was seen to require increasing levels of funding in itself – the apparent shortcomings in public sector outcomes notwithstanding. Beliefs such as these among the British populace were at least partially responsible for Conservative election success in 1979 and the far-reaching changes enacted in the public sector as a result.

However, according to the public services managers interviewed for this chapter, the solutions sought to these problems have produced a public sector in which the focus on means continues to predominate and in which ends are still neglected. That is, the public sector is still too means rational, still too masculine, at least according to these twelve women. Service delivery and quality of working life continue to suffer from the masculine emphasis on control (now regarding the use of resources in public service procedures), quantification and reductionism (reducing procedures to how much they cost to see whether they can be done more cheaply – assessing everything in monetary terms), objectivity (making judgements about procedures based on 'factual' numerical information), linear logic (if we manage our procedures more cheaply and more efficiently, this will result in better achievement of our objectives), decisiveness (investing in more profitable public service activities – such as paediatrics – as opposed to those that soak up resources – such as psychiatry) and competitiveness (struggling to make procedures cheaper than those provided by others in the marketplace). In the new public services, the importance of masculine means rationality apparently produces an emphasis on quantitative indicators of economy and efficiency as opposed to qualitative assessments of likely outcomes. This is despite the fact that, as Alvesson and Billing (2000: 150) point out, although feminine values may not be as appropriate in capitalistic organisations focused on profit making, they are obviously apposite in 'caring' organisations that provide for central human needs – as the public services can be seen to do.[2]

In general, then, these respondents imply that economy and efficiency have become the new public sector watchwords but that, despite a related emphasis on monitoring of service delivery and accountability, effectiveness is still being compromised. Masculine-oriented means continue to dominate feminine-oriented ends. But, and importantly, means now seem to translate into doing the job as cheaply as possible as opposed to doing it 'by the book' regardless of whether that was the most effective approach (the 1970s model). The symbol of 'due process' has been replaced, suggest these women, by the symbol of 'saving money', and so public sector workers still 'look to existing symbols for guidance in resolving ethical dilemmas, rather than examining the moral assumptions which underpin such symbols, and feel reassured by the notion of order which [they impose] upon outcomes' (Pratchett 2000: 120–1).

In these accounts, the masculine 'system goals' of efficiency and economy are prioritised over and above feminine 'mission goals' of effective delivery of services in health, education, welfare and so on (Lawton 1998: 55–6). The respondents' comments suggest that the public services are still failing to achieve what Dunsire (cited in Farnham and Horton 1999: 39) identifies as the all-important balance between resource efficiency and goal effectiveness. Moreover, the growing pressure on staff, and the problems associated with remuneration, could be seen to result in further depressive effects on service provision, not to mention higher labour turnover (costly in itself). It is also important to remember that, if the consumerist ideology continues to take hold, then the means-focused threat to quality of service that these respondents identify is potentially even more problematic – as suggested by Belinda in a remark about our 'total obsession' with our health. Melissa's suggestion that public service staff are increasingly demoralised by rising expectations with regard to customer care, which in turn may well impact on that care, is also relevant here. As Taylor and Waghorne (1998: 145) suggest, setting standards of service without providing what is necessary to meet them, whether finan-cially or in terms of human resources, is counterproductive in a very real way – and Wright (1997: 11) makes the valid point that, if citizens are becoming consumers, then might this not also mean that public servants are becoming producers

> motivated by the logic and the rewards of the private market place[?] …
> [I]n those circumstances, many hard-working and underpaid officials,
> previously driven by a commitment to the public good, will demand proper
> remuneration: if they receive it, costs will rise; if they do not, the most
> likely scenario, they will have little incentive to give their best.

Nonetheless, attacking what appears to be a continuing emphasis on mas-culine values in the public services may be problematic, primarily because masculinity is not all bad. As Alvesson and Billing (1997: 202) point out, masculinity tends to get things done because of its focus on processes and tasks, and many advances (in medicine, say) have come about as a direct result of a masculine ethos. We can recall at this point the respondents' sense that some improvements had come about as a result of a greater emphasis on the use of resources in the public services. In general, though, these women agree that, in the contemporary public sector, just as in the past, 'public servants are rarely afforded the opportunity to reflect carefully upon the competing value imperatives which inform a given situation, freed from the constraints and structures of the institutions which impose order and structure on daily life' (Pratchett 2000: 122). What also emerges very strongly from these women's accounts is their commitment to what they see to be the bottom line of public services – delivery of high quality service *and* caring for staff. Ironically, this has resulted for some of the respondents (Olivia and Hilary) in a desire to leave the sector altogether.

For these respondents at least, then, public services management is a complex and perhaps essentially contradictory activity, which requires a high level of individual commitment at the same time as an ability to live with ambiguity. What is also interesting is their implied sense that, despite the growing similarities between private and public, management in the public sector still retains a particular identity of its own, and presents more difficulties than the same activity in the private sector.

Appendix: respondents' details

Belinda heads up an NHS substance misuse team.
Brenda is a year tutor on a university Master's programme.
Harriet is year tutor on several undergraduate degrees and also manages an
    undergraduate degree course.
Helen oversees a suite of university degree and diploma programmes.
Hilary is an NHS staff nurse, and until recently had operational responsibility
    for a small division of the intensive care unit where she works.
Holly manages a team that oversees community service within a local proba-
    tion service.

Marie looks after a section of her university's profit-making arm, which focuses
on raising money from non-government sources.

Meg oversees community-based teams as well as inpatient units in her role
as an NHS service manager.

Melissa manages a local government council housing team.

Olivia heads up a local government housing benefit team.

Rachel manages a regional child care division in the social services.

Tracey looks after a communications team in local government, as well as
being responsible for strategy and policy in that area.

Acknowledgement

Arguments based on the same broad data set appeared as: Brewis, J. (1999)
'How does it feel? Women managers, embodiment and changing public sector
cultures', in Whitehead, S. and Moodley, R. (eds), *Transforming Management:
Gendering Change in the Public Sector*, London: UCL Press, pp. 84–106.

Notes

1 Tracey, on the other hand, argued that users of local government services are
   not consumers because they do not have a choice whether to utilise the relevant
   provision. Here she echoes Rachel's comments on social services users.
2 A more detailed development of issues raised here with regard to masculinity,
   femininity and management will appear in Brewis *et al.* (forthcoming).

References

Alvesson, M. and Billing, Y. D. (1997) *Understanding Gender and Organizations*, London:
Sage.
—— (2000) 'Questioning the notion of feminine leadership: A critical perspective on
the gender labelling of leadership', *Gender, Work and Organization*, 7 (3): 144–57.
Brewis, J. and Linstead, S., with Fulop, L. (forthcoming) 'Gender and management',
in Linstead, S., Lilley, S. and Fulop, L. (eds), *Global Organizational Behaviour and
Management*, Basingstoke: Palgrave.
Farnham, D. and Horton, S. (1999) 'Managing public and private organizations',
in Horton, S. and Farnham, D. (eds), *Public Management in Britain*, Basingstoke:
Macmillan, pp. 26–45.
Flynn, N. (1997) *Public Sector Management*, London: Prentice Hall.
Horton, S. and Farnham, D. (1999a) 'The politics of public sector change', in Horton,
S. and Farnham, D. (eds), *Public Management in Britain*, Basingstoke: Macmillan,
pp. 3–25.
—— (1999b) 'New Labour and the management of public services: Legacies, impact
and prospects', in Horton, S. and Farnham, D. (eds), *Public Management in Britain*,
Basingstoke: Macmillan, pp. 247–58.
Keeling, D. (1972) *Management in Government*, London: Allen and Unwin.
Lawton, A. (1998) 'Business practices and the public service ethos', in Sampford, C.

and Preston, N. with Bois, C.-A. (eds), *Public Sector Ethics: Finding and Implementing Values*, Leichardt, NSW: Federation Press, pp. 53–67.

Merton, R. K. (1957) *Social Theory and Social Structure*, New York: The Free Press.

Morris, D.S. (1998) 'Moving from public administration to public management', in Hunt, M. and O'Toole, B. J. (eds), *Reform, Ethics and Leadership In Public Service: A Festschrift in Honour of Richard A. Chapman*, Aldershot: Ashgate, pp. 55–66.

Painter, M. (2000) 'Contracting, the enterprise culture and public sector ethics', in Chapman, R. A. (ed.), *Ethics in Public Service for the New Millennium*, Aldershot: Ashgate, pp. 165–83.

Peters, B. G. (2000) 'Is democracy a substitute for ethics? Administrative reform and accountability', in Chapman, R. A. (ed.), *Ethics in Public Service for the New Millennium*, Aldershot: Ashgate, pp. 127–39.

Pollitt, C. (1993) *Managerialism and the Public Services: Cuts or Cultural Change in the 1990s?*, Oxford: Blackwell.

Pratchett, L. (2000) 'The inherently unethical nature of public service ethics', in Chapman, R. A. (ed.), *Ethics in Public Service for the New Millennium*, Aldershot: Ashgate, pp. 111–25.

Rouse, J. (1999) 'Performance management, quality management and contracts', in Horton, S. and Farnham, D. (eds) *Public Management in Britain*, Basingstoke: Macmillan, pp. 76–93.

Taylor, A. and Waghorne, M. (1998) 'Public sector managers, public sector workers and ethics: A trade union perspective', in Sampford, C. and Preston, N., with Bois, C.-A. (eds), *Public Sector Ethics: Finding and Implementing Values*, Leichardt, NSW: Federation Press, pp. 137–48.

Weber, M. (1968) *Economy and Society: An Outline of Interpretive Sociology*, Volume 1 (eds G. Rothand and C. Wittich), New York: Bedminster Press.

—— (1994) 'Bureaucracy', in Clark, H., Chandler, J. and Barry, J. (eds), *Organisation and Identities: Text and Readings in Organisational Behaviour*, London: Chapman and Hall, pp 225–31.

Wright, V. (1997) 'The paradoxes of administrative reform', in Kickert, W. J. M. (ed.), *Public Management and Administrative Reform*, Cheltenham: Edward Elgar, pp. 7–13.

9 Hard nosed or pink and fluffy?

An examination of how middle managers in health care use the competing metaphors of business and care to achieve desired outcomes

Ann Young

Introduction

It is striking when listening to health care managers describing their work how they move frequently between metaphors of caring and those associated with a business-oriented approach. They talk of caring, of sharing, of the values of service, of being 'pink and fluffy'. In contrast, they clearly appreciate the pressures on them to respond to business expectations, to be efficient, to argue finances, to 'blacken their hearts' in the way they manage others.

This separation of health care work into a caring component and a business orientation has always existed but has become a critical issue in Europe in the last 15 years. Over this period, various global and demographic changes have destabilised European economies with a knock-on effect on the funding of welfare systems in general and a political willingness to introduce into many health care systems new variations on the central control versus competitive market models.

However, a change in rhetoric does not necessarily lead to new values and hoped-for results. As Lowe (1993) pointed out, policy should be judged by its actual impact. This sentiment was echoed by Baldock (1993: 24), who argued that the delivery of welfare relied on relationships between organisational forms and outcomes and that the organisation was 'the mechanism by which political commitments and intentions are turned into welfare outcomes'. It is the organisational process of translating strategy into action that is the focus of this chapter.

The aim of this chapter is to examine the effects of a contractual and managerialist approach to health care on middle managers' perceptions of power. Three contrasting groups of middle managers were interviewed: National Health Service (NHS) nurse managers, NHS finance managers with an accounting background and nurse managers from private hospitals. It was thought that the first two groups would illustrate how the introduction of general management and managed markets into the NHS had affected the managerial mode of operating, with the expectation that the finance managers had seen their control increase as a result and that the nurse managers would have experienced a marked shift in how their power operated, away from a traditionally warm influencing mode. The independent sector managers were expected to be more hard nosed and business oriented in their totally marketised organisational setting.

The results were not quite as expected. It was striking that all three groups had faced massive and frequent imposed change and repeated restructurings. Although the trigger for these in both the NHS and the private sector included the response to market forces, it was the restructuring that seemed to have affected them most. All the managers studied, with very few exceptions, were able to exercise choices of whether they played the 'pink, fluffy' card or the hard business one. This seemed to be mediated through the uncertainty over role boundaries, the ability to identify several 'bosses' and the use of gender. This applied across all three groups and demonstrated an interesting use of ideology as a value system, as rhetoric, as justification and as resistance.

The chapter is divided as follows. The starting point is the notion of unavoidable conflict. This seems to be best described by using the concept of ideological mismatch. How people deal with these potential conflicts is examined through interviews with three contrasting groups of middle managers; managers in an NHS trust with a nursing qualification, finance managers in the same trust with an accounting background and a group of nurse managers from private hospitals. The influence and use made of professional and managerialist ideologies are identified for each group. In addition, the appreciation of gender as an aspect of work relationships raises the issue of these ideologies being gendered constructs. The findings are then drawn together by looking at managers' perceptions of change, both organisational and personal. Finally, the continuing usefulness of the notion of ideology as a theoretical framework is discussed. Some suggestions are made as to further ways that this might be developed.

Unavoidable conflict?

In the Western world, advances in technology and ageing populations have been triggers to escalating costs for providers, while high unemployment and, again, demographic change have also been significant.

Early efforts to seriously address the problem involved calling for cost containment. Initially constraints were imposed on doctors' fees and prescribing rights and new building and the purchase of new equipment was limited (Ham 1994). However, by the mid-1980s, the failure of such measures encouraged politicians to move to an approach focusing on the efficient use of resources. This involved strengthening management, providing budgetary incentives and reviewing the scope of services to be provided.

In 1984, Margaret Thatcher wanted to break 'with the debilitating consensus of a paternalistic government and a dependent people' by introducing management practices from the private sector (Lowe 1993). With the introduction of general management in the NHS, the language changed. Talk was around productivity and efficiency, business plans and budgets, with devolvement of responsibility to a lower hierarchical level. However, it is debatable how far cultural change subsequently shifted from a highly professionalised system to a general managerialist one.

The next attempt was the introduction of the purchaser–provider split and managed markets. There is a great deal of literature on the implementation of market-like mechanisms in many countries (Moran and Prosser 1994) and the purchaser–provider split is now common throughout Europe. The intention has been to create a system more sensitive to the needs of the users as well as to provide a countervailing force to the power of the providers (Ham 1997). On the whole, European health care has tried to avoid 'the worst of all worlds' (Ham 1997) in order to get the best trade-off between markets and bureaucracy.

However, one of the main restrictions to change has been the power of the professionals. As McCarthy and St George (1990) comment, pressure to change has most definitely not come from the medical profession, though, even so, while the state needs doctors, they need the state. It is certainly likely that the medical profession has had to lose some ground in the face of external regulation over individual salaries or payments as well as through central budgets and non-financial measures of quality audit and managed care.

Although there are suggestions that professional power is declining, with serious challenges being faced through the deskilling of some traditional areas of work, alongside the growth of more assertive and critical consumers (Moran and Wood 1993), other evidence suggests continuing professional domination. The techniques used by professionals seem to follow two routes. First is the 'invasion' of management posts by doctors and nurses who, although to some extent being management trained, do not identify themselves with 'the prevailing managerialist predilection for economic rationalism' (Harrison and Pollitt 1994). Second is a refusal by doctors either to become involved in or even to recognise the validity of managerial authority (Parker and Dent 1996). Harrison and Pollitt (1994) suggest that three approaches are available to challenge the professionals to become incorporated or to change the environment. The development of new managerial posts for physicians does improve the likelihood of professional cooperation, although it also creates potential problems over managing the dual commitment (Hoff 1999; Hoff and Mandell 2001).

It seems inevitable that a result of changes to health care systems along the lines discussed above will be a restructuring of organisations. The general trends in both private and public sector organisations are to reduce bureaucracy, remove layers and encourage multi-skilling and flexibility of the workforce (for example, see Handy 1985; Peters 1988). However, the top-down implementation, seen in the UK in both public and private systems, does not always lead to desired outcomes (Beer *et al.* 1990).

Lowe (1993) also makes the point that policy is often left ambiguous at the centre, allowing quite marked discretion to local purchasers and professional providers. This is apparent in the UK, and relevant to the research described in this chapter, where the looseness of structures has facilitated a number of idiosyncratic personal approaches.

Whatever pattern is adopted, conflicts seem to be unavoidable. Bureaucracy versus democracy, central control versus local knowledge, equity versus market forces, professional power versus management control, all are key dilemmas in the creation of an effective health care system. These tensions will continue to affect health care organisations and the way that managers working within them can manage. Calling on respective ideologies around managerialism, markets and professionalism might help to explain how managers at the micro level reflect the macro changes being imposed. The chapter now moves on to consider this through an examination of the interview material collected.

The interviews with middle managers

The interviews took place in a hospital setting in order to facilitate public/ private sector comparisons, there being no community private provision that was comparable to the NHS. Managers with accounting and nursing backgrounds were chosen as these are probably two of the three most influential groups in health care (the doctors being the other group).

The numbers of managers interviewed was fairly small. While the quantitative data was indicative only, the qualitative analysis proved effective in highlighting differences as well as similarities (Strauss 1987). A disappointment was the lack of any female finance managers; one was located but did not have a professional qualification and therefore was not included in this study. However, there was nothing from her interview that was contrary to the findings described in this chapter. The personal profiles of the managers are listed below:

Managers with a nursing background – NHS

1   Nurse general manager, outpatients; female, white, late 50s.
2   Senior nurse, quality; female, white, 42 years old.
3   Lead nurse, medicine/resuscitation officer; female, white, 38 years old.
4   Infection control nurse; male, white, mid-50s.
5   Senior clinical nurse, accident and emergency; male, white, late 30s.
6   General manager, paediatrics/director, community child health; male, white, early 50s.
7   Deputy general manager/nurse adviser for children's services; female, white, mid-30s.
8   Lead nurse surgery/ward manager; female, white, mid-50s.
9   General manager, critical care; female, white, approximately 40 years old.

Managers with a finance background – NHS

1   Finance manager, planning and control; male, white, late 20s.
2   Contracts manager; male, white, 30 years old.
3   Financial services manager; male, white, approximately 30 years old.
4   Assistant director, financial management; male, white, 37 years old.
5   Deputy director of finance; male, white, early 50s.

Managers with a nursing background – private care

1   Matron; female, white, 50s.
2   Outpatients and day care manager; female, white, late 30s.
3   Ward manager; female, white, late 30s.
4   Matron; female, white, late 30s.

It was thought that the two groups working in the NHS trust would illustrate how the introduction of general management and a contractual environment into the health service had affected the managerial mode of operating, with the expectation that the finance managers would have seen their control increase as a result, and that the nurse managers would have experienced a marked shift in how their power operated, away from a traditionally warm influencing mode. The independent sector nurse managers were expected to act as a control group, with perceptions of power in a totally marketised organisational setting and with, overall, an emphasis on a harder and more forceful management style than that seen in their NHS counterparts.

Translating policy into outcomes

The subtitle of this chapter includes the concept of 'desired outcomes'. These are likely to be highly controversial in the light of competing professional and managerial groups. This section examines middle managers' views of the changes being imposed, the outcomes required and actually achieved, and relevant organisational structures set in place for the changes.

Most of the public sector managers interviewed had strong ties to the NHS, developed over many years. They had been living its history and understood the implications of general management and managed markets. They had all felt the increasing pressure to cut costs with the loss of middle managers' posts and the devolvement of budgets. The implementation of the reforms of the 1990s had impacted on middle managers' roles through monitoring and meeting contract numbers, reporting patients' charter targets and setting up audit tools in the clinical as well as the financial arena.

Middle managers in the private sector were also well informed. They understood the increasing competitive pressures on the company as well as the knock-on effects of the NHS changes. These translated into a much greater awareness of patient power and a change to a more customer-driven service away from a purely profit-making focus. Quality control and cost reductions through careful assessment and monitoring of patients, as well as across the board budgetary restrictions had been experienced.

Although all managers were clear on the broad targets to be achieved by their organisations, there was some uncertainty in the NHS over how these should translate into action. Several managers criticised strategy as being 'airy-fairy'. Nursing targets were one area in which there was a lack of clarity.

Information on actual outcomes has always been difficult to ascertain as measurement in health care has been, and continues to be, an imprecise science, both on what to measure and how to measure it. Reaching any conclusions from the interviews is therefore very tentative.

There were indications that targets in the NHS trust were not always met. In relation to contracts, dealing with a heavy and variable accident and emergency workload was continually affecting the contracts for non-emergency care. Nurse managers admitted ignoring requirements and finance managers had instigated systems to 'move the money around' depending on activity levels rather than contract numbers. Some massaging of numbers also took place in the reporting of patients' charter targets, for example, on outpatients waiting times. As one manager put it, 'I've discovered that they sample the figures.'

It was potentially easier to manage outcomes in the private sector through the selection of which patients to treat or, more to the point, not to accept as potentially incurring above average costs. However, there was a hint of difficulties around achieving certain outcomes. First, the local planning cycle was seen as a 'paper exercise' as inevitably budgetary restrictions were imposed during the year. Second, certain policies would be initiated but left up in the air when another project became the focus of 'head office'.

What was common across the organisations studied was the frequent restructuring both of hierarchies and of individual roles that had taken place. Workloads had grown heavier as both public and private organisations had become flatter. Implementation was thus taking place in a turbulent and often uncertain environment.

'Piggy in the middle'

Middle managers are, almost by definition, caught between other groups of workers. It might be surmised that, with shifting values, the nature of the trap has changed.

It was the middle managers with line management responsibility who felt most in the middle and, of these, those with a nursing background rather than an accounting one. Three of the most senior managers interviewed (two from a nursing and one from a finance background) were comfortable with this state of affairs. 'I like being in the hubbub of the hospital, being operational to a degree,' was one comment, while another was happy being called 'the interpreter'. 'I can interpret the business-speak into health language, and health language into business-speak.'

However, most managers found being in the middle increasingly stressful, and this applied equally across public and private sectors. For example, one manager stated, 'I could only stand up and shout how wrong it was, but I still had to go outside to face the workers and put on this management front.'

Nurse managers were having to become more financially and business oriented. One saw the NHS culture as very much financial versus professional, while another, from a private hospital, described her feelings about this as follows:

> There have been times when, as a manager, I felt it's a bit cut-throat, a bit hard. Other times, I've thought, good ... this is the right thing to do. ... The more responsibilities you are given, the more demands that are put on you, the harder it is to be 'pink and fluffy'. And that has become very difficult in the last two years.

By contrast, for finance managers, being 'stuck in the middle somewhere' seemed to refer to the problem of isolation from the clinical side.

During the interviews, managers' comments indicated commonly accepted perceptions of how they were seen by others. A number of these fit neatly into stereotypes. Almost without exception, the managers in both public and private sectors positioned themselves alongside their professional background. The nurse managers saw themselves as being patient oriented, even when in a role no longer requiring a nursing qualification, while finance managers also called on conventional stereotypes of finance people being mistrusted and blamed for putting the block on things. There was also the view that in order to move further into management, middle managers must 'blacken their heart'.

Tactical manoeuvres around more senior managers

An examination of how the interviewees managed their bosses threw up some interesting information on the number of bosses as well as the types of behaviour adopted.

Seventy-two per cent of the managers saw themselves as having more than one boss. Officially they could usually, but not always, name their nominated line manager, but the informal hierarchy was sometimes more important to them in the way they worked. There was some difference between the groups. In the NHS trust, this applied to 90 per cent of managers with a nursing background and 60 per cent of finance managers, but to only 50 per cent of nurse managers in the private hospitals. One NHS manager identified four possible bosses, but she had, like two-thirds of her nurse manager colleagues in the trust, two discrete jobs, by comparison with only 25 per cent in the private sector and none of the finance managers.

This is not to say that these managers did not have multiple responsibilities. All managers, whether nursing or accountancy, public or private sector, had gone through so much change with frequent restructuring that jobs were on the whole a hotch-potch of earlier roles, responsibilities from other managers moving on and totally new activities imposed as a response to contracts, customer care and quality management in a market context. Such a situation seemed to give scope for considerable freedom, particularly in the NHS trust.

Although nearly all managers presented rational argument (either profes-sional or business based) as being the way to win what they wanted from senior people, this was clearly a major oversimplification. The use of history, gender, blackmail and playing one boss off against another were tactics that were admitted quite frequently (the use of gender will be dealt with separately as it coloured a number of other relationships). As well as selecting appropriate arguments, managers would also choose which boss to approach depending on what they wanted. 'For empathetic support I go to X as he has the experience; for a hard-nosed response, I approach Y as he wields more leverage at executive level', came from a finance manager. Not surprisingly, the manager with four bosses found this quite useful as she could confound the corporate directors with clinical arguments quoted from her medical managers, and vice versa, playing one powerful person off against another.

The policy ambiguity that exists at macro level is interpreted at micro level as managerial discretion. Although there was overall acceptance of the line manager's 'power of veto', there was also perception that some senior managers' attention was focused elsewhere, for example 'in the business side of things' which gave space even if not any active support. Thus, a number of managers openly accepted the need to be devious. They had developed skills of choosing the right arguments for a certain situation as well as the right boss. These skills were particularly noticeable in the managers with a nursing background as they could call on both caring and business rhetorics, the finance managers being restricted by the stereotypes already noted. Although the scope for managerial discretion was probably greater in the NHS than the private sector, which had firmer formal structures and less ambiguity, this did not prevent managers in the latter from acting in as 'political' a way as their public sector counterparts. Further insights on the conflicting ideologies manipulated by these middle managers may come from exploring their relationships with that most powerful of professional groups, the doctors.

Managing medical power

Doctors were seen as very powerful by both nursing and finance managers. Therefore, relationships with them had to be managed with great care and face-to-face conflict avoided if at all possible. As one nurse manager put it, 'Be a nurse for the right reasons, not to challenge the doctors because they'll win, they'll always win.'

As already touched on, calling on medical influence could help the managers get their way with their own superiors. Several examples were given of using medical/manager alliances to achieve desired ends. The nurse managers were the most likely to have frequent contact with doctors. One manager had, over the years, developed some strong networks with consultants and had on occasion used their support as a lever. 'You can prime them up a bit.' Unusually, a finance manager was also able to use his alliance with doctors, forged through the specialist role he was fulfilling over contracts. But they provided a strong source of influence as 'they are talking [about] human life [in a way] that I can't do because I'm not a nurse or a doctor.'

Getting doctors to change required different strategies although it was seen as a crucial element in the successful management in health care. 'The key lesson I've learnt is that to manage the service you need to be able to manage the consultants. If you can manage them, you're halfway there.' Spending time working with them on special projects built trust and gained cooperation. As a result of this approach, one nurse manager had ended up managing a group of doctors with their full consent.

It was sometimes necessary to resort to devious tactics. In one situation, the consultants' lives had been made very comfortable by a group of nurses who had been around a long time: 'They made them [the consultants] tea, fixed them carrot cake, put a plaster on when they fell over, carried their bags every morning and patted them on the head when they went home.' By rescheduling of shifts and upsetting the equilibrium, one manager purposefully increased the consultants' discomfort until they were prepared to accept some new solutions that helped to make their lives better again. In a number of one-to-one conflict situations, female nurse managers with male doctors also used certain gender stereotypes (see below in the section on gender games).

By contrast, the finance managers used techniques that were much more 'hands off'. For example, the pattern in the NHS has been to devolve budgets to directorates, which, for the clinical areas, would usually be headed by a consultant. As one finance manager explained, 'We delegate the decisions and then, suddenly, they haven't got the time, they haven't got the technical ability that they should have to deal with a lot of these issues. So it sort of gets pushed back!' The finance managers interviewed had been quite happy to pick this up again rather than to help the doctors understand what they had to do. After all, control over money was a way of counterbalancing (to some extent) the professional power of the clinical staff.

The state of affairs described above must, however, be seen as uncertain. As NHS doctors decide to become 'incorporated' with the growth of new dual roles, they might well become as skilful as the nurse managers in moving between professional and managerialist rhetorics for the furtherance of their own ends. However, at the time of interview, it seemed that they felt secure enough in their medical power not to move very far in this direction.

In the private sector, nurse managers' perceptions gave the impression of slightly more equal relations with doctors than in the NHS. The relationship of doctors with the respective organisations was in fact very different. In the NHS, managers and hospital doctors were all employees, while the nature of the contract between consultants and private hospitals was much more a business one. As nurse managers pointed out, consultants were customers as users of hospital facilities and resources. To a marked extent the managers felt that their control over staff and internal decision making was less open to question by the doctors than in the NHS.

Because of the strength of medical power, there was the hint of middle managers turning to the use of gender as a resource. As this was also seen in the management of their relationships with superiors and occasionally subordinates, the various manifestations are described next.

Gender games

The hard, masculine face of management and finance and the softer, more caring side of nursing are widely acknowledged stereotypes. In addition, doctors are usually envisaged as male and nurses as female. Such perceptions seem to have either resulted in or been used to underpin certain behaviour. The managers interviewed illustrated the adoption of several gendered relationships, parent/child, lover or partner and single-sex solidarity, as well as image manipulation through the use of gender.

The role of mother was either taken by or ascribed to a number of female managers with a nursing background. This could involve subordinates or doctors and be a loving or controlling figure. The loving mother tried hard to care for her staff and make them happy and saw this as very important. 'I remember a patient saying to me, the staff are so happy. I was so pleased.' There was one example of a male nurse manager putting one of his bosses in a maternal role:

> I would almost describe my relationship with her as a mother/son relationship ... and as I moved on and moved through things, sometimes I've cut the strings, sometimes she's cut the strings and told me I've got to get on with that rather than go to her.

Some managers acted out controlling maternal roles. One manager repeatedly called her staff, many of mature years, 'girls', and when they came to her door to ask permission for something, her response was 'Well, no, you can't, ... and we sit and have a talk about things.' The same manager adopted a similar role with consultants who accused her of being 'nursish', meaning that 'nurses are on this earth to stop doctors doing what they needed to do.' Another manager felt that she had no option but to take this role with a consultant. 'He had a temper tantrum in front of me. I treated him like a child and won.'

Parental roles were not consciously adopted by the male managers although one of the older finance managers was known as 'uncle' throughout the organisation. He enjoyed taking a supportive role with subordinates whether he was their line manager or not. Otherwise, the finance managers were notable for their reticence on the subject of subordinates. When pressed, they seemed more concerned with monitoring and control than with the valuing and personal growth that was typical of most managers with a nursing background.

Roles of lovers and partners are described next. These were played out between female nurse managers with male superiors. One manager described the use of her feminine wiles as 'smiling, thank you very much … gets an awful lot done.' This manager had been happy to adopt the female role in that particular management team. 'Right from the beginning they said that they needed me to be the pink and fluffy one, the person who's really there for the team.'

Several female managers seemed to adopt a nagging wife role with their male bosses whose power was indisputable. In a way, they both played games of having more power than was in fact the case. The first said, 'My boss says I don't need any assertiveness training … that's because I have a need to put him in his place sometimes. He's very authoritarian at times.' The other rather jokingly said, 'I have power over my boss. He does what I say. He has a bad conscience.' She put this down to him being the hard money man, again calling on established gendered stereotypes.

The use of gender in the formation of informal organisational power blocs is a frequent occurrence in any work setting. Examples of this were seen in the NHS trust.

The boys or lads were mentioned several times by the finance managers. One felt he had been accused of 'sorting out jobs for my boys', another used the term to differentiate different groups, 'the maintenance boys', the union 'lads'. Of the nurse managers, one male talked of playing football once a week with 'some of the boys' who were very senior in the organisation. He saw it as a way of networking 'although I am always conscious of what I am saying'.

A similar 'women's club' had also been set up but, for female managers, the informal male groupings were often experienced by them as exclusion. 'There were a lot of forums that the consultants went to that we (two female managers) were excluded from because we weren't one of the boys. And we didn't have a voice.'

A big difference between the managerial groups interviewed was the conscious use made by the nurse managers of their professional background and the image manipulation that some of these managers embarked on in order to achieve desired outcomes. Most saw the professional qualification as giving them credibility with both general managers and doctors. One took drastic action to enforce this. She found that, when in a suit, she was ignored by the doctors, so 'I put my frock on, and when I'm in a frock, I'm a nurse.' Although this worked for her, another manager felt that wearing her dress and frilly hat triggered condescending behaviour from the doctors. So she wore a business suit and 'they were horrible to me.' She then wore a very smart dress which was a little softer while not being like a nurse uniform and felt that this sidelined both the condescension and the aggression that had been triggered by seeing her as the hated business person. Not surprisingly, this image manipulation through clothing was mentioned only by women.

To summarise, gender seemed to be involved, either consciously or unconsciously, where the distribution of power was perceived as being unequal. Women managers seemed to draw strength from maternal and sexual images when faced with more powerful male doctors and senior managers. Although potentially subject to abuse, such acts are going to be discernible in many unequal relationships. The male managers felt little need to call consciously on these images, reinforcing the inferior position of women in the work force. Certainly, in the NHS trust, there were no women above the management level of those interviewed (excepting the medical staff).

Such findings underpin the point that gender is still a powerful determinant of behaviour at work. Already identified has been the key role of different professional values on managers. This section demonstrates that managerialist and professional ideologies are themselves highly gendered constructs.

Reflection on the interview results

First, a comparison between management styles in the public and private sectors is made followed by a comparison of management styles between professional groups.

Although there was a complete and expected separation between the public and private managers' perceptions of their organisational cultures, this difference failed to influence their management styles. In the private sector, there was slightly less room for manoeuvre around organisational structures. There was a firmer and more clearly defined hierarchy, tighter systems and some constraints on managerial discretion. The different contractual relationship with the doctors modified without changing techniques of managing medical power but how managers dealt with superiors and subordinates was markedly similar in both sectors. Finally, the size of the respective organisations probably had an influence on power groupings, a private hospital being a smaller and more discrete unit than some of the clinical directorates found in the NHS trust.

The difference in managerial behaviour between the two professional groups selected was (amazingly) consistent. To a large extent, these seemed to fall into line with expected stereotypes of financial management being hard and masculine and nursing management being caring and feminine, even with the inclusion of several male managers in this group. This finding applied across both public and private sectors with remarkable cohesion of managerial styles between the nurse managers.

While indicative of different professional values, this difference could not be wholly supported by ideological arguments. The research had hypothesised that the NHS nurse managers would have had to operate in a harder, less warm way, similar to that expected in the private sector. Although there was some confirmation in that the nurse managers in both sectors had had to learn the skills of getting their way in a more financially oriented and contractual environment, they had also retained their traditional softer mode. Of particular interest was the way in which they were often able to move purposefully between the two styles, of great value to them when facing the continuing power of clinical arguments.

The finance managers did not have this option except in rare instances in which they could call on medical support or develop warmer, more influencing, skills. On the whole, they came across as a rather isolated group whose power had mainly been enhanced as the NHS shifted to a greater business-oriented approach by picking up the pieces that nobody else wanted or knew what to do with. A critical factor in management control continued to be the power of the doctors whatever their contractual status.

The following and final section will enlarge on the effects of change, reflecting back on the middle managers' interpretation of the macro explanation offered at the start of this chapter.

Implications of imposed change for a professional workforce

The point was made earlier in this chapter that managers play a key role at organisational level in ensuring successful implementation of policy. It was suggested that organisational structures and cultures would shift to a more businesslike approach, affecting the style of management found at middle manager level. But, as it turned out, managers' comments on how they saw managerial change demonstrated a wide diversity of opinion.

For the private sector, managers thought that management values had shifted from very hard financial ones to more professional and caring ones, although the financial driver was still present. This they saw as coming from the executive level, at which a female chief nurse had recently been appointed and charged with 'putting the love back in.' However, in relation to their jobs, most saw the need to get tougher or tighter, although claiming to retain the soft, caring side of themselves. 'It's that strange balance of being there for people and yet being able to think on your feet, to get out of situations and to be ahead of situations that could happen.'

In the NHS, there were even more mixed messages. Some were as expected, with an emphasis on becoming harder, but several managers indicated that in some ways they had been able to adopt softer management styles. One had learnt to become more tolerant, saying of decisions to be made, 'Let's think about this, let's sleep on it and if we really want to go for it, let's go for it tomorrow, but let's not really go for it today.' Another manager compared old, autocratic styles of nurse management with today's teamwork and influencing styles. A number were continuing to use warm, caring modes and consciously resisted the pressures on them to become harder.

A tentative conclusion to be reached is that the introduction of a business-like approach to health care at policy level does not automatically alter the behaviour of middle managers, although they do have to take it into account to some extent. The managers in this study had learnt to find ways around the pressures being imposed on them, whether in the public or private sector. This particularly applied to those with a nursing background but some finance managers were also finding it more effective to call on caring rhetorics than to rely solely on a harder style.

In both sectors and professional groups, several felt that having to cope with so many changes had given them the confidence to work in a number of different ways. However, the downside was anxiety and uncertainty, the finance managers being particularly prone to these emotions.

Conclusion – ideology as a theoretical framework to explain middle managers' behaviour

In today's UK health care services, it is probable that there are two main competing ideologies, managerialism and professionalism. The arguments in support of this will not be included here but, as Young (1997) concluded, it is debatable from the evidence whether managerialism can succeed in undermining professionalism through the imposition of clinical audits and managed care or whether professionalism will continue to dominate through an emphasis on service and expert knowledge. Of particular interest to this chapter is the view of Abercrombie *et al.* (1990) that subordinate groups are capable of generating beliefs and values that run counter to seemingly dominant ideologies. The very 'middleness' of the managers interviewed seemed to put them in a position in which their allegiance could be either to the 'top' or to the 'bottom' of their organisation, with potential uncertainty over which way they might jump!

What was clear from this research was the ability of middle managers, particularly those with a nursing background, to use professionalism as a way of enhancing their own power. However, when it suited them, they were also able to move into managerial arguments if that would get them what they wanted. In short, they used ideology rather than let it use, or be used to dominate, them. This chapter demonstrates the way in which managers alternated between using ideology as a value system, as rhetoric, as justification and as resistance. For some, using alternating ideological arguments caused serious discomfort and their response might be to shift ideological allegiance, for example from professional to managerial values. At times, there was the suspicion that a caring rhetoric was used to get a required response as it seemed immoral to argue against it. Others were comfortable wearing different 'hats' in an instrumental way without having to maintain a total allegiance. In retrospect, appropriate ideological arguments were used to justify this instrumentality. Finally, a number of middle managers in this study demonstrated quite clearly their ability to question changes being imposed on them and used ideology as a tool of resistance. It is, therefore, worth considering an alternative perspective on ideology, proposed by Gilbert and Mulkay (1983), namely that ideology does not necessarily determine actions but provides a vocabulary or repertoire that participants may employ to justify, evaluate and explain their actions. They see ideology 'as an interpretative resource subjectively used rather than as a dominant ideology' (ibid.: 28).

Separately, but to some extent integrated, is a third ideological strand, that of paternalism. Male domination in health care is of long standing and it was of interest how the female managers attempted to undermine this through the use of gender games. However, such games were not actually going to lead to any major threat to senior male managers and male medical staff. On the whole, as Anyon (1983) explained, such activities are likely to be low profile and individual. Generally, the behaviour of the two professional groups tended to follow a gendered path. As highlighted in a range of literature, gender underpins most of our activities and the different professions have built on this with the incorporation of certain stereotypes that are still strong in spite of legal and other measures to change them (see Hugman (1991) for a comprehensive summary of gender and the caring professions). However, some women managers were able to dip in and out of using the conventional stereotypes. It was interesting that several female managers made the point that they were not 'gentle, loving sorts of people'.

With this somewhat complex matrix of ideological influences, further development of an ideological explanation of managerial behaviour needs to move from an interpretation of ideologies as discrete entities to one that can explore the inter-relations between them. I suggest that the concept of ideological articulations as proposed by Gramsci (1971) and developed by Mouffe (1979) might be particularly useful in progressing the analysis I have initiated here

References

Abercrombie, N., Hill, S. and Turner, B. (1990) *Dominant Ideologies*, London: Unwin Hyman.

Anyon, J. (1983) 'Intersections of gender and class: Accommodation and resistance by working class and affluent females to contradictory sex role ideologies', in Walker S. and Barton L. (eds), *Gender, Class and Education*, Lewes: Falmer Press, pp. 19–37.

Baldock, J. (1993) 'Patterns of change in the delivery of welfare', in Taylor-Gooby P. and Lawson R. (eds), *Markets and Managers: New Issues in the Delivery of Welfare*, Buckingham: Open University Press, pp. 24–37.

Beer, M., Eisenstat, R. and Spector, B. (1990) *The Critical Path to Corporate Renewal*, Cambridge, MA: Harvard Business School Press.

Gilbert, N. and Mulkay, M. (1983) 'In search of the action', in Gilbert, N. and Abell, P. (eds), *Accounts and Action: Surrey Conferences on Sociological Theory and Method I*, Aldershot, Hants: Gower, pp. 8–34.

Gramsci, A. (1971) *Selections from Prison Notebooks* (ed. and trans. Q. Hoare and G. Nowell Smith), London: Lawrence and Wishart.

Ham, C. (1994) *Management and Competition in the New NHS*, Oxford: Radcliffe Medical Press.

Ham, C. (ed.) (1997) *Health Care Reform: Learning from International Experience*, Buckingham: Open University Press.

Handy, C. (1985) *The Gods of Management*, revised edn, London: Pan Books.

Harrison, S. and Pollitt, C. (1994) *Controlling Health Professionals: The Future of Work and Organisation in the NHS*, Buckingham: Open University Press.

Hoff, T. (1999) 'The social organisation of physician-managers in a changing HMO', *Work and Occupations*, 26 (3): 324–51.

Hoff, T. and Mandell, J. (2001) 'Exploring dual commitment among physician executives in managed care', *Journal of Health Care Management*, 46 (2): 91–111.

Hugman, R. (1991) *Power in Caring Professions*, London: Macmillan.

Lowe, R. (1993) *The Welfare State in Britain since 1945*, Basingstoke: Macmillan.

McCarthy, M. and St George, D. (1990) 'Prospects in health care for the UK', in Casparie, A., Hermans, H. and Paelinck, J. (eds), *Competitive Health Care in Europe*, Aldershot: Dartmouth Publications, pp. 377–92.

Moran, M. and Prosser, T. (1994) *Privatisation and Regulatory Change in Europe*, Buckingham: Open University Press.

Moran, M. and Wood, B. (1993) *States, Regulation and the Medical Profession*, Buckingham: Open University Press.

Mouffe, C. (1979) 'Hegemony and ideology in Gramsci', in Mouffe C. (ed.), *Gramsci and Marxist Theory*, London: Routledge and Kegan Paul, pp. 168–204.

Parker, M. and Dent, M. (1996) 'Managers, doctors and culture: Changing an English health district', *Administration and Society*, 28 (3): 335–61.

Peters, T. (1988) *Thriving on Chaos*, London: Macmillan.

Strauss, A. (1987) *Qualitative Analysis for Social Scientists*, Cambridge: Cambridge University Press.

Young, A. P. (1997) 'Competing ideologies in health care', *Nursing Ethics*, 4 (3): 191–201.

10 Ministering angels and the virtuous profession

Service and professional identity

Heather Höpfl

'No interaction with the patient'

The paper had its origins in a small pilot study which was conducted after the completion of a large-scale cross-national study of life and work values in the UK, France and India, conducted at Lancaster University in the late 1980s. The pilot study drew on the findings of the cross-national study and, in particular, used the research instrument developed for the study in order to undertake a preliminary investigation of professional identity in nurses. The principal research instrument for the larger study was the repertory grid technique (Kelly 1955; 1963; Fransella and Bannister 1977) and to test the research instrument a small pilot study was conducted with a group of nurses from the Royal Lancaster Infirmary. The sample group consisted of only ten nurses. The pilot study was extraneous to the main study and concerned with emergent methodological issues. However, the results of this small piece of research were intriguing and deserved further examination. The purpose of the grids was to detect principal constructs related to the attitudes and values of a given occupation. Clearly, there are issues related to the selection of an appropriate research instrument and the repertory grid is not without its critics. In particular, the repertory grid has been criticised from a number of different positions for the problems associated with the framing of the constructs in the elicitation process and for the use of statistical methods in its analysis. However, one appealing feature of the grid is the fact that it provides the opportunity to get behind assumptions that are taken for granted and well-rehearsed attitudes. Consequently, the grid provides a means of tapping social constructs that are not part of the stock of responses which can so easily become the substance of interview data.

Without wishing to give undue endorsement to the technique, the repertory grid provides a useful tool for the preliminary isolation and detection of issues for further elaboration. A reasonably accessible introduction to the tool can be found in Kelly's 1963 book *The Theory of Personality: The Psychology of Personal Constructs*.

However, having said this, it would be inappropriate to give any weight to the small sample of nurses' grids in the pilot study. Nonetheless, a broad outline of the findings is pertinent to this discussion. The grids revealed that the primary 'component', that is the principal means by which nurses discriminated between the activities/tasks they performed in their work lives, was construed in terms of those tasks that they saw as central to the job and those that they saw as peripheral. The bipolar component 'central' to 'peripheral' was made up of a collection of constructs that included 'related to treatment', 'care', 'therapy' and, by implication, their opposites. This is not perhaps so surprising. However, when read in conjunction with the second component, which was 'involves interaction with patient' to 'does not involve interaction with the patient', an interesting pattern of nurses' tasks began to emerge. This second principal component was made up of a group of constructs that included 'talking to the patient', 'assisting the patient', 'taking responsibility for the patient' (Figure 10.1).

It appeared from this small sample that a surprising number of nurses' tasks fell into the quadrant described by 'peripheral to the job' and 'does not involve interaction with the patient'. Such activities might be related to administrative tasks and training responsibilities but also included activities that would usually be expected to involve interaction with patients such as 'bed making'. 'Taking a patient's temperature' was construed as central to the job but as involving no interaction with the patient. Other activities that were construed as peripheral but involving interaction included 'escorting patients', 'eliciting personal details' and 'serving food'. Nurses identified the most important quadrant on the grid as being that concerned with core nursing activities ('central to the job') and with interacting with patients. They could label the quadrant in terms of 'treatment' and 'care' but, in fact, relatively few activities actually fell into this space. Many of the activities that might be expected to occur in this quadrant, 'applying and removing dress-

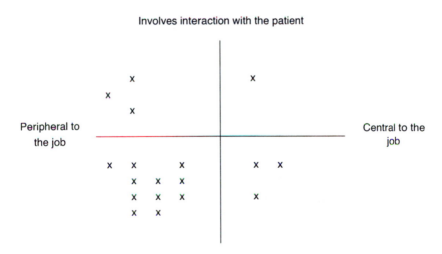

Figure 10.1   Repertory grid constructs: Nurses RLI (Royal Lacaster Infirmary).

ings', 'injections' and, as mentioned above, 'taking a patient's temperature' had migrated either into or towards the 'central'/'no interaction' quadrant. 'Bathing patients' and 'preparing patients for operations' remained securely in the 'ideal' quadrant.

When confronted with the initial findings from the grid, the nurses were surprised by the discrepancy between their perception of the essential characteristics of their work and the extent to which other activities predominated in their day-to-day work tasks as indicated by their consensus grid (the aggregate grid of the six nurses in the study).

However, they quickly interpreted the discrepancy as indicative of the way in which the occupation had changed and to the increasing bureaucratisation of the National Health Service (NHS). In short, their emotional and vocational attachment to their work was located in the tradition of 'service and dedication' to nursing as a vocation. Their satisfactions, they claimed, came from the opportunity to work with patients on essential nursing tasks. Their routine jobs were increasingly removed from that ideal. Only by routinising some aspects of patient care, (essential nursing tasks performed without interaction with patients) could they manage to perform across the range of tasks required of them. Dissatisfaction was expressed with tasks that were both peripheral and did not involve interaction. Despite the small sample, the emergent issues indicated that a specific study of nurses' attitudes and values might yield some interesting data on the implications of organisational change for occupational perceptions within a particular group.

Representing the nurse

A more extensive examination of nurses' attitudes using the repertory grid was proposed in collaboration with Julia Hallam, Department of Politics and Communication Studies, University of Liverpool. Hallam had undertaken a systematic study of 'images' of nursing in the twentieth century and had given specific attention to changes in the notion of service. She has argued that nurses have moved from a position of subordination and moral control to one in which they seek professional recognition and acknowledgement of their training and skills (Hallam 1995). In effect, nurses appear to be seeking to rid themselves of the image of 'ministering angels' in order to attain a perception that not only implies professional competence and skill but also represents nurses as workers with material needs: to break the association between service and subservience. As long as the public image of the nurse is that of an 'angel of mercy' superhuman expectations are not unreasonable. Nursing has been dirty work with a noble significance.

The notion of nursing as a vocation supported by a moral commitment to service and dedication is a significant social perception, not least among nurses themselves. Until comparatively recently, nurse training has conformed to its historical antecedent as the charitable work of religious orders: the nursing 'sister'. Similarly, nurses were expected to live in nurses' homes with at least the pretence of a strict moral code of behaviour. Men were excluded from nurses' homes and their grounds, a curfew was operated and there were strict rules of conduct with severe penalties for contravention. Nurses were not allowed to become engaged or marry while in training. A hierarchy of initiation existed with stringent rules of interaction between levels. An almost Trappistine silence was required of the lower ranks and a respectful attitude to superiors *sine qua non*. Training was rigorous and procedures were to be followed with exactitude. 'Knowing one's place' and knowing 'when to speak' are phrases that frequently recur in comments by older and retired nurses when talking about their training.

The notion of nursing as a vocation was reinforced by the values of the total institution – conformity in dress and demeanour, separation of the sexes, geographical segregation of initiates. Service and subservience were inextricable concepts. This was further reinforced by the system of training that offered periods of college-based courses that were interspersed with lengthy periods of on-the-job training on the ward. This style of training confirmed the role of *training by initiation* with duties and experiences geared to providing exposure to dirty and unpleasant aspects of the job. Migration up the hierarchy involved a movement away from contact with 'dirt'. Ward responsibilities, in this sense, were always a managerial task in that the ward sister was responsible for preserving order, the performance of necessary tasks and the keeping of records. This chapter seeks to provide a preliminary examination of nurses' commitment to 'service', in order to examine possible differences between male and female nurses, to identify emergent hierarchical differences, and to offer some tentative comparisons between nurses and other defined groups.

Shifting images

Hallam, in her article 'The changing image of the nurse' (Hallam 1995) and in her book *Nursing the Image* (Hallam 2000), provides a fascinating account of the background to the current crisis in nursing identity and, indeed, in nursing recruitment. Hallam's work and her collaboration on a publication for the European Network of Organisational Psychologists provided a great many insights into issues of identity and experience in the changing nature of nursing as an occupation. Hallam, who herself had previously been a nurse, is also a specialist on film and representation and has recently produced a book on *Realism and Popular Cinema* (Hallam and Marshment 2000). Her experiences and analysis provide a remarkable context for understanding shifting notions of service in the nursing profession. Her book is a detailed and valuable contribution to the field. In this chapter, only the outline of her work is presented as it contributed to our joint publication (Höpfl and Hallam 2000). Hallam explains that in the post-war period, the British government, through the Ministry of Labour, produced information on most careers for dissemination to schools, labour exchanges and career offices. *Nursing and Midwifery Services (Women)* was Number 33 in the 'Careers for Men and Women' series. Hallam points to the introductory paragraph of this pamphlet, which seeks to demonstrate how the 'arduous' work and responsibilities of the training period are offset against the numerous advantages to be gained by qualifying. This is when 'the field of opportunity is open so wide that a nurse can give her best service' and find 'the deepest personal satisfaction' (Höpfl and Hallam 2000). As in other publications around this time, there is an emphasis on the value of nursing experience for the possible future roles of wife and mother, while stressing that 'opportunities for work are not necessarily limited by marriage'. On this latter point however, as Hallam (2000) indicates, the literature is remarkably silent; nurses who married in training were invariably dismissed, and it was virtually impossible to combine marriage with a career. In the tradition of the vocational commitment of the convent, advancement in nursing required a renunciation of worldly concerns and pleasures.

By the early 1950s, however, there was a clear change. Hallam shows how in *Your Chance* (published in 1950), the familiar image of the nurse has lost much of its classical rigidity and seriousness; the nurse on the front cover looks invitingly out of the picture at the reader as she glides by with her tray – a soft, feminine image. She has well-defined eyebrows, an open mouth, she is smiling – and looks remarkably similar to the picture of a figure found on the dust cover of a highly popular series of nursing books for girls, the Cherry Ames stories. These US books became 'bestsellers' in the post-war period and, Hallam (2000) argues, they were written for a young female audience at the beginning of their adolescence. The books depict nursing as a job rather than a profession, a worthwhile and satisfying job but one in which the notion of service is clearly limited to serving male doctors and male patients. This is both a significant change and a different depiction of service. The opportunities offered by nursing training in these books are the personal satisfactions of fun, travel and adventure. The life of service and professional values is not part of this image. Hallam (2000) tells how the recruitment brochure picks up on these associations in an obvious attempt to appeal to the lower middle-class and working-class readership of the novels. It was also meant to dispel public assumptions about nursing as charitable work undertaken by upper-class young women, poorly paid, hard and dirty work that leaves no time for fun and romance. The front cover attempts to make nursing look more exciting and appealing, promising not only a worthwhile job but the possibility of 'a career with status and prospects', and an opportunity to change your social position 'in service to the nation'. The nationalisation of the health services had created an increased demand for nursing services, which revealed a severe shortage of trained staff. Hallam (2000) has traced the ways in which changes in educational entry requirements were opening up the possibility of nursing as a career to lower middle-class and working-class girls. The promise of social mobility in service to the nation undoubtedly offered a tantalising incentive to some to enter the profession. What Hallam is demonstrating by recourse to this literature is that a clear shift in the ethos of service becomes apparent, *away* from ideas of vocational commitment to the profession and *towards* serving the nation through a commitment to the emergent NHS. This change in the conception of service is highly significant. Nursing was becoming less popular as a career and there was an acute shortage of qualified nurses, despite the fact that the educational requirements for entry that had been suspended during the war had not been reinstated. White (1985) sees the failure of the General Nursing Council to reinstitute the pre-war entry requirement as symptomatic of a change in attitude among nursing leaders, who, according to White, were no longer concerned with the good of the profession but with the common good.

Consequently, Hallam argues, nationalisation had changed the constitution of nursing's ruling body, the General Nursing Council, altering the balance of power in favour of the former municipal hospital sector. Matrons from the former voluntary sector, long accustomed to leading the profession and projecting the public image of nursing, found themselves outnumbered and over-ruled by the managerial ethos of the matrons from the municipal sector. This change, along with the admission of men to both the General Nursing Register and the Council, had a profound effect on nursing's public image throughout the 1950s. The commitment from the municipal sector matrons to serve the newly nationalised Health Service slowly displaced the reified, or, in terms of the notion of the construction of a professional identity, the perhaps 'personified', notions of service to the profession itself. *Your Chance* reveals the strength of the managers in enacting government policy at this time and the growing commitment among many senior nursing staff to support the more egalitarian ethos of the newly formed Health Service (Hallam 2000; Höpfl and Hallam 2000).

Angels and gods

Throughout the 1950s and 1960s the construction of nursing as a vocational profession fractured into a more complex set of occupational images. Hallam (2000) makes the point that public projections of the nurse as an 'angel', an image of asexualised feminine values of self-sacrifice, obedience and moral purity, underwent a stark change. Professional nursing had advocated and used the 'angel' image to advance its claims to a 'separate but equal' professional sphere to that of medicine and to bolster its own claims of autonomy and authority. But in a public service economy in which nursing is regarded as a right rather than a gift or a privilege, there was a growing dislike of the ideology of the white, female, middle-class sacrifice and moral authority that the image of the angel represented. Images of nurses as petty authoritarians, 'battleaxes', and sexually frustrated spinsters became increasingly common in popular culture. The fracturing of the angel image into parody and pastiche is most apparent in popular films such as the *Carry On* series that was a big box office attraction throughout the period. Hallam has made a careful study of the role of film in recruitment literature and draws attention to such films as *Carry On Nurse*, *Carry on Matron* and *Carry On Doctor*, in which nursing is mercilessly lampooned for its petty authoritarianism, impotency, incompetence and frivolity (Hallam 2000). Other films, such as *The Feminine Touch*, show nurses tending to the needs of their doctor boyfriends while doctors administer the tender loving care at the bedside, traditionally given by nurses. 'Doctors are deified as godlike saviours, superseding the ministering angels in the holy order, who become handmaidens to medical men' (Hallam 1995). Service, thus, is redefined and the nurse placed in the hieratic service of medicine as personified by the doctor.

According to Hallam (2000) nursing's romance with medicine reached a high point in the late 1950s, when the publishers Mills and Boon capitalised on the demand for romantic images and launched their international paperback enterprise with an ongoing series of doctor/nurse romantic novels. Throughout the 1960s, the newly developing international image markets in publishing and television programmes made spectacular US images of godlike medical men increasingly available to British audiences. Nurses became background figures in small-screen melodramas, while on the big screen they were satirised as petty authoritarians and sexually frustrated spinsters, or depicted as promiscuous objects of male sexual fantasy and desire. The combination of 'machismo' and 'melodrama' in many of these prime-time television shows and films clearly reworked 1950s ideas about nursing as a service to the community into a 1960s ethos of self-abnegating servility to medicine and medical men, which rendered screen images of nurses virtually silent. Nurses are visible only as handmaidens or as decoration and sexual spectacle.

Medical procedures

A similar shift in the notion of service is also apparent in the recruitment literature. Hallam (2000) shows how in *SRN* (published in 1965) black and white photography and dramatic lighting was used to give documentary authenticity to pictures of modern hospital work. Pictures of life and death struggles foreground complicated medical procedures undertaken over the lifeless bodies of disinterred patients. Increasingly, nurses were shown serving the new technologies of medical cure rather than undertaking the traditional tasks of nursing care. Assisting the doctor in his work was represented as the finest work a nurse can do – an idea constantly reinforced in the medical romances of the time. In other words, nurses *achieved* their identity by being *called* into the service of potent medical men (Hallam 1995).

By the late 1960s, the recruitment literature for professional (state-registered nurse – SRN) training and practical (state-enrolled nurse – SEN) training had polarised, with the former emphasising the 'high-tech' drama of modern curative medicine and the latter favouring popular fantasies of the relationship between nursing and femininity. The drama of documentary realism was used to attract the professionally inclined (middle-class) reader, while discourses of service and vocationalism embedded in subtexts of doctor/nurse romance and motherhood were used to attract practical (working-class) girls through mythopoeic imagery and emotional associations. The disappearance of images of nurses in authority from anything other than teaching roles, while perhaps creating a more friendly picture of nursing work, also lowered the threshold of expectation of those coming into nursing. The future, as a qualified nurse, became a distant reality compared to the sense of drama and immediacy created by documentary-style photography and the subtextual promise of fun and romance.

Female subordination and male medical power

The highly romanticised image of nursing reached its zenith in the late 1960s with recruitment literature such as *A Girl Like You* but was publicly contradicted by media images of anger and dissatisfaction among nurses themselves. Hallam argues that this was the first time that nurses had vociferously complained about their outmoded working conditions, outdated pay scales and obsolete working practices. Unionised nurses raised sufficient support among the general nursing population and the trade union movement to press these complaints at the highest level of government. The campaign gave nursing a voice and raised the public profile of a profession that since the 1950s had been increasingly submerged beneath images of female subordination and male medical power.

Nursing entered the 1970s a fragmented and divided profession and Hallam traces the significance of this for the professional. In particular, she shows how the separate factions, each with their own power bases, found it difficult to reconcile their differences. The two-tier structure of training reinforced differences in status, attitudes and outlook. State-registered nurses, trained for specialist positions, either in management or education and training, tended to regard nursing as a profession; enrolled nurses, trained to do the hard and dirty work of day-to-day patient care, tended to regard nursing as a job. Registered nurses were trained to instil vocationalism in others, while protecting their own professional status as managers and specialists; enrolled nurses were trained to obey orders and instructions, while respecting 'hands-on' experience as the criterion for promotion and advancement.

One of the most significant developments that Hallam identifies is the separation at the top of the nursing hierarchy. The power and authority at one time invested in the voluntary hospital matron separates into two separate nursing identities: one with the power to 'hire and fire' nursing staff in the interests of serving 'the common good' of the NHS but with no authority in the specialist areas of nursing knowledge and education; the other an 'authority' in a chosen specialist area, promoting the ethos of serving the patient but whose power is limited to developing the speciality and participating in nurse education and research. In spite of recent changes in nurse training that are slowly being introduced throughout Britain in part to address the problem of fragmentation, these divisions in identity and status between different nursing factions continue to inform beliefs and attitudes among nurses practising today. Within this context, a shift in the notion of service to one of *service provision* reveals the conflicts between ideologies of service that are grounded in professional values of personal responsibility and control, egalitarian values based on bureaucratic control and entrepreneurial values rooted in competitive enterprise. This shift of emphasis is highly significant in relation to the position of nurses and is taken up in the next section. This will deal with how the implications of Hallam's work on the representation of the nurse inform notions of service and, in relation to a managerial culture, seeks to throw light on different interpretations of who is served: the patient, the state or the common good.

Service vs. entrepreneurialism

There have been a number of studies of the attitudes and values in nursing in recent years (White 1985; Ackroyd 1993; Hallam 1995), each making a different contribution to an understanding of the nursing profession. Ackroyd (1993) rightly points out that there are difficulties from the outset of any such study not least the problem of ascertaining the key issues for investigation. It was this specific problem that prompted the investigation which reported here. The research attempted to identify concerns for further examination during 1995–6. Consequently, the report here is on 'work-in-progress' from research conducted at Halton General Hospital, Runcorn. Fifty nurses at the hospital were asked to complete a career orientations inventory (Schein 1990) and the results were processed according to sex, age, grade and length of service. The inventory identifies 'career anchors', the specific attachments that individuals bring to their career choices: the criteria that are important and those that are less important. The instrument is rather crude but it provides a common basis for comparison and raises issues that can be used for further discussion, for semi-structured interviews, and so forth. The choice of career anchors as a preliminary analytical tool offered the opportunity to identify nurse perceptions of occupational values and to discern gender and other differences. The inventory produces a classification based on a range of scaled responses. Eight career anchors are defined and respondents' answers indicate individual preferences in relation to occupational characteristics. The results are shown in Table 10.1.

The overall results for all fifty subjects in the study indicate that in simple averaging, the common career anchor in the nurses' commitment to their work is related to a notion of service and dedication. Clearly, this outcome is not without interpretative difficulties. However, leaving these aside for the moment, it is possible to point to a considerable emphasis on the role of 'service' as an occupational value for nurses of all grades, male and female, in the study. There is an emotional attachment to this value that relates to the perception and, indeed, self-perception of the occupation as a vocation. Of course, it is difficult to discriminate between the notion of service to the patient and service to the common good, from service to service provision, as

Table 10.1   Career orientations

	Nurses			MBA
	All No. 50	Men No. 5	Women No. 45	No. 50
Technical/functional				
Managerial				*
Autonomy/independence				
Job security	*	*	*	
Geographical security				
Service dedication	*	*	*	
Pure challenge				*
Lifestyle	*		*	
Entrepreneurship				*

Hallam (2000) identifies in her work. However, if service is taken in this context to mean an action or actions performed for the 'other' either as a personal or abstract act, this provides an understanding of the values and motivations of nurses as utilitarian.

Nonetheless, however much the appeal of the primacy of service and dedication might be, when individual ratings are taken into account rather than a crude aggregation, the predominant central concern in the data is with job security. This is the highest rated career anchor for all nurse subjects irrespective of sex, rank or length of service. There were only five men in the study, all in their thirties and in lower professional grades. However, their ratings were remarkably similar. They differed from the larger women's sample in only one respect: the inappropriately termed 'lifestyle' career anchor that relates to the balance between work and domestic life was less evident. Men attached less importance to the acquisition of technical occupational skills than women. There was no evidence to suggest that career anchors changed with length of service or with professional grade, consequently a female nurse aged 59 with 41 years service produced a remarkably similar ordering to a female nurse aged 31 with 6 years service. Profiles conformed to a consistent pattern. Thus, whereas for women the predominant career anchors were service, job security and lifestyle, in that order, for men it was job security and service. The lowest scoring anchors were, for both groups, entrepreneurialism, pure competition and managerial concerns (in ascending order), while for the men in the study, entrepreneurialism, autonomy and independence, competition and managerial concerns were low rated.

The emergence of common professional values is not perhaps surprising. However, it presents an interesting comparison with the career anchors of women clerical workers – at least as represented in a small study (sample size eleven, all women and not included in the table above) and, more strikingly, with Master of Business Administration (MBA) students of both sexes (sample size fifty, twenty-eight men, twenty-two women; see Table 10.1). These studies, conducted with MBA students at Bolton Institute in the mid-1990s, and with clerical staff also at the Institute, are not intended to constitute a thorough and scientific study of the career anchors of clerical workers and MBA students. Rather, they are intended to provide some indications regarding primary orientations towards work. Male MBA students produced a central constellation of anchors, which included pure competition, entrepreneurialism and managerial concerns, precisely the lowest rated anchors of the male nurses. Women MBA students included autonomy and independence, in conjunction with entrepreneurialism and managerial competence. It is also apparent that, for some women MBA students, geographical immobility was a factor. The career anchors of women clerical workers, however, are not dissimilar to those of the nurses, with a primary emphasis on service, job security and lifestyle. Consequently, despite the crude research instrument, it appears that it is possible to discern occupational constellations of anchors. There are a number of issues that emerge from this observation not least the problem of interpretation. To identify common occupational patterns is relatively easy. To offer accounts of how such profiles might emerge is more difficult.

Clearly there are issues that relate to the ways in which a professional identity is constructed, to the relationship between personal preference and career choice and to the construction of occupational identity through a process of *bricolage* and occupational mythopoesis. Personal predisposition and career choice are clearly not unrelated and once an individual has entered a particular career, socialisation into that career would indicate convergent values among its members. The occupational identity can be produced as an artefact by a process of *bricolage* (Linstead and Grafton Small 1990) and supported by transformational metaphors that both confer and confirm identity (Fernandez 1986). The professional 'identity' of the nurse can thus be viewed as an artefact that is produced and reproduced by a mythopoeic process and presented in the service orientation of the career anchors inventory. The question that this poses is the extent to which such constructions are detrimental to the power position of nurses. It is apparent that there is a relationship between service and subservience that permits the manipulation of the service role.

Patience and patients

Pertinent to this it is interesting to note that the words passion/patience/ patient (the virtues and object of service) are derived from the Latin (*patior*) meaning to suffer, to support, to undergo, and, in an obscene sense, to submit to another's lust, to prostitute oneself. A passion is to be borne or suffered. The bearing of a professional role similarly becomes a matter of passion and, such that nursing provides a specific exemplar of this, of personal sacrifice. Consequently, to enter the nursing profession requires that one takes on a role, supports the appropriate frame of action, submits to changes, and bears up (Höpfl and Linstead 1993).

The self-perception (perhaps, indeed, self-deception) that is apparent in the production of the service identity appears to be devoid of competitive, entrepreneurial and control needs. By implication, such a position is extremely vulnerable. Nurses have sought to reinforce the technical exactitude of their work, to give emphasis to the managerial demands that are placed on them and to underscore their commitment to service and dedication. However, such values carry fundamental contradictions and this leaves nurses open to the exploitation of their ambivalence. Their career orientations are radically different from those of potential managers and, by their attachment to service values, their political position is radically weakened. Virtue it seems is not rewarded but 'managed'. In this sense, whether the construction of the professional identity of the nurse is a facet of socialisation or the result of mythopoesis, which both precedes and succeeds entry into the profession, is irrelevant to the apparent consequences. For these suggest that the adoption of a service commitment creates a vulnerability to the machinations of more entrepreneurial/managerial identities. Superficial analysis appears to indicate that the increase in the number of men in nursing has not, as is often claimed, accelerated the position of nurses towards a more militant position. Rather, it would seem that men are attracted to nursing for similar reasons to women. Arguably, recent moves towards job enlargement for nurses in the UK provides clear evidence of their increased exploitation under the guise of respect for their professional competence although with a managerial emphasis on *service provision* this might be viewed by managers simply as a better use of resources. However complex the issues that relate to the interpretation of the construction of the professional identity of nurses, it is important to bear in mind the political implications of their core professional values and their susceptibility to exploitation. This analysis is not confined to changes in the nursing profession and so is intended as a prompt to reflect on other occupations that have been subject to such changes.

In the past, nursing as an occupational identity has been given coherence by the emphasis on professionalism and a high valorisation of the notion of service. In contrast, the modern nursing curriculum is being shaped by the academic demands of the higher education system and practical training is now seen as the applied aspect of this training. Changes in the language of nursing, away from notions of 'serving the patient' to providing 'care management facilities' are indicative of a more abstract definition of service with implications for the relationship between nurse and patient. This is evidenced by the small survey at the beginning of this chapter that shows many practical activities involving patients being performed with 'no interaction with the patient'. It is also found in the widespread use of this type of terminology in nursing journals: for example in the account of the nurse's role within 'nursing care delivery' (Jinks 2000); or of 'drivers and barriers to service development (in mental health provision) in London' (Hills 2000); or a study of 'factors that influence nurses' customer orientation' (Darby and Daniel 2000). With such evolving notions of professionalism and its associated move away from contact with the patient comes the construction of 'care' and of 'service' as abstract categories rather than as practical performatives. The imagery of nursing is now a very complex *bricolage* of service, professionalism, academic standards, managerial expectations and failing compensations. Nurse managers are expected to know as much about budgets and operational management as they do about patient care (Lindholm *et al.* 2000). In the last 10 years, the rhetoric of increased professionalism, with its implicit extension of workload, has begun to wear thin and the gulf between service and cosmetic definitions of service level agreements has further opened up this gap (Darley 2000). The introduction of the dubious and contested concept of empowerment into the NHS is unlikely to contribute to greater freedom for nurses but is, on the other hand, likely to contribute to a greater sense of dissatisfaction. The greater militancy of nurses attests to the changing perception of the occupational role (Höpfl and Hallam 2000).

Care and care management

Historically, the articulation and representation of the image of nursing has served a variety of regulatory and recruitment functions. The construction of the role around a changing notion of 'service' has put nursing into a weak and fragmented position. Its very ambivalence between 'service' and 'self-interest', between 'professionalism' and 'personal choice', and its high moral tone has paralysed personal and political action and led to an increased detachment from the day-to-day responsibilities of the job. In other words, the cult of 'service provision' and the language of 'care management' have removed the nurse increasingly from the satisfactions of the job. In this respect, the gendered aspect of the work is to do with the way in which such construc- tions are devised, imposed and used as instruments of regulation within the profession. This chapter is not about gender per se. Rather, it is about the privileging of male constructions over female acts. In this sense, the argument is concerned with differences between masculine and feminine rather than male and female. The male and female nurses were much the same in the survey reported earlier in the chapter. Likewise, the men and women in the MBA study produced very similar results. These groupings show occupational characteristics rather than gendered ones. This chapter, in contrast, looks at the way in which 'good order' and regulation within the nursing profession is a masculine construction. By an emphasis on rhetoric and on categories and definitions, as in many other professions, nursing and nurse management has privileged discourse over doing and the definition of care over caring. This is because there is a widening gulf of meaning between abstract representations, of image and of roles, and the day-to-day experiences of people doing their normal work. In nursing, this has serious implications as the notion of care for the person becomes translated into care for the fulfilment of an abstract set of categories that form part of an evaluative system of care management. In other words, there is a separation into care for the regulation, the 'law' and for the patient, the 'body' in a very literal way. As Eagleton argues, 'The law is male, but hegemony is a woman; this transvestite law, which decks itself out in female drapery is in danger of having its phallus exposed'(Eagleton 1990: 58). This is apparent in the ways in which nursing has sought to create the feminine 'other', or, if you like, the *anima*, in notions of care and satisfaction: customer care, care management systems, 'client satisfaction' (Darby and Daniel 2000) and so called 'care delivery'. So, nursing has constructed itself in images of nursing and service, in diagrams and charts, in texts and metrics that seek to support such representations. In its representations, nursing has sought to give itself a 'body' both in terms of the manipulation of images of the nurse and in terms of its commitment to care. However, as Eagleton says, it is a male construction that seeks to represent itself as female. It is the law pretending to be a female body and it is exposed as a phallus. In other words, the commitment to care is bound to fail because it is merely a construction: it is not a real body. The female 'other' it seeks to present is a male construction and, therefore, the disillusionment within the profession is, in part, the ability to see the phallus. It is little wonder, therefore, that notions of quality and care, the ubiquitous valorisation of staff, and the appeal to 'professional values' have more in them of melancholy than of matter. In a recent paper in the *Journal of Nursing Management*, Fedoruk and Pincombe (2000) argue that 'in the emerging health care system of the new century, nurse executives practices will focus on achieving change rather than predictability in organisational outcomes'. At heart, this is a recognition of the need for more female-centred management practices. Indeed, arguably, the leadership qualities that are needed in the twenty-first century are precisely feminine ones. Managerialism has led to a loss of contact with the human values and the privileging of order and regula- tion over experience and personal knowledge. There has been a search for the lost 'otherness' that has resulted in the construction of quasi-value systems in nursing, in teaching and in commercial organisations (see Cooper 1983). Such constructions are bound to fail. Nursing is a most interesting occupation to study in this respect because what in other occupations become mere ciphers for these dynamics, in nursing they are played out in the contested arena of day-to-day interactions, values and conflicts.

On being liberated from the constructions

The intention of this chapter has been to offer some preliminary findings regarding perceptions of nurses' identity and their implications for the politi- cal position of nurses. It is important for occupational groups to confront the ways in which they construct their professional identities as the basis of their political praxis: men and women in work enterprises have to be liberated and to liberate themselves from imprisonment by the predominant deifications and reifications (Sievers 1994: 306)

For these dominate and regulate their behaviour and actions. There are implications here for human resource development, which require fuller attention to changes in occupations and the sense of identity that attaches to them. The changes in nursing have led to a crisis that might have been foreseen with more attention to the nature of the identity of the nurse and, in particular, a greater appreciation of the understanding of what constitutes a professional identity. Other occupations and those in charge of their destinies might learn some valuable lessons by examining the effects of changes on nurse identity.

References

Ackroyd, S. (1993) 'Towards an understanding of nurses' attachments to their work: Morale amongst nurses in an acute hospital', *Journal of Advances in Health and Nursing Care*, 2 (3): 23–45.

Cooper, R. (1983) 'The Other: A model of human structuring', in Morgan, G. (ed.), *Beyond Method, Strategies for Social Research*, Beverley Hills: Sage, pp. 202–18.

Darby, D. N. and Daniel, K. (2000) 'Factors that influence nurses' customer orientation', *Journal of Nursing Management*, 7 (5): 271–80.

Darley, M. (2000) 'Rhetoric or service', *Journal of Nursing Management*, 8 (4): 191–92.

Eagleton, T. (1990) *The Ideology of the Aesthetic*, Oxford: Blackwell.

Fedoruk, M. and Pincombe, J. (2000) 'The nurse executive: Challenges for the 21st century', *Journal of Nursing Management*, 8 (1): 13–20.

Fernandez, J. W. (1986) *Persuasions and Performances, The Play of Tropes in Culture*, Bloomington, IN: Indiana University Press.

Fransella, F. and Bannister, D. (1977) *A Manual for Repertory Grid Technique*, New York: Academic Press.

Hallam, J. (1995) 'The changing image of the nurse', *Research, Film and Video Tape Conference*, Bolton Business School.

Hallam, J. (2000) *Nursing the Image*, London: Routledge.

Hallam, J. and Marshment, M. (2000) *Realism and Popular Cinema*, Manchester: Manchester University Press.

Hills, B. (2000) 'A comparison of senior nurses and managers views on the development of mental health services in NHS Trusts in London', *Journal of Nursing Management*, 8 (5): 291–96.

Höpfl, H. and Hallam, J. (2000) 'The changing image of the nurse: Issues of identity and experience', in Le Blanc, P. Peters, M. Buessing, A. and Schaufeli, W. (eds), *Organizational Psychology and Health Care: European Contributions*, München: Rainer Hampp Verlag.

Höpfl, H. and Linstead, S. (1993) 'Passion and performance, suffering and the carrying of organizational roles', in Fineman, S. (ed.), *Emotion in Organizations*, London: Sage, pp. 76–93.

Jinks, A. M. (2000) 'What do nurses do? An observational survey of the activities of nurses on acute surgical and rehabilitation wards', *Journal of Nursing Management*, 8 (5), 273–79.

Kelly, G. A. (1955) *The Psychology of Personal Constructs*, New York: Norton.

Kelly, G. A. (1963) *Theory of Personality: The Psychology of Personal Constructs*, New York: Norton.

Lindholm, M., Sivberg, B. and Udén, G. (2000) Leadership styles among nurse managers in changing organizations, *Journal of Nursing Management*, 8 (6): 327–35.

Linstead, S. L. and Grafton Small, R. (1990) 'Theory as artefact: Artefact as theory', in Gagliardi, P. (ed.), *Symbols and Artifacts: Views of the Corporate Landscape*, Berlin: de Gruyter, pp. 387–419.

Schein, E. (1990) *Career Anchors*, San Diego, CA: University Associates.

Sievers, B. (1994) *Work, Death, and Life Itself: Essays on Management and Organisation*, Berlin: Walter de Gruyter.

White, R. (1985) *The Effects of the NHS on the Nursing Profession 1948–61*, London: Kings Fund.

Part III

Identity and biography

11 Gendered narratives of the management of residential care homes

John Chandler

Introduction

This chapter focuses on the issue of how social care can be managed by providing two distinct – and gendered – life histories of people involved in managing private residential care homes. From these are derived two 'ideal-types' of the management of social care which, while derived from a study of the residential care setting, could be applicable elsewhere in the public, private and voluntary sectors.

Despite the drive to promote 'care in the community' and a move away from residential provision in large-scale institutions, residential care continues to be important. There has, however, been a marked change in the pattern of provision (Johnson 1984; Glennerster and Hills 1998). Whereas in the period up to 1980 the majority of residential places were in the public sector, private and voluntary homes now provide the majority of residential places for the elderly, the younger physically handicapped, those with learning difficulties and those with mental illness. The 1980s and 1990s saw the privatisation of residential care, not its decline (the number of residential places went up in this period). This trend, moreover, was not confined to the UK but was also occurring in many European countries simultaneously (Baldock 1993). Of course, much of the care provided for in the private and voluntary sector is publicly funded, part of the blurring of the boundary between public and private sectors.

The distinction between private, voluntary and public residential homes is widely used in the literature on residential care, but what does this distinction signify? It is tempting to see homes in the private sector as differing from those in either the public or voluntary sectors in one crucial respect, from which others follow: the existence of the profit motive. From this may be thought to stem all sorts of evils: low wages and poor conditions; cost cutting, which jeopardises health and safety or renders those in care isolated and bored; the termination of care where there is no longer sufficient profit to be made; or the hiking up of rates to vulnerable clients who cannot easily 'shop around'. It seems easier, perhaps, to accept people profiting from cornflakes than care. But a moment's thought suggests we need to be cautious about how we see these private homes. For one thing the literature on small businesses suggests that there are a number of motives for setting up a business other than profit (Scase and Goffee 1980). And even if profit is an important consideration, then poor standards of care and poor treatment of staff may not be the best means of securing it.

But the intention here is not to engage in an evaluation of the relative merits of private and public provision. The aim is much more modest: to examine, through just two case studies, two different approaches to managing private residential care homes. In doing so I will look at these homes through the narratives of a woman and a man, who are respectively a manager and a proprietor of two different homes.

This is not the place to debate the merits of 'life history' and narrative research or its application in any detail (Josselson and Lieblich 1993; Musson 1998), but some brief points concerning the method are pertinent. First, it is recognised that the narratives presented here are not simple representations of 'reality'. They have been constructed by the author from interview data that is itself the result of a complex discursive performance. Second, they represent just one way of writing the narratives – narratives that are themselves contingent upon a particular researcher asking particular people particular questions at a particular time and place. These 'stories' are, then, a (re)presentation of the efforts of two people involved in running residential care homes to account for how they do so – and how they fashion an identity accordingly (Ochberg 1994: 114). Furthermore, in presenting and publishing these accounts the stories become capable of being appropriated by others in the work of constructing identities (Giddens 1991: 10–14). Through them we can come to see, and perhaps refashion, a range of possible managerial identities.

It is to the two narratives that I now turn.

Frank[1]

I interviewed Frank in the 'training room' of a residential home housing twelve elderly people, close to the centre of a large town. The room was well appointed and businesslike, with black and grey dominating the colour scheme of the coordinated furnishing and decor. Frank appeared to be in his late forties and was dressed in a light-grey suit. He seemed keen to talk about both himself and the home, and the interview, which was tape recorded, lasted more than 2 hours. Frank was the proprietor rather than the designated manager of the home, but his role seemed akin to that of the owner manager of a small business. Though not present at the home all the time he said staff were used to seeing him 'four or five times a week'.

Frank could be seen as the very embodiment of managerialism, an example of what Rose (1989) was addressing in examining how 'the personal and subjective capacities of citizens have been incorporated into the scope and aspirations of public powers' (Rose 1989: 1). Frank's own description of himself was of a former National Health Service (NHS) general manager who was 'now utilising planning and management skills to develop [his] business interests'. His talk was peppered with the language of business and management: 'operating systems', 'customer focus', 'vertically integrate the market', 'marketing advantage', 'quality control procedures'. Asked about where his knowledge of management came from he mentioned management training in the NHS as well as ideas coming from management journals, books and videos:

> *In Search of Excellence* [Peters and Waterman 1982] ... there was a video and a book. That was a real inspiration to me. I really identified with that and these comments about why Disney is so good ...

Frank seemed proud of the home's achieving ISO 9000 (a quality assurance standard), something he initiated. He claimed to have written the required operating procedures and gave the following reasons for aiming for this standard:

> It was a marketing advantage. No one else has it. Also it's a very good management tool in terms of ... control. ... As proprietor of the business, even though you are not physically here every day, the fact that your policies and procedures [are there] and that you do the audits of all the procedures. ... You can be quite distant in terms of hierarchy or physically distant and still control all elements of the business. ... So it's a very good management tool, particularly for an autocrat.

Frank continually brought the interview back to the issue of quality. He said his home was 'striving for excellence' and the procedures were, as he expressed it, mechanisms for attaining and assuring quality. This quality emphasis and his explicit reference to Peters and Waterman would appear to align him with 'new wave' management thinking (Wood 1989; Ferlie *et al.* 1996: 13), however his comments also vividly demonstrate how this can come close to a traditional Taylorist form. In constructing the procedures, he says:

> It starts with values [echoes of Peters and Waterman's (1982: 279) 'value-driven' management here], then you get on to how jobs will be done. So you can even control how a table's laid through [ISO 9000] and if staff don't do it then ... the procedure's failed and they haven't complied, so I take it up with the manager as a non-compliance.

As in Taylorism the procedures encapsulate the 'one best way', staff are trained in it, compliance is monitored and enforced and monetary incentives, as well as discipline, are used to motivate workers (staff receive 'enhancement' of their wages once they demonstrate compliance with the standards set).

But if Frank can be seen as the epitome of neo-Taylorist managerialism, he was, on the evidence of this interview, also shaped by other influences.

Frank described his origins as 'growing up on a post-war housing estate with the backside hanging out of my trousers'. He entered nursing and qualified as a registered mental nurse (RMN) and a registered general nurse (RGN). He described his early career as a 'conventional progressive career in health service ... through the nursing ranks into general management'. As someone whose political beliefs were 'left of centre' he saw the irony in his career advances coinciding with Conservative reforms of the NHS in the 1980s. He described his last few years as a NHS manager as a time of considerable pressure, and stress:

> You're attempting to reconcile the irreconcilable very often. ... I think that was a lot to do with my nursing background, my first discipline. You're aware you have to reduce your budget. In the last year I think I had to knock £8m. off the revenue budget ... It would cause me real conflict in the consequences of those changes. It's quite easy to close a ward. ... I think people that may not have been from a caring discipline – from say an accounting discipline – they could have kept that as rational and deliver it. The problem I had was that I could deliver it but I was torn by the actual consequences of that action. I knew people were suffering or not having access to facilities that morally I think they should have.

He also reported other symptoms of stress at the time – irritability, lack of sleep, constantly feeling tired. In the end he felt he had to leave:

> I was absolutely brassed off with the political dynamics of the health service. ... We were delivering covert agendas all the time and I found that, to me, was contrary to my own value system. It caused all sorts of conflict. ... An issue arose ... an issue of principle. You can have them when you're 45 and you've got the safety of a pension ... So I said I'd leave to save any embarrassment or any public utterances.

Having left he was:

> determined I wanted to go into business ... I felt the only way I could practise my management skills unencumbered was by operating my own business.

He looked at a number of businesses:

> fish farms, pet shops, wholesaling. I just knew I wanted to go into business. I was a little bit brassed off with the concept of being involved with care because it, in a general sense, because it takes a real toll on, you know, to be committed. ... But among the business transfer deals I looked at three or four residential homes ... . But if I tell you that ... [I] was absolutely shocked rigid with what I perceived as the apathy, the lack of real customer focus on the client, the greed, the overall dinginess, shoddiness of the

operation. I was determined with almost a zeal that I could impact the industry by buying a home, operating a home ... within my own model.

This is not to say his motives were entirely altruistic. In opting for a residential home as a business he was selecting 'one of very few businesses that, when I looked at it, it added up. There was a return.' Above all, though, the impression he gave was of wanting to manage a business in his own way – and that involved making his values explicit and ensuring they were implemented in the business. He suggested these values were enshrined in the home's charter of client's rights and informed the procedures he laid down:

> That's why I control procedures. That's why I write them, that's why I implement them, that's why I change them. Because at every [level], no matter how trivial – purchasing food, laying tables – you can keep consolidating the basic values.

These values included giving clients the opportunity to exercise choice. This was put into operation in the laundry procedure, for example, which he described as follows:

> Residential clothing will be washed as frequently as necessary and always at the immediate request of the resident. If the resident does not wish to put their own cleaned clothing away, care staff will do it: give the resident choice.

When asked whether everyone in the home shared these values the response was:

> Well, could you not share these values? ... You don't just give [staff] a manual and say you must do things this way. That would take all initiative away. They know the philosophy. They know what I expect. They absorb the values. ... We've only had a couple of incidents in 3 years where I've had real doubt whether staff accord to the same values.

> *What happened in these cases?*
> They left.
> *They left, or you dismissed them?*
> They left.

Carol

Carol was the manager of a residential home for thirty residents with learning difficulties in a rural location. I interviewed her in her office, which was tidy but not excessively so. There were what I took to be family pictures on the shelves, and Carol was dressed quite casually. She seemed relaxed and was very easy to talk to. We were interrupted on two occasions, once by a member of staff and once by a resident. On each occasion there was friendly banter between Carol and these others.

Carol had spent the bulk of her working life at the home. She started when she was still at school, working at weekends. There was a period of 2 years working with animals immediately after leaving school, but after this she returned to the home and had been there ever since – 16 years in total. In that time she had, as she put it, 'done every job there is here except gardener/handyman'. This long association with the home also represented a long association with a high proportion of the residents and staff, since most of the residents were said to have been there 15 or 20 years and most of the staff for many years, too. She described the place as:

> a very homely home. Everybody feels … it's like as if it's an extended family. It's not like going to work to be quite honest. They're part of your life and you do grow very very attached to them because they're all long-stay residents … . You become their family where they haven't got family and you become part of their life and they become part of yours. … I wouldn't want to work in any other residential setting because I know it wouldn't be the same. It wouldn't have the same atmosphere; the staff wouldn't get on so well together. Most staff have been here 10 years plus so you work as a team, and they, as well as the residents, become part of your family.

Her commitment and attachment to the residents came across very strongly throughout the interview. One resident had recently died and her grief was mixed with anger, provoked by the response of others outside the home:

> A florist actually said, 'Oh, do you have to pay for the flowers?' I said, 'No – we *want* to.' It was all 'Well he's only someone you look after, its only your job.' But he's not. To me it was like losing your uncle, a granddad, or something like that. He's part of my life and he's gone … and all the staff found that difficult.

But there were compensations in the job, too, not just from the attachment to others but in the possibility of achieving something:

> The fact that you're actually developing something. You're helping to develop skills with people that perhaps, otherwise, they wouldn't have the chance to. They do basic educational skills, basic learning skills, basic living skills. And all those goals you set and achieve, it's as if you're achieving the goals as well, yourself, because you're helping them.

The impression given was that similar values of care were present here, as in Frank's home, but not institutionalised in such a highly proceduralised or formal way. Carol had just completed a national vocational qualification

(NVQ) assessor's course in care, but she said she did not learn much from the course about care that she did not already know, and although she would be happy for her staff to go through NVQ training, she did not think they wanted to or that it would make a difference. This did not mean she did not manage the staff or ensure they were trained. But if Frank's managerial style was neo-Taylorist, Carol's seemed very different. When staff come from other homes, she said:

> It can be difficult to get them round to your way of thinking. They want a list of what's to be done and when, whereas we don't really work like that. We work around the residents and with the residents … . The main difficulty is helping people to understand that any achievement – albeit he learns to write his name in 7 years, which is one we've had recently – is an achievement. It's like climbing Everest for that man … . But to help staff to understand that it's Mount Everest for them as well, because he may have done it, but without them he wouldn't have.

Carol described the process of appointing new staff. First she interviewed them and took them on a tour of the home; then she gave them 1 month's trial. She described how she looked for clues in the prospective member of staff interactions with the residents and observed, for example, how residents responded to their arrival each day: 'The main thing is the resident's views.' Active attempts to manage the way care was delivered in the home could also be seen in the coaching she gave to staff (although she never used this or any other fashionable management term). For example in seeking to encourage staff to offer residents choice and independence, she spoke of occasionally having to jog her staff's memory:

> You'll get, 'Oh, he'll have toast.' I'll say, 'Have you asked him.' 'Oh, he always has toast.' 'But he might not want toast today.'

This and several other examples were delivered in a highly nuanced way that managed to demonstrate, even in the retelling, how something close to a scold could be delivered with a degree of distancing humour. But correction could take a number of forms:

> Perhaps you'd call me a spy as such. [She laughs.] I try not to let my presence to be known too much, or not that I'm there watching you. And then perhaps if someone is doing something wrong, I'll sit down and have a chat to them, or perhaps the member of staff that they're working with … perhaps you could persuade them. We never try to make anything seem too, 'Oh my God, I've made a mistake, now I'm in trouble.' We don't really have that atmosphere.

And yet, occasionally there was a perceived need to be stricter – something she recognised could cause difficulty:

> People seem to think, 'Oh, she's very friendly, and she'll give advice personally and towards their work,' and all of a sudden you're saying, 'Now, I have talked to you about this before, and now I am going to have to formally tell you that this can't go on.' And you'll get a little bit of animosity for a day or two and then they settle down. But people need to understand that, as much as I'll be their friend outside of work and I'll help them with most things, this is a business and has to be run a bit as a business.

But if it was a business, this did not seem, from Carol's perspective, to be incompatible with care. Indeed, she gave the impression that profit was not the issue for her or the proprietor. She speculated that the proprietor would probably 'like to get rid of it but can't':

> It's attachment to the people. It's strange and I don't think you'd come across it anywhere else. It's their home and you're not going to take it from them. And you're not going to let someone else come in and do whatever to them.

The present proprietor, it should be noted, used to be the manager and he took over ownership after the previous proprietor 'went bust due to other financial dealings' (i.e. unconnected with the home).

Carol described herself as the proprietor's protégée. She described him as:

> A placid man, very caring, but he wouldn't tell you he was. Very, very easy going. … He'd help anybody and he'd like to see people treated fairly no matter what their position in society, their academic position, anything. He'd treat anybody as you'd wish to be treated yourself. And I think that's rubbed off on me.

But although she reports saying to the proprietor, 'I'm getting more like you every day,' she also said there were differences: he was more 'paternalistic' whereas she was keener on the resident's 'charter of rights'; she was prepared to stick up for things she thought right, where 'he'd give up'.

Carol, then, presented herself as a relational manager, who was clearly deeply concerned about the care of residents, with care involving being supportive but also seeking to develop the individual resident's abilities as much as possible, as well as allowing them to exercise choice. She would appear to operate in a participative way: 'I do try to take other people's ideas and opinions', and she provided a number of examples in which she had taken the opinion of residents and staff into account (e.g. over the choice of food and its suppliers). In presenting the home as an extended family in which there was mutual regard and attachment connecting residents and staff, she also displayed an awareness of having to balance friendliness and discipline, individual rights and collective concerns. She illustrated the latter with the example of baths. While recognising the importance of individual choice and autonomy she said that if a resident was to choose not to bathe: 'I'm sorry, but they will have a bath. … Persuasion is a wonderful thing. And bribery.'

In all this, one is tempted to see not the embodiment of managerialism but an older idea from which the idea of managing is in part, perhaps, derived: managing a household or home – or even that of motherhood. But if Carol seemed to be more than a good enough mother to staff and residents, she also demonstrated some of the ambivalence that can be characteristic of motherhood (Hollway and Featherstone 1997). Asked about her career aspirations she said she would hope to leave in around 10 years, once her son was out of school, and open a bed and breakfast and build up to having a string of bed and breakfasts or hotels:

> I do like it here, but when I'm 40 I think I've got to think about myself rather than working for someone else. So that's when we move on. … There again you might come back in 15 years time and still find me here. It'll be a wrench leaving here at any time … [but] basically I'm running a business for somebody here but I'm not getting a share of the profits. I'm running it for a wage. I need to be at some stage doing it for myself.

But she would not want to own her own care home. The reasons she gave for this are interesting, a mixture of the calculative and the affective: 'Because it plods on [as a business] … you're not going to get very high from doing that.' But also:

> [As a business] bed and breakfasts are easier, you can turn off at the end of the day. I'm not saying I don't like it. I never turn off here, but I'm attached to the thirty people here and probably will be until the end of my life or until the end of their lives. I don't want to make that commitment to people again and I'm not the kind of person that could make that commitment and break it. … I don't want to make that kind of commitment to another set of people, and another set, because there is only so much of me to go round.

Discussion

What do these accounts reveal about the management of residential care? First, it would seem that managing care in the private residential setting is not intrinsically inimical to putting a high priority on 'care'. The private form may, of course, have a number of possible drawbacks: private businesses can and do go bust, proprietors can and do sell the businesses on – with uncertain consequences. Given such uncertainties, it might well be argued that the private sector is an inappropriate context for the care of such vulnerable groups. But leaving this 'uncertainty' question aside, the findings suggest that it is not the public or private ownership that matters so much as the way the home is managed – a finding consistent with studies of privatisation in other sectors (Bishop and Kay 1988; Parker 1993).

It is, then, perhaps appropriate that the literature on social welfare has, in recent years, become preoccupied with management and managerialism. This reflects perceived changes in the nature of welfare organisations, with writers such as Clarke and Newman (1997) arguing that there has been a trend towards the 'managerial state', with managerialism challenging the dominance of bureau-professionalism. Most of this discussion has focused on the impact on public sector organisations, but with writers also pointing to the growth in contracting and subcontracting it no longer seems appropriate to study only public sector organisations. It becomes increasingly important to consider the nature of private sector provision of welfare services.

This chapter, of course, presents findings from interviews with just one manager and one proprietor of two different but relatively small private residential homes, and no claim to typicality can be made. Indeed, both respondents presented their own approach as being unusual. If they are of interest, it is because they suggest contrasting ideal-types. Frank's way of managing could be said to be based on managerialism, conceived as a discourse or ideology (Clarke and Newman 1977; Rose 1989; Pollitt 1993) and which can be seen as neo-Taylorist in form. The other case, represented by Carol, demonstrates an approach to management in which everyone in the home (residents as well as staff) seems to be a part of the process of managing the home. This is not to say there is no division of labour, giving Carol a somewhat different role to others, but it does suggest that making the home 'work' as a caring community involves everyone contributing ideas and work. As Carol puts it: 'I'm not in charge. I'm not "up here, I'm in charge."' She does, of course, actively manage the home but she does so by sharing the task of managing with others. Managing is not something that is her sole responsibility and prerogative. Conception and execution are woven together, not sharply separated. And this is not based on management theory but through the everyday practice of living and working together (a practice that of course draws on the rhetoric of family, business, rights and care and cannot but be influenced by its social and historical context). This seems to be a relational management without managerialism, if managerialism is understood to be either a discourse or a legitimating ideology.

This distinction between management and managerialism is an important one. Managerialism can, at its most general, be seen as a discourse about managing work. As such, it represents a body of knowledge that is presented as technical and rational and that speaks of how to organise, direct and control work. Having its origins in classic texts, such as Taylor (1947) and Fayol (1949), it explicitly justifies a division of labour in which managers carry out certain functions on the basis of technical knowledge of the best way. We must be careful, however, not to accept managerialism's own account of itself. The relationship between managerialism, management and manager is not as simple as managerialism itself would have it. As Hales (2001) and Reed (1989) have argued (see also Burton 1993; 1998), and as Carol illustrates, management is a social process involving coordination, goal setting, control and decision making. As Hales (2001: 7) has put it:

> those called managers are not necessarily responsible, even collectively, for every part of the management process. Since separation of the management process is often incomplete or has been reversed, non-managers can and do engage in some form of management, if only of themselves. Management is not exclusive to managers. ... Moreover managers may also carry out technical functions relating to the work process and, like any other employees, may engage in various non-work activities while 'at' work.

So, whereas managerialism as a body of knowledge undoubtedly to some extent creates managerial subjects (Hollway 1991: 188), Carol illustrates that those called managers are not always subject to these effects. Her case also illustrates that management does not necessarily have to be separated from execution: those, like Braverman (1974), who emphasise the social development of a division of labour based on the separation of conception from execution are in danger of exaggerating the influence of managerialism and equating what managers do with what Taylor and others say they must do. If, however, management is a social process it is something that has to be negotiated in practice in the day-to-day interactions with the managed. Just as studies of 'street level bureaucrats' and professionals suggest they do not simply follow the formal rules (Lipsky 1980; Hudson 1989), so we can expect managers as people to practise management in ways that cope with day-to-day exigencies and may or may not correspond to what comes out of business schools or managerial texts. And if managing is a negotiated activity, it is likely to be shaped by individual biographies, with how people enact the role of manager being influenced by their experience of being managed, their age (Arber and Ginn 1995) and their roles as parents and partners. No wonder, then, that studies of managers (e.g. Pahl and Pahl 1971; Scase and Goffee 1989; Marshall 1995) reveal a range of individual negotiations of the role, as well as, quite frequently, low levels of attachment to it.

In focusing on how two individuals approached managing residential homes it is perhaps not surprising, then, that their individual biographies should influence their work. Frank's nursing background and his own dissatisfaction with his previous managerial role would appear to be a powerful influence on his attitudes and behaviour, beyond the influence of a managerial discourse. Carol's experience of working within the home for many years before becoming 'promoted' to manager, together with the example of her former manager, whose protégée she was, likewise seemed to shape her approach. These cases, while no doubt unique in their detail, nevertheless can be taken to suggest a general point: that we cannot understand what managers do solely with reference to a discourse of managerialism. If, as individuals, these people are both an effect of power and its vehicle (Foucault 1980: 98), their subjectivity is actively constructed through the (inter)play of discourses and experience. These people have constructed their self-identity as managers as a reflexive project of the self (Giddens 1991: 185). In this process these two individuals seem to have found different ways of reconciling management, enterprise and care for vulnerable groups.

But what of gender? A number of authors (e.g. Acker 1990; Collinson and Hearn 1996) have drawn attention to the gendered nature of organisation and management – and in analysing these cases it would seem appropriate to address this issue. The differences between Frank and Carol can readily be related to the literature on gender difference. In the terms introduced by Gilligan (1982), Frank seems to be the embodiment of the 'logic of justice' – the rationalistic, rule-governed male – while Carol similarly seems to exemplify the 'ethic of care' – a much more relational approach. Frank's narrative also seems to exemplify a 'masculine' form of management in its 'instrumental pursuit of the control of social relations' (Kerfoot and Knights 1998: 8). He could be seen as 'aggressively competitive, goal driven and instrumental in pursuit of success' (ibid.: 8). Even while embracing 'care' as an important value, Frank seems concerned to reduce it to a set of rules and abstract principles that can serve to control how the work of care is done. In terms of the literature on leadership, Frank seems to exhibit the 'transactional' or command-and-control style, which Rosener (1990) has argued is more commonly associated with males, and Carol the interactive or relational style associated with females.

Any interpretation of the differences between Frank and Carol in terms of gender difference has its problems and dangers, however. In particular, it might be objected that it does little to unsettle the feminine/masculine dualism or to emphasise how existing gender relations are socially constructed and potentially unstable (Butler 1990). But this study need not be seen as supporting one side of the gender difference/similarity debate over another, since two cases in themselves tell us little (Chodorow 1978; Gilligan 1982; Butler 1990; Powell 1993). If there is a danger of appearing to reinforce gender stereotypes, it should be recalled that Carol, in common with the women in Lunneborg's (1990) study, did not just demonstrate the stereotypically 'feminine' qualities, such as a 'nurturing' approach to co-workers, but also those that might be seen as more stereotypically masculine – being ambitious, 'tough' and forceful when necessary.

It is, in any case, entirely possible that there might be women who manage like Frank and men like Carol – indeed, telling these stories may suggest each as a possibility for men and for women. This stance, in turn, might be objected to on the grounds that it implies a degree of individual choice and agency that may be illusory. However, in arguing for a position that sees individuals as shaping their own identities, I recognise that they do so under certain conditions and constraints and employing certain socially available discursive resources. All I would claim is that we are all engaged in a 'reflexive project of the self' (Giddens 1991) and that this chapter, at best, may serve men and women in their reflexive practice. Of course the stories could have other effects and serve to reinforce dominant views of masculinity and femininity (see also Gabriel (1998) on the 'dangers' of stories) but this would be a simplistic reading of the narratives, which are richer than this and suggestive of a wider range of possibilities.

In identifying Frank with managerialism and managerialism with masculinity, nor do I wish to be taken to imply that managerialism is 'bad' in so far as it is 'masculine'. If Kerfoot and Knights (1998) are justified in equating dominant conceptions of management with a particular form of masculinity that is associated with control, instrumentalism, 'rationalism', and is 'aggressively competitive' it is not, to my mind, its 'masculine' form that is the problem but the consequences of such a form. The test of its desirability, or otherwise, is in terms of how women and men are treated – as groups and individually – and how relations of inequality and domination are reproduced.

On these terms the choice between Frank and Carol's model of management is by no means clear-cut, at least on the evidence I have collected. However, I think it highly likely that Frank's approach, because it is so 'rule governed', will provide little autonomy and capacity for innovation for those subject to it. As such work in Frank's home is more likely to resemble Braverman's 'degraded' work and be contrary to the care worker's 'emancipatory interest' (Habermas 1972). It is also likely to silence the voice of the women who do the work of caring in Frank's home. Conversely Carol's approach seems more closely to resemble Habermas's 'ideal speech situation', through which consensual norms can emerge in situations free from domination. Of course, this may be to make the contrast too marked. There are relations of power in Carol's home: 'I'm sorry, but they will have a bath.' And the operation of familial and other discourses themselves reproduce gendered power relations. Nevertheless, care workers and residents would seem to have more scope here for negotiating the patterns of behaviour and interaction in which they are involved, and as a result there may be more scope for learning and development.

However, the speculative nature of such comments reveals a real limit to the research: without examining the narratives and lives of care workers and residents, these stories remain partial and tell us little of the consequences. Yet another serious limitation lies in relying upon interviews with managers, which may well be self-justificatory. How are we to know that their apparent preoccupation with care is not simply a rhetorical mask? This is, undoubtedly a problem with this kind of study, and a good case could be made for insisting that if we are to understand management, we must never simply take managers own account of themselves. If management is a social process in which even those who are not labelled managers are involved, then surely we must seek to hear from as many of those who are participating in management as possible. From this point of view, all we can hope to gain from these two managers is a partial view. But are not all views partial, and is not the question rather whether these views are interesting or not? We might agree with Rhodes (2000: 25), who, in an article sympathetic to the use of narratives in organisational research, advises: 'don't believe everything/anything that you read/write.' If, however, at one level, this is unexceptionable, it may serve to underestimate the power of stories in providing people with the means of shaping and reshaping their identities.

Even if it is accepted that these two accounts of managing organisations are worth telling, however, there is the question of whether they have a more general relevance, beyond the world of residential care homes. Clearly it would be wise to be cautious, and it is important to stress the characteristics of the organisational forms in which these management approaches are taking place. Here the issues of ownership and the profit motive seem to be less significant than might have been expected, but a range of other factors could be important: the small-scale nature of the organisations, the residential setting, the nature of the work done, and the very direct and personal relationships between the proprietor, manager and staff. There is a prima facie case for thinking that all these factors would seem relevant in making Carol's relational management approach a realistic possibility, suggesting it may not be easily emulated elsewhere. It has often been recognised in the past that size matters in organisations in a number of different ways (Child 1984). If small is more likely to be beautiful (Schumacher 1974), perhaps we need to do more to focus on organising in smaller scale settings.

However this may be, the account of management in two residential care homes presented here suggests two sharply contrasting approaches to managing. One has been described as neo-Taylorist in form, the other as relational management without managerialism. Both seem to represent a way of 'managing to care', even within the constraints of running these homes as private businesses. While the neo-Taylorist management approach may have merit, the alternative would seem to represent at least as attractive an option – one consistent with the dignity, job satisfaction and development of staff and residents alike and lacking the dangers of domination that may be associated with neo-Taylorism. Of course, either of these forms works within a set of resource constraints, which places limits on the standards of care that can be provided for residents and the levels of pay that can be given to staff, suggesting that concentrating on approaches to management only takes us so far.

A further conclusion of this modest study is that the form management takes in a particular organisation is powerfully shaped by the biographies of those involved. While managerialism may well be a powerful discourse 'governing the souls' of managers and managed alike, there is still much unevenness in its impact and it is subject to active negotiation and interpretation by those involved. We must therefore continually seek to look beyond the rhetoric of managerialism and refuse to be dazzled by it. For while managerialism as a gendered discourse and as an ideology is important, so too is human agency. And Carol could be an inspiration.

Acknowledgements

I would like to thank Jim Barry and Mike Dent for their comments on successive drafts of this chapter: it is the better for them, but any errors or inadequacies that remain are my responsibility.

Note

1   Names and incidental details have been changed to protect anonymity.

References

Acker, J. (1990) 'Hierarchies, jobs, bodies: A theory of gendered organizations', *Gender and Society*, 4 (2): 139–58.

Arber, S. and Ginn, J. (1995) *Connecting Gender and Ageing: A Sociological Approach*, Buckingham: Open University Press.

Baldock, J. (1993) 'Patterns of change in the delivery of welfare in Europe', in Taylor-Gooby, P. and Lawson, R. (eds), *Markets and Managers: New Issues in the Delivery of Welfare*, Buckingham: Open University Press, pp. 24–37.

Bishop, M. and Kay, J. (1988) *Does Privatization Work? Lessons From the UK*, London: London Business School.

Braverman, H. (1974) *Labor and Monopoly Capital*, New York: Monthly Review Press.

Burton, J. (1993) *The Handbook of Residential Care*, London: Routledge.

Burton, J. (1998) *Managing Residential Care*, London: Routledge.

Butler, J. (1990) *Gender Trouble: Feminism and the Subversion of Identity*, London: Routledge.

Child, J. (1984) *Organization: A Guide to Problems and Practice*, 2nd edn, London: Harper and Row.

Chodorow, N. (1978) *The Reproduction of Mothering*, Berkeley, CA: The University of California Press.

Clarke, J. and Newman, J. (1997) *The Managerial State: Power, Politics and Ideology in the Remaking of Social Welfare*, London: Sage.

Collinson, D. L. and Hearn, J. (eds) (1996) *Men as Managers, Managers as Men: Critical Perspectives on Men, Masculinities and Managements*, London: Sage.

Fayol, H. (1949) *General Industrial Management*, London: Pitman.

Ferlie, E., Asburner, L., Fitzgerald, L. and Pettigrew, A. (1996) *The New Public Management in Action*, Oxford: Oxford University Press.

Foucault, M. (1980) *Power/Knowledge: Selected Interviews and Other Writings 1972–1977*, Brighton: Harvester.

Gabriel, Y. (1998) 'The use of stories', in Symon, G. and Cassell, C. (eds), *Qualitative Methods and Analysis in Organizational Research: A Practical Guide*, London: Sage, pp. 135–60.

Giddens, A. (1991) *Modernity and Self-Identity: Self and Society in the Late Modern Age*, Cambridge: Polity Press.

Gilligan, C. (1982) *In A Different Voice: Psychological Theory and Women's Development*, Cambridge, MA: Harvard University Press.

Glennerster, H. and Hills, J. (eds) (1998) *The State of Welfare*, 2nd edn, Oxford: Oxford University Press.

Habermas, J. (1972) *Knowledge and Human Interests*, Heinemann: London.

Hales, C. (2001) *Managing Through Organisation: The Management Process, Forms of Organization and the Work of Managers*, London: Thomson Learning.

Hollway, W. (1991) *Work Psychology and Organizational Behaviour: Managing the Individual at Work*, London: Sage.

Hollway, W. and Featherstone, B. (eds) (1997) *Mothering and Ambivalence*, London: Routledge.

Hudson, B. (1989) 'Michael Lipsky and street level bureaucracy: A neglected perspective' in Barton, L. (ed.), *Disability and Dependency*, London: Falmer Press, pp. 42–55.

Johnson, M. (1984) 'Privatising residential care: A review of changing practice and policy', in Laming, H. (ed.), *Residential Care for the Elderly: Present Problems and Future Issues*, London: Policy Studies Institute, pp. 52–63.

Josselson, R. and Lieblich, A. (1993) *The Narrative Study of Lives*, Volume 1, Newbury Park: Sage.

Kerfoot, D. and Knights, D. (1998) 'Managing masculinity in contemporary organizational life: A 'man'agerial project', Organization, 5 (1): 7–26.

Lipsky, M. (1980) *Street Level Bureaucracy: Dilemmas of the Individual in Public Services*, New York: Russell Sage Foundation.

Lunneborg, P. (1990) *Women Changing Work*, New York: Bergin and Garvey.

Marshall, J. (1995) *Women Managers Moving On: Exploring Career and Life Choices*, London: Routledge.

Musson, G. (1998) 'Life histories' in Symon, G. and Cassell, C. (eds), *Qualitative Methods and Analysis in Organizational Research: A Practical Guide*, London: Sage, pp. 10–27.

Ochberg, R.L. (1994) 'Life stories and storied lives' in Lieblich, A. and Josselson, R. (eds), *Exploring Identity and Gender: The Narrative Study of Lives*, Volume 2, Thousand Oaks, CA: Sage, pp. 113–44

Pahl, J. M. and Pahl, R. E. (1971) *Managers and their Wives*, Harmondsworth: Penguin.

Parker, D. (1993) 'Ownership, organizational changes and performance' in Clarke, T. and Pitelis, C. (eds), *The Political Economy of Privatization*, London: Routledge, pp. 31–53.

Peters, T. and Waterman, R. (1982) *In Search of Excellence: Lessons From America's Best-Run Companies*, New York: Free Press.

Pollitt, C. (1993) *Managerialism and the Public Services*, 2nd edn, Oxford: Blackwell.

Powell, G. N. (1993) *Women and Men in Management*, 2nd edn, Newbury Park, CA: Sage.

Reed, M. (1989) *The Sociology of Management*, London: Harvester Wheatsheaf.

Rhodes, C. (2000) 'Reading and writing organizational lives,' Organization 7 (1): 7–29.

Rose, N. (1989) *Governing the Soul: The Shaping of the Private Self*, London: Routledge.

Rosener, J.B. (1990) 'Ways Women Lead', *Harvard Business Review*, 90: 119–125.

Scase, R. and Goffee, R. (1980) *The Real World of the Small Business Owner*, London: Croom Helm.

Scase, R. and Goffee, R. (1989) *Reluctant Managers: Their Work and Lifestyles*, London: Routledge.

Schumacher, E. F. (1974) *Small is Beautiful: A Study of Economics as if People Mattered*, London: Abacus.

Taylor, F. W. (1947) [1911] *Scientific Management*, New York: Harper and Row.

Wood, S. J. (1989) 'New wave management?', *Work, Employment and Society*, 3 (3): 379–402.

12 The problematic professional

Gender and the transgression of 'professional' identity

Deborah Kerfoot

Introduction

Much of the research that has taken place under the heading of gender at work over the last decades has been concerned to locate women's experience in the context of the paid labour market and to advance our theorising of women's continued differential status in terms of pay and employment opportunities. Many contemporary studies of women in the professions and 'professional women' have likewise focused on 'moving up' the corporate ladder or in 'professional' arenas as evidence of their continued progress in the enclaves of organisational life, both in public and private sectors alike. Coupled with interest in the transition of public sector organisations towards modernisation, marketisation and managerialism (see, for example Pollitt 1990; Hood 1995; Clarke and Newman 1997), several academic commentators have begun to explore further the contours and (re)configurations of gender in contemporary organisational sites (Gherardi 1995; Ledwith and Colgan 1996; Collinson and Hearn 1996; Whitehead and Moodley 1999).

Following insights on subjectivity and identity drawn primarily from post-structuralist analysis, this chapter seeks to develop the continued interrogation of gender in managerial work, drawing on vignettes from research interviews on management and managerial practices in two public sector organisational settings. In seeking to problematise managerial work, the chapter examines the links between managerial work and professional identity, and the way in which the practices of organisations serve to reproduce and reinforce predominant conceptions of what 'counts' as professional work. In the context of management and managerial work, this has come to be bound up with an idea(l) of purposive-rational and largely instrumental behaviours towards self and others. Disguised as a mechanism for displacing the self when organisational concerns so dictate, the concept of the manager as professional is at once a paradox: for managerial identity is dependent continuously on 'success' in controlling, quantifying and examining others both as professional practice and in pursuit of a sense of 'professional' identity. The chapter discusses gender in relation to the professional ideal, and elaborates the discussion of 'the professional' with reference to masculinity and management practice.

Professionalising management?

The growth of management and large-scale organisations is perhaps the most significant feature of contemporary society and has facilitated much in the way of academic and other theorising stemming from early excursus, in classical management theory at least, to Weber's 'seminal' ideal-type bureaucracy. Control of the pre-capitalist workplace had centred around family-based control and craft and/or guild regulation, whereas larger theocratic ideology promoted the submission of all to authority 'particularly the highest authority' (Bendix 1956: 47) in the form of a sovereign deity. With the emergence of capitalist systems of production, these pre-capitalist means of controlling work organisations and their members came to be perceived as insufficiently rigorous at the level of control over both the processes and products (Marglin 1974; Clawson 1980). As the emerging factory system came to supplant pre-capitalist systems of regulation, early forms of simple, direct controls achieved prominence. Coupled with a corresponding ideology of entrepreneurial pre-rogative acting to legitimate the controls of capitalist factory owners,

> (t)he personal power and authority of the capitalist constituted the primary mechanism for control ... . Alone or perhaps in concert with a few managers, he watched over the entire operations of the firm. He supervised the work activities directly; he maintained a close watch over his foremen, and he interceded immediately to solve any problems, overridding established procedures, firing recalcitrant workers, recruiting new ones, rearranging work schedules, reducing pay, handing out bonuses, and so forth.
>
> (Edwards 1979: 25)

Typical of the philosophy of capitalist prerogative was a concomitant belief in 'naturally' identifiable leaders and of a form of social and organisational Darwinism whereby capitalist superiority was evidenced by the accumulation of capital. From this flowed the notion that capitalist systems, as capitalist employers, could best serve the larger economic and social interest through the maxims of profit accumulation, expansion and closely regulated workplaces (see Storey (1983) for discussion).

However, processes of industrialisation in the mid-nineteenth century, together with the growth and development of ever larger capitalist enterprises, signalled the demise of the effectiveness of simple controls and spurred interest in bureaucratic rules and procedures as mechanisms for regulating increasingly complex organisations. Here, a legitimating ideology of fairness and impartiality, coupled with a rearticulation of modernist conceptions of order, rationality and efficiency, spawned interest in the development of managing as a discrete activity and precipitated the development of 'modern' management. In similar vein, MacIntyre (1981) regards 'the manager' as an emergent group as both the outcrop and embodiment of a bureaucratic form of organisation:

for MacIntyre the ascendancy of bureaucratic organisations can be attributed to the decline of institutions such as the Catholic Church and the monarchy. The seduction of bureaucracy and of modern management thus lay in its appeal to notions of order, effectiveness, productivity and efficiency, and the realisation of instrumental goals by means of controlling others in the space left 'vacant', so to speak, by other mechanisms of social and organisational regulation. While my concern here is less to periodise precisely the genesis of the modern conception of management than to contextualise the discussion of professional identity that follows, it is important to note that the transition/ transformation of workplaces towards bureaucratic organisational forms and processes remains the topic of debate. For example, in some feminist discussion (Kanter 1977; Ferguson 1984), bureaucracy is seen to be less connected to the production of mechanisms for organisational efficiency and effectiveness than to the reproduction of inherently gendered cultures of subordination, dominance and female ghettoisation.

As a historically situated form of managing, and as a control mechanism for managers themselves, professionalism arose in tandem with the growth and proliferation of bureaucracies. Extending a degree of discretion to key staff and, at least notionally, more autonomous workplace relations, professionals are held to have the capacity for increased self-direction and self-regulation. In other contexts, numerous studies have depicted professional standing as something played out by occupational members who sought to 'professionalise' their work in the search for greater personal and collective autonomy and enhanced material and symbolic rewards (Larson 1977). Similarly, talk of the professions more generally and in connection with social class spawned interest in the investigation of specific groups of professionals and of the changing nature of professional work. Hanlon (1999), for example, charts the struggle to redefine professionalism in relation to the law, charting the legal profession as becoming fragmented and increasingly assessed on managerial and entrepreneurial criteria. For still other commentators, professionalism is both a rhetorical device and an ideological resource 'to legitimate the claims various expert groups and their representatives make on society's material and cultural base' (Reed and Anthony 1992: 596). Larson (1977) portrays the processes of professionalising by occupations as a market strategy to create or enhance monopoly controls over certain aspects of their work and draws attention to the ways in which key groups mobilise in relation to constructions of expert knowledge. Professionalising strategies by groups of workers in the face of increasing employer and/or state control have been the substance of debates, of varying persuasions, across a broad range of academic commentary.

In the contemporary context, the rubric of professional management practice in any number of organisational locations retains a variety of elements from techniques of closure (by means of control over entry portals for example); through processes of accreditation and certification, such as may be offered by bodies such as the Institute of Personnel and Development (IPD) in the personnel and human resource fields; to specified codes and methods of disciplinary procedure. Pollitt (1993) draws attention to the linkages between the professionalising of management and the emergence in the late twentieth century of 'managerialism' defined as: 'a set of beliefs and practices, at the core of which burns the seldom-tested assumption that better management will prove an effective solvent for a wide range of economic and social ills' (ibid.: 1).

This appeal to, and for, professional legitimacy – the trained, 'qualified', certified, self-regulating management expert – has been generative of the conditions for heightened uncertainty among management, not least at the level of the knowledge base of managers themselves. In any variety of public sector settings, the concern for service and product quality, flexibility and internal markets, together with a trend towards marketisation more generally, has combined to create the conditions for challenges to managerial legitimacy and managerial knowledge in equal measure. At one and the same time, the contemporary transformation in management theory and practices towards greater entrepreneurialism on the part of so-called 'professionalised' managers has signalled a diminution of the role of the manager as rule-bound, hierarchically driven and controlled 'organisation man' (Whyte 1956). In combination, managerial philosophy has shifted wholesale from a predominant concern with regulating day-to-day aspects of the employment relationship towards a more diffuse array of practices seen as enhancing commitment and cooperation in organisations in the direction of the consumer of public sector services. With regard to the work of managers themselves, this desire to apprehend the ultimate 'value added' of employees, by means of harnessing their creative potential in the name of managing, has rendered middle managers in particular more 'exposed' both to their superiors and subordinates alike. The demands on many managers in the contemporary public service sector are such that services are far more intensive with respect to labour than in manufacturing contexts, thereby heightening the emphasis on managers to both devise and deliver the required degree of control and coordination.

Alongside the continuous monitoring, individual and interpersonal scrutinies of 'audit culture' in many organisations, target-driven output/performance management practices have achieved prominence in arenas of the public sector hitherto untouched by the exposure to the competitive pressures of newly created markets (see Kerfoot and Whitehead (1998; 2000) for case study example). In sum, while there is plainly little dispute that these pressures towards work intensification and heightened job insecurity have had an impact upon lower hierarchy staff, attention has latterly turned towards an extension of the analysis in the direction of empirical studies of managerial labour. Not least in terms of their own immediate job prospects, managers are clearly implicated in the processes of sustaining the idea(l) that managerial work necessitates a degree of 'expertise' in whatever guise. Whether this is benign complicity or active strategy on the part of (insecure) managers is of less significance perhaps than the effects of the new managerial/professional configuration on organisationally reinforced modes of social relation. In this regard, Fournier (1999) contends that professionalism can be viewed as a disciplinary technique, made real on the part of organisational members by means of their attachment to notions of professional competence that delineate them from 'mere' subordinates. This consideration of professional identity can be interrogated in terms of the inter-relationships between a diverse range of factors. In earlier work exploring the linkages between gender and managerial work (Kerfoot and Knights 1996), I have contended that contemporary managerial work represents, reflects and reproduces ways of thinking and behaving that can be identified as being in line with a dominant form of masculinity. While emphasising the multiplicity and diversity of masculinities, the analysis of masculinity is used to convey certain ideal-type features, such as disembodiment, instrumental rationality and a preoccupation with control, that are commonly though variably reproduced in managerial discourses. The following section pursues aspects of this investigation of gender in relation to professional identity, drawing on vignettes from interviews with female managers in two public sector sites.

(Re)constructing the professional

This section traces aspects of the process by which two women managers in different organisational sites took part in the construction of professional identity. The interviewees were noteworthy in several regards. First, and most notably perhaps, is the degree of experience each had of her respective field and her long-standing attachment to and employment history in the public services. 'Rich' accounts of public sector change could thereby be accessed at the level of the minutiae of day-to-day experiences of those who had 'grown up' through it. Common to both accounts was the belief that the public sector had become 'more akin to' the private sector generally and that the decline of funding and pressures for efficiency and cost-effectiveness of service delivery had had a deleterious effect upon levels and quality of service to end-users. Further, both women felt that the pressure to adopt market models had introduced unnecessary competition, had had a detrimental effect on morale of staff at all levels and a largely, although not universally, negative effect on managers ability to retain a public service ethos. As Karen expressed it, the services needed, in her opinion, to 'keep sight of why we were there – and what we were doing it for – in the first place'. Equally, the implication for the women as managers was that generic, professional managerial skills had increasingly come to take precedence over other service-specific skills and over 'caring' in its widest sense.

The women participated separately in a number of semi-structured in-depth interviews and discussions over a period of months. First, informal contact with the women outside of their organisations was maintained throughout, enabling a fuller account of particular workplace transitions to be drawn, away from the gaze of senior management. Second, and a coincidental characteristic of the accounts of both respondents, was that each was experiencing a period of challenge and/or difficulty in relation to her work circumstances. The nature and timescale of the interviews was such that it became possible to unravel in some detail the women's embodied experience of moments of tension with respect to her work. Third, each responded to her perceived 'crisis' in terms of particularised rearticulations of professional competence, drawing upon her ideas of what it meant 'to be professional' as a mechanism for structuring her reactions and behaviours in line with the professional ideal. For reasons of confidentiality and anonymity, the women are given the pseudonyms Brenda and Karen. Aspects of the factual description of given workplace practices in their accounts are partially changed to prevent identification of the relevant local authority region.

Brenda

Brenda is 53 and is currently acting manager in a local authority residential care unit. Her more (hierarchically) senior colleague at work is temporarily removed from service following leave of absence on unspecified medical grounds. There is neither evidence nor clear suggestion that the colleague will return at any point. Brenda is newly in post and is thereby doubly uncertain of both her employment position, in terms of the ultimate outcome of her colleague's indisposition, and her own feeling about taking over the post if invited to apply. The unit provides primarily full-time fully residential care for, on average, twenty-two elderly people. Occasional short-stay respite care is offered when staffing and other circumstances, often the availability of a bed, allows. This is usually arranged by means of liaison with members of the local social services team, the members of which also oversee the release of 'vulnerable' elderly patients from long-term hospital inpatient stays. Such patients are, in practice, seldom referred to the unit in which Brenda is employed as there are questions surrounding the viability of what is referred to in the unit, as elsewhere in the authority, as 'wastage', in cost-accounting terms, of beds only temporarily filled. Brenda has a particular interest in this practice since her work history in the field, spread over 15 years with the same local authority, has encompassed a variety of care roles, always with elderly clients. A previous post saw her with responsibility for overseeing welfare benefit and personal care provision for the elderly in their own homes following hospital discharge, and called upon her to liaise with a wide spectrum of care providers: tendered services employees and their representatives (broadly referred to colloquially as 'home help' in a variety of forms); medical and social services professionals; clients' families; and, of course, the clients themselves. Brenda is thus well placed to be able to 'map' changes in the provision and delivery of care in the authority over a considerable period and well versed in the requisite variety of skills and expertise that her work requires. It is in part this depth of knowledge that is the source of her ambivalence towards the unit manager post, were it to be fully vacated. Although cognisant of what she would be 'in for' if she got the job, as she puts it, Brenda is engaged by the promise of seniority, social status and responsibility that was denied to her in the days, many years earlier, when she was 'just a housewife'.

An additional source of ambivalence for Brenda however, relates to an area of her personal history known neither to any of her colleagues nor to her superiors in the authority. Prior to the 15-year employment history sketched here, Brenda has had no other paid work, having taken care of her husband (from whom she is now divorced) and two sons, now adults of 31 and 33 years of age. She has also cared for her mother, as her only surviving parent, until the onset of her mother's mental decline and admission to a care unit run by the same authority in which Brenda works. With no previous qualifications of any description, Brenda occupied what free time she had in adult life under-taking college courses, culminating in a period of study as a mature student in higher education. This saw her awarded a first class honours degree in Business Studies and, latterly, a Master of Arts, with distinction in a related field, from two universities close to her home. Her age and lack of work history against her, she was unable to get a job on graduation and so took to concealing what she felt was her overqualified status from prospective employers. This strategy proved immediately effective and Brenda's paid working life began with recruitment as a part-time 'home help' of the type she later went on to manage. The dilemma for Brenda then, in a very real sense, is whether or not to reveal her qualifications in order to enhance her managerial job prospects and 'up' the status of what she regards as her little-recognised range of pro-fessional expertise. Her concern is heightened in so far as a lesser qualified and far less experienced male colleague in a related post had been recently promoted on to a higher managerial pay scale with extended supervisory and other responsibilities. Moreover, this colleague is known to Brenda as having no direct experience of care giving in either personal or professional contexts:

> [Exclamation] Well, then they'd all know wouldn't they? ... All these years on lousy pay [grade] and I could do it blindfold. All he's got is bloody NVQ [national vocational qualification] and some [training] courses! So, I lied, but I'm a liar with two degrees and that's two more than he's got.

Brenda's articulation of her position thereby becomes played out in terms of her professional competence and attachment to processes of accreditation and certification dictated by the authority. She is also concerned about tend-ing to aspects of her appearance, abandoning 'comfy cardigans' in favour of smarter – if impractical – clothes such as tailored jackets. Although for much of her life a carer for others, she downplays or overlooks many aspects of this care-giving experience in elevating the academic credentials about which she had previously been so ambivalent. Having believed her qualifications were an obstacle to job advancement, she (re)constructs and (re)invokes them as mark-ers of her 'rightful' place in the new echelons of professionalised public service care management. In so doing, she at once breathes life into the discourse of managerial professionalism in the public sector and reconstitutes herself in line with its priorities. Implicitly saying, 'Look, I'm a professional too!' Brenda reconfigures aspects of her identity in relation to particularised conceptions of professionalism and the professional ideal. This ideal diminishes the place of hands-on care skills – the embodied, 'texture' of care giving as a human(e) activity – in favour of abstracted conceptions of generic service management capacities far removed from the 'social service of care giving' ethos to which Brenda has been for so long attached.

Karen

Karen is 42 years of age and presently employed as an education welfare manager in a neighbouring local authority region to Brenda. Following graduation from university, she initially trained as a primary school teacher, drawing on her degree in Religious Education and Applied Social Studies. This has provided the starting point for an albeit discontinuous work history (by virtue of almost 2 years child rearing) in various quarters of the education-related field. Following the award of a Post-graduate Certificate in Education (PGCE), Karen entered school teaching in the state sector but quickly found that daily contact with young children dulled the appeal of the work. Before the close of her teaching probationary period, she moved 'sideways' into education welfare with the same local authority region with which she is presently engaged. A divorcee, Karen has raised the only child from her short marriage, a daughter now aged 5, largely single handed. She describes herself as tenacious and hardworking and is clearly keen to provide materially, and symbolically as a role model, for her child in the face of what she regards as lack of meaningful support from the girl's absent father. Managing a team of twelve education welfare officer staff, Karen was appointed to her current job after several years as an education welfare officer herself. The appointment has removed her from the standard authority pay scale for local government officers and on to the first 'rung' of management grades. Annual increments and performance pay, coupled with success at in-house management development courses, should accelerate the achievement of Karen's desire for advancement to the single most senior post in education welfare for her region. Her previous incarnation as an education welfare officer involved her in liaising with schools, teachers, social service units, police and parents in 'chasing up' unauthorised absences by children from school, colloquially referred to as 'truants'. In common with Brenda, Karen is highly experienced and places considerable emphasis on the more subtle social and interpersonal skills requirements her work dictates. She describes these skills in terms of 'having a feel' for the job and prides herself on her ability to work with people at all levels. Here, Karen refers to colleagues and seniors, as well as those with whom she had the most frequent contact as clients – often the most marginalised, economically disadvantaged and disenfranchised members of society. As the vast majority of unauthorised absences from school are condoned by parents, she has been called upon to liaise directly with parents, who were at once hostile to what they saw as interference in parenting their children and to Karen in person as the embodiment of 'authority' in its widest sense.

In terms of recent public sector change, the main issue Karen raises is one of declining service quality, compromised, as she sees it, by demands for accountability and performance monitoring. Although strongly in favour of public scrutiny of all public services and its expenditure, she has become acutely aware of the way in which accountability has come to be reconfigured in the form of market mechanisms. In post as education welfare office manager for only 10 months, much of Karen's job now consists of trying 'to sell', quite literally, the services of her unit to local schools who 'buy in' an education welfare officer for a pre-arranged period. As the budgets of schools themselves have diminished in practical terms, there is plainly increased pressure on whatever money remains in any school 'kitty'. By the self-same mechanisms of devolved responsibility and accountability, head teachers as, in part at least, controllers of budgets are themselves under pressure to conserve resources, with knock-on effects for expenditure on services such as the one Karen and her team provide. Under what she refers to as the 'old' system, education welfare could, with certain exceptions, largely be accessed on demand. The requirement now to cost out this service as a proportion of any school's budget has meant plummeting uptake of education welfare provision in Karen's region as head teachers are forced to make budgetary decisions and delineate essential from non-essential spending. To this end, Karen now spends a proportion of any working week 'touting for business', as she expresses it, at fairs, in schools and on courses where teachers might be present, trying to persuade teachers and heads of the utility of buying in sometimes only the few hours of her staff's time that they can afford. Given her own budgetary target to work to, Karen must in turn ensure that there is minimal 'slack' or wastage of staff time and that all are as fully engaged as is possible in delivering, on time, within budget and to the satisfaction of schools as consumers of the welfare service. The markers of her 'success' and competence as an education professional are thereby reconfigured. What 'counts' as professional in the context of her work is thus redefined in line with a cost-accounting paradigm of public service. Moreover, additional report writing and increased 'paperwork' have meant that she spends a greater proportion of ostensibly non-work time on work-related activities, with what she regards as detrimental effects on her family life.

Karen's dilemma then, is twofold. In seeking promotion, she expresses a concern to: 'get on, do well and do right by my daughter' but simultaneously finds her quality of (family) life compromised as a result. In trying to make a success of her working life for herself and her child, Karen contributes to the conditions of her own work intensification and reinscribes precisely the 'professional' practice she so dislikes. For it is this professional practice she sees as responsible for ultimately diminishing the quality of the help provided for children in need, in terms of their schooling and educational attainment. This is ironic for Karen, given that under New Labour the educational achievement of children, in general, and school exclusions, in particular, have emerged as salient topics in public debate. Delivering what she regards as largely an abbreviated and truncated version of service under the new regime, Karen is ambivalent in her distaste for the manner in which she feels forced to express her commitment to the new public service professional ideal. In so doing, and with one eye on her own job prospects, she in effect sustains the very conditions within which she silences her own dissent. Moreover, in her concern to demonstrate her commitment to the post to (unspecified) others, Karen has begun to conceal the full extent the demands her role as a single parent place on her. Often unable to complete administrative/paperwork in office time because of the demands of child care and school hours, she has acquired a laptop computer at her own expense, and 'fills in' the remaining work needed to complete certain tasks in the evenings and at weekends. As many of her colleagues also take work home, this is perhaps unremarkable in itself. What is significant however, is more the fact that she has chosen to conceal this part of herself and her behaviour from others in the desire to appear committed and capable of responding to the demands the work throws up. Attempting to 'prove herself' to be professional in the context of public sector management, Karen tries to demonstrate her mastery of the professional ideal by negating elements of herself and what she sees as her own failure or inability to 'hit' the very target work times she has become sceptical of. In wanting 'to be taken seriously as a manager', she feels further compelled to conceal aspects of her own scepticism about the service she and her staff can provide, most often in her day-to-day interactions with the staff themselves. In sum, Karen feels disquieted and destabilised by her own complicity in the processes that diminish, as she sees it, both the quality of service in terms of outcomes for children and their families and the quality of her own lived experience as a mother/woman/manager/professional educationalist.

Discussion: gender and the transgression of professional identity

The above vignettes of identity-construction processes in the context of two public sector sites signal the need to recognise professionalism not as a thing in itself, a discrete entity 'thrust upon' unsuspecting or recalcitrant managers, but as a series of discourses and practices irreducibly bound up in the exercise of power. This conception of power and its operation is in line with Foucault (1980; 1982), in whose work power is seen to exist only in its exercise, operating through the production of particular knowledges. From this theoretical position, power is neither one-directional, nor does it flow from a single source. Power operates in reciprocal relation to subjectivity and identity: in other words, it influences and has an impact upon our sense of who we are as people. Subjectivity thus comes to be constituted, and continually reconstituted through the exercise of power within which conceptions of identity are generated. The women managers here are active subjects. In exercising power and in positioning themselves among competing discourses (such as wife/mother/carer/manager/woman/professional) the women find their own way through a variety of ways of being a woman and a manager, often with unpredictable and unintended consequences. One such consequence referred to here is when Karen feels forced to deny aspects of a primary identification of herself as a mother in order to appear 'committed to the job' and to satisfy what she understands to be the dictates of professionalism in her field. She is thereby transformed into a subject whose subjective sense of meaning and well-being is tied to those social and organisational practices sustained by such power (Knights 1995). At once both subjected to and objectified by the technologies and mechanisms of the professional ideal, managers are clearly 'at the sharp end' of trying to make real the demand to 'reform' the public sector in a variety of contexts, often in much the same manner as are their subordinates. More than this however, managers actively take part in reproducing the conditions within which they themselves construct and are constructed by professional identity. In downplaying her decades of paid and unpaid care-work experience in favour of the formal qualifications she thinks can advance her promotion, Brenda negates her own attachment to the labour and love of caring and reconstitutes herself as the professional manager. Consequently, professional identity is conceptualised as a discursive resource that managers draw upon in the making of themselves as managers. More than this, the managers' very sense of professional identity becomes tied to these mechanisms and technologies of management in the public sector.

Pursuing this (poststructuralist) theorising whereby subjectivity is constructed in relation to discourse, the identity of Brenda and Karen as *women* managers is of significance. Gendered, as other, subjectivities are fractured, historically shifting, continuously unstable and always multiple. Both women are, for instance, mothers as well as managers and each, often unwittingly, expresses this part of her identity in ways that have clear impact on her work. For example, in the case of Brenda, her attempts deliberately to alter her appearance through dress codes indicates another facet of gendered identity construction and calls attention to what I have, in other published work (Kerfoot and Knights 1996) called the masculinity of management practice. Not specifically aligned with men, this conception of management calls attention to the ways in which contemporary organisations are premised on notions of highly instrumental, purposive-rational behaviour – controlling, quantifying, examining and grading. Discourses of professionalism and professional identity thereby constitute both a mode of regulation of the self and proscribe 'what it is to be a manager' in terms of the articulation of specific masculinities and behavioural displays commonly associated with men (see Kerfoot (2002) for elaboration).

Not that all managers (or all men) are typically masculine, however defined. My point is to suggest that the yardstick by which measures of professional competence are generated can be referred to as masculine in that it projects a cultural standard of what counts in the organisation as 'proper' professional practice for both women and men. Masculinity is here conceived of as existing only in practice, having no existence outside the arena in which it is continuously made and remade. Brenda's adoption of more 'formal' dress belies her experience of care giving as stereotypically associated with women and denies caring for the elderly as physical and often very dirty work. In sum, the notion of 'being a professional' can be regarded as mutually interconstitutive of certain constructions of masculinity and of being a manager. The two women here are transgressors of professional identity in that they are, to varying degrees, subjected to, and subjects of, organisationally generated pressures to comply with the dictates of public sector management practice in order to appear successful and competent as professionals. This exemplifies what Gherardi (1995) has referred to as the 'schizogenia' of many women's existence in organisational locales in which organisational affirmations of selfhood commensurate with the professional ideal are overlain by gender 'as both an organisational principle and an organisational outcome' (ibid.: 185). Karen's professional identity is explicitly overlaid but in tension with ideas about her role as mother/manager/woman/family breadwinner. This underscores the concept of identity as gendered, always in process, made and remade in differing contexts. The idea of the precariousness of identity, of identity as in a permanent state of 'work in progress', sits in opposition to a conception of the solidity of identity found in much mainstream management thinking. Such thinking imposes a seamless rationality on the part of selfconscious, 'knowing' managers. By contrast, flowing from a poststructuralist feminist perspective, we can see professional identity as gendered but also as open to resistance, to moments of contestation, transformation and change. For as transgressors of professional identity, the public sector managers interviewed here are both marginalised, as women, by professional practices of organisations and equally capable of subverting prevailing power relations.

References

Bendix, R. (1956) *Work and Authority in Industry*, Berkeley, CA: University of California Press.

Clarke, J. and Newman, J. (1997) *The Managerial State*, London: Sage.

Clawson, D. (1980) *Bureaucracy and the Labour Process*, New York: Monthly Review Press.

Collinson, D. and Hearn, J. (eds) (1996) *Men as Managers: Managers as Men*, London: Sage.

Edwards, R. C. (1979) *Contested Terrain: The Transformation of Work in the Twentieth Century*, London: Heinemann.

Ferguson, K. E. (1984) *The Feminist Case Against Bureaucracy*, Philadelphia, PA: Temple University Press.

Foucault, M. (1980) *Power/Knowledge: Selected Interviews and Other Writings 1972–1977* (ed. C. Gordon), Brighton: Harvester Wheatsheaf.

Foucault, M. (1982) 'The subject and power', in Dreyfus, H. and Rainbow, P. (eds), *Michel Foucault: Beyond Structuralism and Hermeneutics*, Brighton: Harvester Press, pp. 67–81.

Fournier, V. (1999) 'The appeal to 'professionalism' as a disciplinary mechanism', *The Sociological Review*, 47 (2): 280–307.

Gherardi, S. (1995) *Gender, Symbolism and Organizational Cultures*, London: Sage.

Hanlon, G. (1999) *Lawyers, the State and the Market: Professionalism Revisited*, London: Macmillan.

Hood, C. (1995) 'The 'new public management' in the 1980s: Variations on a theme', *Accounting, Organizations and Society*, 20 (2): 93–109.

Kanter, R. M. (1977) *Men and Women of the Corporation*, New York: Basic Books.

Kerfoot, D. (2002) 'Managing the professional man', in Dent, M. and Whitehead, S. (eds), *Managing Professional Identities: Knowledge Performativity and the 'New' Professional*, London: Routledge, pp. 81–98.

Kerfoot, D. and Knights, D. (1996) 'The best is yet to come: Searching for embodiment in managerial work', in Collinson, D. and Hearn, J. (eds), *Men as Managers: Managers as Men: Critical Perspectives on Men Masculinities and Management*, London: Sage, pp. 78–98.

Kerfoot, D. and Whitehead, S. (1998) ' "Boys Own" stuff: Masculinity and the management of further education', *The Sociological Review*, 46 (3): 436–457.

Kerfoot, D. and Whitehead, S. (2000) 'Keeping all the balls in the air: Further education and the masculine/managerial subject', *Journal of Further and Higher Education*, 24 (2): 183–202.

Knights, D. (1995) 'Hanging out the dirty washing: Labour process theory in an age of deconstruction', paper presented at the *13th Annual Labour Process Conference*, Blackpool, April 1995.

Larson, M. S. (1977) *The Rise of Professionalism: A Sociological Analysis*, Berkeley, CA: University of California Press.

Ledwith, S. and Colgan, F. (eds) (1996) *Women in Organisations: Changing Gender Politics*, Basingstoke: Macmillan.

MacIntyre, A. (1981) *After Virtue: A Study in Moral Theory*, London: Duckworth.

Marglin, S. A. (1974) 'What do bosses do? The origins and functions of hierarchy in capitalist production', *The Radical Review of Political Economics*, 6: 33–60.

Pollitt, C. (1993) *Managerialism and the Public Services: Cuts or Cultural Change in the 1990s*, Oxford: Blackwell Press.

Reed, M. and Anthony, P. D. (1992) 'Professionalising management and managing professionalisation: British management in the 1980s', *Journal of Management Studies*, Oxford: Blackwell.

Storey, J. (1983) *Managerial Prerogative and the Question of Control*, Boston, MA: Routledge.

Whitehead, S. and Moodley, R. (eds) (1999) *Transforming Managers: Gendering Change in the Public Sector*, London: UCL press.

Whyte, W. H. (1956) *The Organisation Man*, New York: Doubleday Press.

Index

Printed in the United States
69759LV00002B/207

9 780415 258197